CALIFORNIA

Country Inns and Back Roads

Other books by Jerry Levitin

Country Inns and Back Roads, North America
Country Inns and Back Roads, New England
Country Inns and Back Roads, Britain and Ireland

Country Inns and Back Roads

CALIFORNIA

1994–1995

Jerry Levitin

HarperPerennial
A Division of *HarperCollins*Publishers

COUNTRY INNS AND BACK ROADS, CALIFORNIA.
Copyright © 1994 by HarperCollins Publishers, Inc. All rights reserved.
Printed in the United States of America.
No part of this book may be used or reproduced in any manner whatsoever without written
permission except in the case of brief quotations embodied in critical articles and reviews.
For information address
HarperCollins Publishers, Inc., 10 East 53rd Street, New York, NY 10022.

HarperCollins books may be purchased for educational, business, or sales promotional use.
For information, please write: Special Markets Department, HarperCollins Publishers, Inc.,
10 East 53rd Street, New York, NY 10022.

ISSN: 1060-3786
ISBN: 0-06-273261-7

94 95 96 97 98 ◆/RRD 5 4 3 2 1

CONTENTS

Preface   xiii
Map of North   xviii

NORTH: Upper North Coast   2

Benbow Inn, *Garberville*   3
Carter House, *Eureka*   5
Gingerbread Mansion, The, *Ferndale*   6

Mendocino Coast   9

Agate Cove Inn, *Mendocino*   10
Glendeven, *Mendocino*   11
Harbor House, *Elk*   12
Headlands Inn, The, *Mendocino*   14
John Dougherty House, *Mendocino*   16
Joshua Grindle Inn, *Mendocino*   18
Jughandle Beach Country Bed & Breakfast, *Mendocino*   19
Mendocino Farmhouse, *Mendocino*   21
Pudding Creek Inn, *Fort Bragg*   22
Rachel's Inn, *Mendocino*   23
Stanford Inn by the Sea, *Mendocino*   25
Whale Watch Inn by the Sea, *Gualala*   27
Whitegate Inn, *Mendocino*   28

Mother Lode North   30

Murphy's Inn, *Grass Valley*   31
Red Castle Inn, The, *Nevada City*   32

Mother Lode Central   34

Court Street Inn, *Jackson*   35
Foxes, The, *Sutter Creek*   36
Gate House Inn, *Jackson*   37
Hanford House, The, *Sutter Creek*   39
Heirloom, The, *Ione*   40
Wedgewood Inn, The, *Jackson*   41

Mother Lode South   **43**

    Chateau Du Sureau, *Oakhurst*   44
    Dunbar House 1880, *Murphys*   46
    Serenity, *Sonora*   48

Sacramento   **51**

    Amber House, *Sacramento*   52
    Abigail's Bed & Breakfast, *Sacramento*   53

Sonoma Valley   **55**

    Applewood, *Guerneville*   56
    Campbell Ranch Inn, *Geyserville*   57
    Grape Leaf Inn, *Healdsburg*   59
    Haydon House, *Healdsburg*   60
    Heart's Desire Inn, *Occidental*   62
    Hope-Merrill House, *Geyserville*   63
    Madrona Manor, *Healdsburg*   64
    Timberhill Ranch, *Cazadero*   66
    Victorian Garden Inn, *Sonoma*   68
    Vintners Inn, *Santa Rosa*   70
    Ye Olde' Shelford House, *Cloverdale*   72

Napa Valley   **74**

    Beazley House, *Napa*   75
    Foothill House, *Calistoga*   76
    Larkmead Country Inn, *Calistoga*   77
    Meadowood Resort Hotel, *St. Helena*   79
    Old World Inn, The, *Napa*   81
    Scott Courtyard and Lodging, *Calistoga*   83
    Silver Rose Inn, *Calistoga*   84
    Wine Country Inn, The, *St. Helena*   86
    Zinfandel Inn, *St. Helena*   87

Marin County Coast   **90**

    Casa Del Mar, *Stinson Beach*   91
    Roundstone Farm, *Olema*   92
    Ten Inverness Way, *Inverness*   94

San Francisco and the Bay Area — 96

Alamo Square Inn, *San Francisco* — 97
Archbishops Mansion Inn, *San Francisco* — 98
Inn at Union Square, The, *San Francisco* — 100
Inn San Francisco, The, *San Francisco* — 101
Mansion at Lakewood, The, *Walnut Creek* — 102
Mansions, The, *San Francisco* — 103
Petite Auberge, *San Francisco* — 106
Sherman House, The, *San Francisco* — 107
Spencer House, The, *San Francisco* — 108
Union Street Inn, *San Francisco* — 110
Victorian Inn on the Park, *San Francisco* — 112
Washington Square Inn, *San Francisco* — 114
White Swan, *San Francisco* — 115

Half Moon Bay — 117

Mill Rose Inn, *Half Moon Bay* — 118
Old Thyme Inn, *Half Moon Bay* — 119

Silicon Valley — 121

Hensley House, The, *San Jose* — 122
Inn at Saratoga, The, *Saratoga* — 123
Victorian on Lytton, The, *Palo Alto* — 125

Santa Cruz Area — 127

Apple Lane Inn, *Aptos* — 128
Babbling Brook Inn, The, *Santa Cruz* — 129
Chateau Victorian, *Santa Cruz* — 130
Cliff Crest Bed and Breakfast Inn, *Santa Cruz* — 132
Country Rose Inn Bed and Breakfast, *Gilroy* — 133
Inn at Depot Hill, *Capitola by the Sea* — 135

MAP OF SOUTH — 138

SOUTH: Monterey and Big Sur Country — 140

Gosby House Inn, *Pacific Grove* — 141
Green Gables Inn, *Pacific Grove* — 142
Happy Landing, The, *Carmel* — 143

Jabberwock, The, *Monterey*   145
Martine Inn, The, *Pacific Grove*   146
Old Monterey Inn, *Monterey*   148
Pine Inn, The, *Carmel*   149
Sandpiper Inn At-The-Beach, The, *Carmel*   151
Seven Gables Inn, *Pacific Grove*   152
Ventana Inn, *Big Sur*   154

Central Valley   **156**

Inn at Harris Ranch, The, *Coalinga*   156

Central Coast   **159**

Garden Street Inn Bed & Breakfast, *San Luis Obispo*   159

Santa Barbara Area   **162**

Alisal Guest Ranch and Resort, The, *Solvang*   164
Ballard Inn, The, *Ballard*   165
Bath Street Inn, The, *Santa Barbara*   168
Bayberry Inn, The, *Santa Barbara*   169
Cheshire Cat, The, *Santa Barbara*   170
Inn at Petersen Village, The, *Solvang*   172
La Mer, *Ventura*   174
Los Olivos Grand Hotel, *Los Olivos*   175
Old Yacht Club Inn, The, *Santa Barbara*   177
San Ysidro Ranch, *Montecito*   179
Simpson House Inn, *Santa Barbara*   181
Tiffany Inn, *Santa Barbara*   183
Villa Rosa, *Santa Barbara*   184

Greater Los Angeles Basin   **186**

Channel Road Inn, The, *Santa Monica*   187
La Maida House, *North Hollywood*   188
Salisbury House, *Los Angeles*   189

L.A. Coast and Santa Catalina Island   **191**

Blue Lantern Inn, *Dana Point*   192
Garden House Inn, The, *Avalon*   193

Inn on Mount Ada, The, *Avalon*   195
Seal Beach Inn and Gardens, The, *Seal Beach*   197

Big Bear Region (San Bernardino County)   **200**
Eagle's Nest Bed & Breakfast, *Big Bear Lake*   200

San Diego Area   **202**
Inn, The, *Rancho Santa Fe*   203
Rancho Valencia Resort, *Rancho Santa Fe*   204

PROPERTY INDEX   209
RATES   213
INDEX BY ACTIVITY   217

PREFACE

When I became responsible for revising the late Norman Simpson's Berkshire Traveller series in February 1989, I was surprised to learn that most books on inns and bed and breakfast establishments are written by authors who never visit the inns. In fact, many reviews are simply paid advertisements, written by the innkeepers, and the publisher receives a payment for the inclusion.

You can feel assured that the inns and B&B's in *Country Inns and Back Roads: California* are visited on a regular basis and the reviews are updated each year. And since there is no cost for inclusion, you can be doubly sure that each inn listed is based on its own merits.

However, spending the time on site inspections and finding new properties does not leave me much time to also rewrite each inn each year. If there has been no new information on an inn that meets all my criteria every year, I find myself leaving the write-up untouched. This has caused some inquiry among some faithful readers. If the write-up remains the same over the years, how could the author have visited it? Rest assured, it has been inspected with nothing of significance to add. This is a priority decision by me. I would rather spend the time checking out new inns or visiting those listed than merely rewriting an entry for an inn where the existing information is still true.

I have also noticed that few guidebooks take into account the personalities of the innkeepers. Guidebooks will list facts regarding the inns' settings, locations and interior decoration, but as Norman Simpson believed, the key to a successful inn is the traveler's feeling of being welcomed. An efficiently run, beautifully decorated inn situated on a lovely site will not be listed between the covers of any of the *Country Inns and Back Roads* books if it is missing that intangible human warmth. Of course, to determine that extra ingredient, the inn and its innkeepers need to be visited.

In past years, I have distinguished between full-service inns that serve lunch and dinner and bed & breakfast inns, which serve only the morning meal. These were reviewed in two different books, *Country Inns and Back Roads: North America* and *Bed & Breakfast American Style*, respectively. However, in 1992 I decided to combine the two to list the best of both worlds, plus a few select small hotels that never quite fit into either of the old books. You'll find this new format to continue in the future for *Country Inns and Back Roads: North America* and in my two new regional guides, *Country Inns and Back Roads: New England* and *Country Inns and Back Roads: California.*

The change is based on our nation's traveling habits. Many states and areas within states do not offer many traditional inns, but may have plenty of B&Bs. For example, the West tends to have inns that spread out with cottages or single-story lodges. Classic inns, with the restaurant on the ground floor and the rooms above, are generally found in the East. Why not, then, let you select from one book only?

In addition, many readers told me that going from inn to inn made them crave a respite from the full-course dinners that they were being served each night. For a change, they welcome a B&B or a hotel where many meal options are available.

But all the books in the series still share that *Country Inns and Back Roads* feeling—a hospitality, a warmth that makes you want to return again and again.

Although there are exceptions to every rule, this book generally lists lodgings that have five or more rooms to rent, but no more than 40; a common area where guests can congregate away from the public; private baths; high standards of cleanliness, and innkeeper involvement. The meals are freshly prepared and served in a relaxing atmosphere.

I look for a place that caters to the overnight guest first, rather than the dining guest. This preference eliminates some very fine restaurants with guest rooms above. My ideal is the inn that only serves houseguests. However, financial considerations often require the innkeeper to open the dining room to the general public.

HOW THE BOOK IS ORGANIZED

This book is divided into geographical sections. Each of these sections has its own keyed map showing the approximate location of every accommodation. Of further assistance is the index, which lists the establishments alphabetically, and another index that lists the towns alphabetically and the inn's rates. We have also compiled some new indexes that can help you locate inns offering special activities or amenities.

The paragraphs following the narrative accounts of my visits contain essential information about the amenities offered and nearby recreational and cultural attractions. Reasonably explicit driving directions are also included here.

If you are displeased with one of my selections, or if you feel that a wonderful inn has inadvertently been overlooked, please let me hear from you by using the form printed in the back of the book.

MEAL PLANS

You'll notice references to the following "plans" throughout the text and also in the index of rates. Here are some thumbnail definitions of the terms.

"European plan" means that rates for rooms and meals are separate. "American plan" means that all meals are included in the cost of the room. "Modified American plan" means that breakfast and dinner are included in the cost of the room. The rates at certain inns—commonly known as "bed and breakfasts"—include a continental or full breakfast with the lodging.

RATES

I include a listing of rates in the index. Space limitations preclude any more than a general range of rates for each inn, and these should not be considered firm quotations. Please check with the inns for their various rates and special packages. It should be noted that many small inns do not have night staffs, and innkeepers will appreciate it if calls are made before 8:00 P.M.

RESERVATIONS AND CANCELLATIONS

At most of the inns listed in this book, a deposit is required for a confirmed reservation. Guests are requested to please note arrival and departure dates carefully. The deposit will be forfeited if the guest arrives after the date specified or departs before the final date of the reservation. Refunds will generally be made only if the reservation is canceled seven to 14 days in advance of the arrival date, depending upon the policy of the individual inn, and a service charge will be deducted from the deposit.

It must be understood that a deposit ensures that your accommodations will be available as confirmed and also assures the inn that the accommodations are sold as confirmed. Therefore, when situations arise necessitating your cancellation on short notice, your deposit will not be refunded.

FOR FOREIGN TRAVELLERS

Welcome to North America! Many of you are making your first visit, and we're delighted that you'll be experiencing some of the *real* United States and Canada by visiting these country inns. Incidentally, all of the innkeepers will be very happy to help you make arrangements and reservations at other inns listed in the book.

AUTHOR'S BACKGROUND

Most writers of inn guidebooks have never had the experience of actually owning and operating an inn. I presently own the award winning Inn at Sunrise Point near Camden, Maine, a three-room, four-cottage B&B that is on the ocean's edge. In addition, I owned and operated an urban inn in San Francisco for five years, and I have run a consulting business for innkeepers. In the summer you will find me either visiting inns for the books or at my inn in Camden, Maine.

CALIFORNIA

Country Inns and Back Roads

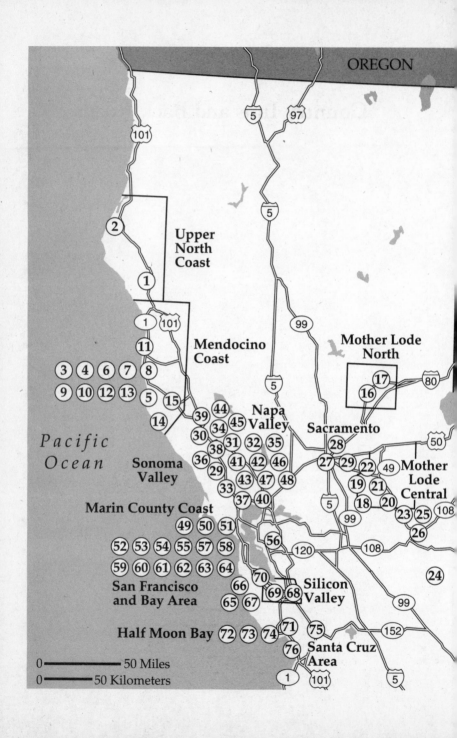

Northern California

1. Garberville, Benbow Inn
2. Ferndale, The Gingerbread Mansion
3. Mendocino, Agate Cove Inn
4. Little River, Glendeven
5. Elk, Harbor House
6. Mendocino, The Headlands Inn
7. Mendocino, John Dougherty House
8. Mendocino, Joshua Grindle Inn
9. Mendocino, Jughandle Beach Country Bed & Breakfast
10. Mendocino, Mendocino Farmhouse
11. Fort Bragg, Pudding Creek Inn
12. Mendocino, Rachel's Inn
13. Mendocino, Stanford Inn By The Sea
14. Gualala, Whale Watch Inn
15. Mendocino, Whitegate Inn
16. Grass Valley, Murphy's Inn
17. Nevada City, The Red Castle Inn
18. Jackson, Court Street Inn
19. Sutter Creek, The Foxes
20. Jackson, Gate House Inn
21. Sutter Creek, The Hanford House
22. Ione, The Heirloom
23. Jackson, Wedgewood Inn
24. Oakhurst, Chateau Du Sureal
25. Murphys, Dunbar
26. Sonora, Serenity
27. Sacramento, Amber House
28. Sacramento, Aunt Abigails's Bed & Breakfast
29. Guerneville, Applewood
30. Geyersville, Campbell Ranch Inn
31. Healdsburg, Grape Leaf Inn
32. Healdsburg, Haydon House
33. Occidental, Heart's Desire Inn
34. Geyersville, Hope-Merrill House
35. Healdsburg, Madrona Manor
36. Cazadero, Timberhill Ranch
37. Sonoma, Victorian Garden Inn
38. Santa Rosa, Vinters Inn
39. Cloverdale, Ye Olde' Shelford House
40. Napa, Beazley House
41. Calistoga, Foothill House
42. Calistoga, Larkmead Country Inn
43. St. Helena, Meadowood Resort Hotel
44. Napa, Old World Inn
45. Calistoga, Scott Courtyard
46. Calistoga, Silver Rose Inn
47. St. Helena, The Wine Country Inn
48. St. Helena, Zinfandel Inn
49. Stinson Beach, Casa Del Mar
50. Olema, Roundstone Farm
51. Inverness, Ten Inverness Way
52. San Francisco, Alamo Square Inn
53. San Francisco, Archbishops Mansion Inn
54. San Francisco, The Inn at Union Square
55. San Francisco, The Inn San Francisco
56. Walnut Creek, The Mansion at Lakewood
57. San Francisco, The Mansions
58. San Francisco, Petite Auberge
59. San Francisco, The Sherman House
60. San Francisco, The Spencer House
61. San Francisco, Union Street Inn
62. San Francisco, Victorian Inn on the Park
63. San Francisco, Washington Square Inn
64. San Francisco, White Swan
65. Half Moon Bay, Mill Rose Inn
66. Half Moon Bay, Old Thyme Inn
67. Half Moon Bay, Zaballa House
68. San Jose, The Henley House
69. Saratoga, The Inn at Saratoga
70. Palo Alto, The Victorian Inn on Lytton
71. Aptos, Apple Lane Inn
72. Santa Cruz, The Babbling Brook Inn
73. Santa Cruz, Chateau Victorian
74. Santa Cruz, Cliff Crest Bed and Breakfast Inn
75. Gilroy, Country Rose Inn Bed and Breakfast
76. Capitola, Inn at Depot Hill

Upper North Coast

Eureka, an old lumbering town on California's beautiful north coast, contains many fine examples of Victorian architecture. Ferndale is now noted for its wonderful antique shops. The entire quaint village is a state historical landmark. Inland and about 40 miles to the south is the town of Garberville, deep in the heart of redwood country. The area code for the numbers listed below is 707.

EVENTS

YEAR-ROUND	Lumber Mill Tours
YEAR-ROUND	Ferndale Repertory Theatre
MARCH	Redwood Coast Dixieland Jazz Festival (info: 442-3738)
APRIL	Rhododendron Festival and Parade (info: 442-3738)
MAY	Bicycle Tour of the Unknown Coast (info: 822-7523)
MAY	All-Kite Regional Championships (info: 442-9245)
MAY	Eureka Rhododendron Festival
MAY	World Champion Great Arcata to Ferndale Knetic Sculpture Race
JUNE	Mid Summer Scandinavian Festival (info: 786-9853)
JULY	Fortuna Rodeo
AUGUST	Paul Bunyan Days: festivities include Demolition Derby, Fire Department Water Fight, Labor Day Parade, Gem & Mineral Show
AUGUST	American Fuchsia Society Show (info: 442-3738)
AUGUST	Humboldt County Fair
SEPTEMBER	McKinleyville Air Show
OCTOBER	Lumberjack Days (info: 826-3011)
NOVEMBER	Bluegrass Festival (info: 725-2378)
DECEMBER	Trucker's Christmas Convoy (info: 445-9211)
DECEMBER	Dickens's Christmas Festival

BENBOW INN
Garberville, California

The owners-innkeepers of the Benbow are Patsy and Chuck Watts, whom I have known for many years. The one outstanding quality that each of them has in such marvelous abundance is enthusiasm, and all of the improvements and additions to this truly unusual northern California inn have been undertaken by them with great joy and love.

"Ever since day one," said Chuck, "we have been very happy and have had a really tremendous time. It's a continuing challenge and we've gotten a great deal accomplished, but I like the idea that the future is big with plans."

"We feel that we are a destination resort-inn, able to accommodate and provide amusement and diversion for all our guests of any age," chimed in Patsy. "We have acquired some fabulous antique pieces, most particularly a magnificent carved buffet for the dining room. We have added a beautiful carved mantel for the fireplace in the lobby and have installed an antique mantel and a fireplace in the lounge.

"We will be having our wine tasting in November, and this has now become a semiannual affair, with many of the California boutique wineries represented."

I first visited the Benbow Inn in 1973 and was immediately intrigued not only with its location in the glorious redwood country of northern California, but also with its design, which shows definite influences of the Art Deco style of the early 1920s. There are also some touches of an English Tudor manor house found in the half-timbers, carved dark wood paneling, solid oak furniture, bookcases, hardwood floors, handsome oriental rugs and truly massive fireplace in the main living room.

Some guestrooms are on the terrace and garden levels with private patios. With four-poster beds, antiques and country fabrics, their decor is most attractive. Three of them have fireplaces and VCRs. Other guestrooms in the main inn had also been handsomely redecorated, and my own room, Number 313, was on the top floor and looked out over the gardens and a wonderful changing panorama of clouds. For those who like to sleep with their windows open you will hear the traffic on Route 101.

The Benbow is, indeed, a destination resort-inn—in addition to swimming, it offers tennis on two tennis courts nearby, a good golf course within walking distance, hiking and magnificent backroading. By the way, it's very accessible by public transportation since the Route 101 buses stop almost at the front door.

At Christmastime there's a twelve-foot tree with teddy bears playing drums hanging from every branch. Under the tree there are Patsy's very special antique, oversized toys. An antique sleigh is on the front porch filled with presents and wreaths. Holly and masses of decorations are all over the inn.

On Christmas Day there is a special two-seatings Christmas dinner and everyone has a wonderful time.

Incidentally, in the fall and all through the holidays, English tea and scones are served in the lobby.

The Benbow also has a film library with over 300 classic films. These are shown every evening. On one of my visits I cheered and wept a little at James Cagney's great portrayal of George M. Cohan in *Yankee Doodle Dandy*.

Patsy, Chuck and Bijou (their Afghan hound, the most photographed canine in northern California) are having a wonderful time greeting guests, sharing their enthusiasm and providing their own bubbling brand of warmth and hospitality. In short, they're model innkeepers. I'm glad they and the Benbow Inn found each other.

———

BENBOW INN, 445 Lake Benbow Dr., Garberville, CA 95542; 707-923-2124.

A 55-guestroom (private baths) English Tudor inn in the redwood country of northern California. King, queen and twin beds available. Non-smoking inn. Air conditioning. On Rte. 101. European plan. Breakfast, lunch and dinner served to travelers daily. Open mid-Apr. to Nov. 28; reopen Dec. 17 for holiday season. Swimming on grounds; golf, tennis adjacent. Hiking and magnificent backroading. Chuck, Patsy and Truffles Watts, owners/hosts.

DIRECTIONS: From San Francisco follow Hwy. 101 north 200 mi. and exit at Benbow.

CARTER HOUSE
Eureka, California

Eureka is an up-and-coming community. I've been visiting it off and on for many years, and it is definitely emerging as an area of considerable interest.

Symbolic, perhaps, of this emergence is the Carter House, a handsome, four-story redwood Victorian home that looks old but was actually completed in 1982. It is an architectural re-creation of the Murphy House, which was destroyed by the 1906 earthquake. Built by the owner Mark Carter himself with three other helpers, the Victorian decor is enhanced by marble and hardwood floors, oriental carpets, potted plants and fresh-cut flowers.

In addition to a lobby, dining room and sitting area, the first floor features a gallery where works of artists are displayed. There are six guestrooms furnished in handsome Victorian antiques, and the two on the third floor offer views of the Eureka marina and the extraordinary Carson mansion. Caveat—they share a bathroom.

Breakfast is served across the street at the Carter Hotel and includes a fresh fruit tart or pastry, fruit compote, assorted fresh homemade muffins, and eggs Benedict or eggs Florentine.

The Carter Hotel is elegant in its own right with each room tastefully done. The small lobby done in modern motif with its plush chairs and couch is where you can sit and have hors d'oeuvres in the afternoon or cookies after dinner. The dining room is adjacent to the lobby and has a fine reputation. I especially enjoyed the creamy sorrel soup with creme fraiche and grilled rabbit, while my wife had the grilled rack of lamb with rosemary sauce.

The Carter House is just a few steps from Old Town Eureka, where there are many beautifully restored turn-of-the-century buildings. This downtown restoration ranks with some of the best I have ever seen and is not as commercial as many.

So, Old Town Eureka and the Carter House are making Eureka a really compelling stop for the traveler on Route 101. If arriving by bus or train, arrangements can be made for a ride to the Carter House in a shiny black Bentley—the Carter House is definitely a class act.

CARTER HOUSE, Third & L Sts., Eureka, CA 95501; 707-445-1390. A seven-guest-room (four private baths) bed and breakfast recently recreated 1884 Victorian mansion in northern California. A full breakfast is served daily; dinner on weekends. Open all year. Conveniently located for guests to visit many of the recreational, cultural and natural attractions of Humboldt County. No pets. Mark and Christi Carter, owners/hosts.

DIRECTIONS: Eureka is approx. 200 mi. north of San Francisco on Hwy. 101, the main north/south highway running the entire length of the West Coast.

THE GINGERBREAD MANSION
Ferndale, California

What a fun place this is! From the moment innkeeper Ken Torbert showed me to the Fountain Suite with its fabulous fireplace, chaise lounge and two old-fashioned Victorian clawfoot tubs, I knew I was in the lap of luxury. In fact, my wife and I couldn't wait to slide into his-and-her firelight-illuminated bubble baths after a hard day of touring.

If the Fountain Suite is occupied, there are eight other spacious rooms to inhabit here, including the deluxe Gingerbread Suite with its "toesy-to-toesy" tubs, or the romantic Rose Suite or Lilac Room. Each is unique and elegantly furnished with antiques. The rooms are spacious and papered in delicate patterns. Attention to detail is obvious. "We're sticklers for all the little things that make our guests comfortable," Ken confided to me. The hand-dipped chocolates waiting at the bedside were two of those little details.

Ken has created a showplace with his inn. The small village of Ferndale, often called the Victorian Village, is something of a marvel in itself. Many examples of Victoriana still exist here, harking back to the late 1880s when Scandinavian, Swiss-Italian and Portuguese dairy farmers prospered and built splendid homes known as "Butterfat Palaces" in the Eastlake, Carpenter Gothic and Queen Anne styles. Ferndale has, in fact, been designated a State Historic Landmark.

None of these homes is more of a standout than the Gingerbread Mansion. The spectacular peach and yellow showplace is a combination of the Queen Anne and Eastlake architectural styles accented by elaborate woodwork around turrets, gables and porches. Three-story fuchsias, boxwood topiaries and a fountain with two camellia trees add to the inn's English garden.

Originally built as a doctor's residence in 1899, the home was later enlarged and used as a hospital. Its checkered past also includes stints as a rest home, an American Legion Hall and an apartment building. Ken rescued the structure in 1983, enventually expanding it to nine rooms and suites with private baths, plus four parlors.

The furnishings are Victorian, yet comfortable. A number of fireplaces offer cozy spots for relaxing. Afternoon tea and cakes are served in the parlors, where there are books, magazines and a mind-boggling thousand-piece jigsaw puzzle of the inn.

Ken takes exceptional care in running the inn. His full breakfasts are served family style in the formal dining room overlooking the marvelous garden and fountain. Two large lace-covered tables are set with green depression glass. Home-baked goodies, including his special chocolate zucchini bread, local cheeses, cakes, breads, baked egg dishes, fruit, fresh-squeezed orange juice and rich brewed coffee are the fare.

Dinner suggestions are freely given and include recommendations to local restaurants. Leave for dinner early to explore the village. I found all sorts of interesting shops, including businesses that have been in operation since the 1880s: the pharmacy, the local newspaper, a wonderful old mercantile store, as well as a shop full of old and rare books, a candy factory, a blacksmith, and many crafts shops and galleries.

THE GINGERBREAD MANSION, 400 Berding St., Ferndale, CA 95536; 707-786-4000/1-800-952-4136.

A nine-guestroom (private baths) Victorian mansion in a historic landmark Victorian village in northern Calif., five mi. from the Pacific Coast. Queen beds; rooms with both queen and twin beds available. Breakfast and afternoon tea included. Recommendations and reservations made for restaurants within walking distance. Open year-round. Garden, games, puzzles and bicycles on premises. Unique village for sightseeing, shopping, antiquing, visiting crafts shops, art galleries, museum, repertory theater, coastal drives, Avenue of the Giants (redwoods), river activities, festivals and many other events nearby. No pets. No smoking. CCs: Visa, MC. Ken Torbert, owner/host.

DIRECTIONS: From Hwy. 101, take Fernbridge exit and continue five mi. to Ferndale.

Mendocino Coast

Mendocino is a picturesque village with many well-preserved 19th-century buildings and homes. The architecture reflects the New England roots of the town's settlers. If you drive to Mendocino by way of Highway 128, you'll pass through Boonville and get a good look at the budding wineries of the newly revitalized Anderson Valley. The other approach, along the coast highway, will take you through fishing villages and the town of Gualala. Don't be surprised if you find some recognizable scenes in the town of Mendocino since "Murder, She Wrote" is filmed here. The area code for the numbers listed below is 707.

EVENTS

YEAR-ROUND	Skunk Train (info: 964-6371)
DECEMBER–JANUARY	Grey Whales' migration south
FEBRUARY–MARCH	Winter storms, big Pacific waves
MARCH	Mendocino Whale Festival (info: 1-800-726-2780 or 964-3153)
MAY	Food & Wine Festival (937-0113)
MAY	Mendocino Heritage Day Celebration (1-800-726-2780)
JUNE, END OF	World's Largest Salmon Barbeque, Fort Bragg (964-6598)
JULY 4TH	Mendocino Village (964-3153)
JULY, MIDDLE TO END	Mendocino Music Festival (info: 964-3153)
SEPTEMBER, MIDDLE	Winesong: Wine & Food Tasting (info: 964-5185)
DECEMBER, MIDDLE TO LATE	Christmas Festival (964-3153)

SIGHTS
Anderson Valley wineries
Botanical Gardens
Pygmy Forest
Village of Mendocino

AGATE COVE INN
Mendocino, California

We have visited many memorable inns, but Agate Cove is near the top for its spectacular and secluded view of the Pacific Ocean and the rugged coastline, all near the little northwestern California community of Mendocino, a National Historic village.

With their B&B guests in mind, Jake Zahavi and Sallie McConnell added an expansive living room overlooking the ocean to their main house, which was built in 1860. Here, guests are treated to a sumptuous breakfast, including fresh fruit, juice, fresh baked breads, coffee, tea and special omelets with a choice of fillings, as well as other good things cooked on an antique wood stove. With the surf crashing on the rocks below and exploding into colorful mists, it is a breakfast experience not to be forgotten.

Guests stay in modern cottages amidst Pacific cypress and abundant apple trees, whose products may serve the breakfast table all year long. Each cottage has a separate entry with parking nearby, and they all have either a king or queen four-poster bed, some with canopy tops, country type wallpaper and antique quilts. All but one has a fireplace and a view of the ocean.

This is also an inn with a new garden area and all but one cottage has an outside deck with flower boxes and deck chairs, so you may either wave to your neighbor, stroll across the lawn for some pleasant conversation or stay put and read the San Francisco paper that is delivered to you each morning.

AGATE COVE INN, Box 1150, 11201 N. Lansing St., Mendocino, CA 95460; 707-937-0551.

A 10-guestroom (individual and double bungalows with private baths) seaside B&B on the rugged Mendocino coast in northwestern California. Franklin fireplaces, heating, TV, coffee makers, king or queen beds, and ocean views. Complimentary big country breakfast. Open year-round. Fine galleries, antiques, artisans and craftsmen in shops, excellent restaurants in village and nearby. No pets. Two dogs in residence. Smoking outside. CCs: Visa, MC, AE, DI. Jake Zahavi and Sallie McConnell, owners/hosts.

DIRECTIONS: From Hwy. 1, take Lansing St. exit westward toward ocean.

GLENDEVEN
Mendocino, California

This section of northern California on Highway 1 is rapidly becoming a weekend and midweek vacation area for residents of the Bay area. The drive up the coast with its tremendous cliffs and headlands is most spectacular. Glendeven is actually in Little River, just a mile and a half south of the historic coastal town of Mendocino, with its interesting shops, galleries and restaurants.

Innkeepers Jan and Janet de Vries told me that the original farmhouse, barn and watertower were built by Isaiah Stevens in 1867. I must say that he picked a very gracious location and today this Victorian house is a cheerful bed-and-breakfast inn.

The center of activity is in the main farmhouse living room, with a fireplace, a baby grand piano, and windows facing south affording an extraordinary view of the well-tended garden and the bay. Both Jan and Janet de Vries are designers and are involved in contemporary arts and crafts, as evidenced by the ceramics, the paintings and the numerous gallery notices.

The guestrooms have quite unusual furnishings with a generous number of antiques as well as contemporary decorations. The Stevenscroft rooms and

Eastlin suite have their own fireplaces and decks. All guestrooms have views of the bay or the gardens. A refurbished barn has been converted into a two-story suite, perfect for four.

The continental breakfast is generous, including fresh orange juice, fresh fruit or baked apple, muffins, morning cakes, coffee, tea, and baskets of brown hard-boiled eggs.

GLENDEVEN, 8221 North Highway 1, Little River. CA 95456; 707-937-0083.

An 11-guestroom (nine private baths) bed-and-breakfast elegant farmhouse/inn on a headland meadow overlooking Little River Bay. Queen, double and twin beds. Open year-round. Most convenient for enjoyable excursions to the northern California coastal towns and many nearby parks and beaches. No pets. CCs: Visa, MC. Jan and Janet de Vries, owners/hosts.

DIRECTIONS: Either follow coastal Hwy. 1 all the way from San Francisco, skirting the shores of the Pacific, or follow Hwy. 101 to Cloverdale, Rte. 128 to Hwy. 1, and then proceed north to Little River.

HARBOR HOUSE
Elk, California

This is another good place to greet spring, because spring comes lustily and vigorously in this part of the world, and the sea in its many moods washes ashore gently or raucously, but the rhythm never ceases. I awaken in the morning to look through the trees to the great rock formations that seem to have been thrown almost helter-skelter from the end of the headlands. Helen and Dean Turner, the innkeepers, had thoughtfully provided a very comfortable chair in the window, with a perfect view of the sea stacks and tunnels, which, along with the arches, caves and small islands, provide an unusual view from the inn.

This particular group of rock formations was at one time a staging area for the loading and the unloading of lumber schooners. Fortunately, the story of this community has been graphically presented in the unusual brochure of the inn, with dramatic photographs showing just the scenes that I have described.

The subtitle for Harbor House on the rustic sign on Route 1 is "By the Sea." Fewer words are more apt than these. Although the main entrance is on the highway, the immediate focus of all the attention is in the rear of the inn, which looks out over the Pacific, and almost every guestroom has this view.

The main building of the inn was built in 1916 as an executive's residence. The construction is entirely of virgin redwood from the nearby Albion Forest. In fact, it is an enlarged version of the "Home of Redwood" exhibit building of the 1915 Panama-Pacific International Exposition in San Francisco.

Guestrooms in the main building and adjacent cottages are individually heated and have private baths. Fireplaces and parlor stoves are stocked with wood, and some of the accommodations have sun decks.

I reflected that were it not for the dominance of the sea, the view from the *other* side of the house across the meadows and into the low coastal hills could be thought of as very beautiful.

Because Helen and Dean Turner have always had a great deal of involvement and interest in the arts, from time to time Harbor House presents programs by soloists and chamber music players. The living room with its wood paneling provides an ideal atmosphere. As Helen says, "So many artists live on the coast and an intimate concert in the living room is a wonderful way to hear them." Also, Helen tells me, "Sometimes these concerts are spontaneous and informal, as a talented guest sits down at the Steinway or picks up the guitar."

Our dinner was the nice, slow, mellow kind I love and get so rarely. It was such pleasant, unhurried service. We were free to be alone together or speak to others if we wished, a wonderful blend of solitude and society.

We got wonderful pictures of all the colorful flowers and scenery. Beautiful as the pictures are, they do not capture what it was like to be there, or explain why I felt homesick when I had to leave.

HARBOR HOUSE, 5600 S. Hwy. #1, Box 369, Elk, CA 95432; 707-877-3203.
A six-guestroom, four-cottage (private baths) seaside inn, 16 mi. south of Mendocino, overlooking the Pacific. King and queen beds available. Fireplaces in four cot-

tages and five rooms. Breakfast and dinner served daily to houseguests. Open year-round. Private beach, ocean wading, abalone and shell hunting, fishing, and hiking on grounds. Golf, biking, boating, ocean white-water tours, deep-sea fishing and canoeing nearby. No pets. Two cats in residence. No credit cards. Dean and Helen Turner, innkeepers.

DIRECTIONS: Elk is approx. three hrs. from Golden Gate Bridge. Take Hwy. 101 to Cloverdale, then Hwy. 128 west to Hwy. 1. Continue on Hwy. 1 south six mi. to Harbor House.

INN EVENTS: SEPTEMBER 7 OR 14—Great Day in Elk
  NOVEMBER—Thanksgiving Feast
  DECEMBER—Christmas Feast and Special Holiday Decor

THE HEADLANDS INN

Mendocino, California

"I seem to be remembered for our breakfasts," stated Sharon Hyman, owner of The Headlands Inn along with her husband, David. My breakfast at the inn was indeed a memorable event. Responding to a subtle knock around 9:00 A.M. my first morning at the inn, I retrieved the heaping breakfast tray which, along with the morning newspaper, had been set outside my door. I wrapped myself in the thick terry bathrobe provided by the inn and set the meal on a table close to the wood stove. Pouring a cup of coffee, I sat down to enjoy this

private offering. Steam rose from a plate with Florentine ham rolls smothered in a creamy cheddar cheese sauce. If that weren't enough, there was also a baked pear in a carmel ginger sauce topped with vanilla yogurt and gingerbread muffins. What a wonderful idea: breakfast in bed or, in my case, by the fire every morning.

Being an early riser, I had already lit the fire in my fireplace to cut the early morning chill typical of the Northern Pacific coast. My room, called the Betsy Strauss room, had a bay window that overlooked beautiful English gardens and the waves crashing on the rocks in the cove where the big river flows into the ocean.

Not only was I surrounded by natural beauty, but the inn itself has quite a history to relay. Originally built as a barber shop in 1868 on Main Street for John Barry, the local barber, a second story was added to the Victorian structure several years later to create living quarters for John's family. In 1884, it became a restaurant and hotel. Late in the 1800s, the ownership changed once more, and the house was moved to its present location. (Keep in mind that moving a house in those days was quite a sight to see. Large logs were used as natural rollers, and with a team of horses pulling the sturdy structure over them, you can be sure it was the local entertainment for the day.) Around 1924, John Strauss and his wife, Bessie, purchased the house, and it was their family home until 1979. The history has been kept alive by naming the rooms after past owners.

Today the house has four capacious guestrooms and a private cottage with an unusual embossed tin ceiling. All have their own wood-burning stoves. There are two parlors, one on each floor, filled with casual antiques. The front parlor has an Austrian piano, dating from the 1800s that still boasts a wonderful tone. Guests are encouraged to play. During holidays and summer weekends the piano is played by talented local youth while afternoon tea is served. Tea is offered each day with an array of cookies and nuts. The upstairs parlor has a small refrigerator, tucked away in an armoire, available for guests.

Owners David and Sharon discovered Mendocino while passing through on a camping trip and loved the quaint little village and exquisite natural beauty of the area. Two years later, in October 1992, they were able to purchase the Headlands Inn and fulfill a shared vision. Sharon's career in interior design and marketing and David's in sales and management have prepared them for this venture.

I discovered everything is within easy walking distance of the inn. Many novelty shops and art galleries displayed local talents. I had been told that some famous artists live here, enjoying their anonymity within the small village. Restaurants featuring varied cuisine could be spotted along the main streets, and even in some back alleyways. At the rugged coastal cliffs, paths wove downward to beaches below. A walk along the Headlands, just west of town, showed me the magnificent fury of the ocean, waves spewing white water high as they crashed against rock obstacles. In nearby state parks, one can hike or go horseback riding within dense groves of redwood trees many centuries old. During my visit, I took a short drive north to the larger town of Ft. Bragg and toured the Botanical Gardens, rich in color and foliage.

THE HEADLANDS INN, P.O. Box 132, Mendocino, CA 95460; 707-937-4431.

A five-guestroom (private bath) Victorian saltbox on the corner of Albion and Howard Sts. Complimentary breakfast served at your door each morning. King and queen beds. Wood-burning fireplaces in each room, plus ocean views. Open year round. Two-night minimum stay on weekends, three or four days during holidays. No smoking. Ocean beaches, shopping, art galleries and restaurants a short walk away. Hike in the redwoods or canoe on Big River. Short drive to a small golf course. No pets. No CCs. Sharon & David Hyman, owners/hosts.

DIRECTIONS: Take Hwy. 1 along the coast to the village of Mendocino. At traffic signal, go west. Turn onto Howard St. and proceed to intersection of Howard and Albion Sts.

JOHN DOUGHERTY HOUSE
Mendocino, California

The fog was slowly rolling inland as I crossed the bridge into the town of Mendocino. The small size of the town made simple work of locating the tradi-

tional blue and white saltbox built by John Dougherty in 1867. With only six guestrooms, I was looking forward to the privacy it offered.

Owners David and Marion Wells were on hand to welcome me. "I'll take you to your room," David offered. "Tomorrow, when you've had a chance to settle in, I'll give you the grand tour."

My room was the connecting historic Water Tower, patriotically topped with an American flag. Once used to supply water to the house, it has been renovated into a guestroom with high beamed ceilings, a sturdy four-poster bed and a wood stove. The fire was already burning. There is an adjacent sitting room and a private bath. Complimentary chocolates and wine were set out on the antique table. I resisted their temptation as I unpacked, convincing myself they could serve as dessert later.

David had told me that restaurants and shops were within easy walking distance, so I pulled on a heavy sweater to ward off the early evening chill and set out to find a place to dine. The streets were quiet; only the fog horn interrupted systematically with its mournful call. I found several restaurants within a short distance, so I decided to continue my explorations, window shopping along the way. I wouldn't be needing my car here.

On my return to the house, a large golden-yellow cat greeted me at the front door, leaning against my legs and purring. "That's Triston, the head inn cat," Marion said, looking up from her evening book work. "Basil and Coriander are around here somewhere. You can tell I named them, since my favorite hobby is gardening." I had noted the English garden surrounding the house. Now I knew who was responsible for its splendor.

"How did you and David become owners here?" I inquired.

Marion told me they had passed through on a motorcycle trip from Los Angeles to Canada (motorcycles being David's hobby). They fell in love with Mendocino at first sight. In 1988, David left behind a career in restaurant supply sales, and Marion a position as legal secretary, to purchase the historic John Dougherty House. They renovated, decorating in early American style, and continue to add antiques as David finds them. Both have thrived on the transition, mostly because of their natural enjoyment of people.

I bid Marion good-night, stating that I had a date with some bedtime chocolates.

Early the next morning, I found my way to the common room where warmed scones, drizzled in melted butter and accompanied by an abundant platter of fresh fruit, awaited ravenous guests. The common room, set up as a New England "Keeping Room," is graced with stencilled walls, Currier & Ives prints and refinished antiques. A roaring fire and a spectacular view of the Pacific was the backdrop to the friendly conversation. One of the guests invited me to accompany him for a walk to the Mendocino Headlands, which offers overwhelming ocean sights from the high bluffs. I also planned a hike to one of the nearby beaches.

The solitude of the veranda invited me. I wandered out, sipping my coffee, to inhale the scent of salt air mingled with the sweet smell from Marion's garden.

JOHN DOUGHERTY HOUSE, 571 Ukiah St., P.O. Box 817, Mendocino, CA 95460; 707-937-5266.

Historic six-guestroom (private baths) country bed and breakfast. Five woodburning fireplaces. Breakfast included. TV. Queen beds. Open all year. Weekend and holiday minimum stays. Restricted smoking. Short walk to historic village center, shopping, restaurants and beaches. No pets. Three cats in residence. David and Marion Wells, owners/hosts.

DIRECTIONS: West on Ukiah St., approximately one block past post office. House on left side.

JOSHUA GRINDLE INN
Mendocino, California

A New Englander searching for a place to remind him of his home should pay a visit to Mendocino. Not only is the spectacular coastal scenery reminiscent of New England, but many of the wooden Victorian homes resemble those built in the Northeast.

In the 1870s, Joshua Grindle, a native of Maine, came to Mendocino to try his hand in the lumber business. He built a beautiful Italianate house for his bride in 1879 and went to work at a nearby mill.

Californians Arlene and Jim Moorehead, although not New Englanders, were also taken by the beauty of Mendocino and were delighted to be able to buy the Grindle house in 1989, which had already been converted to an inn in 1978.

The Joshua Grindle Inn's five guestrooms in the main house all have private baths and are exquisitely decorated with early American furnishings, etchings and oil paintings. In a cottage adjacent to the inn are two other bedrooms complete with Franklin fireplace. A watertower houses three more guestrooms, two with fireplace.

The parlor off the entrance is beautifully wallpapered, has an antique pump organ and a fireplace decorated with tiles made in England. Here on a chest there is always sherry and a bowl of fresh fruit provided by the Mooreheads. Hospitality abounds in the dining room, where guests may relax at a long pine table while Arlene and Jim serve up a delicious, full breakfast, complete with fresh fruit, homemade muffins, quiche, coffee and tea.

As the inn is only a few short blocks from the main street, it is best to set aside time to walk, browse and explore the many little alleys, paths, shops, art galleries and historic buildings that make up Mendocino.

JOSHUA GRINDLE INN, Box 647, 44800 Little Lake, Mendocino, CA 95460; 707-937-4143.

A 10-guestroom (private baths) attractive Victorian inn on California's northern coast. Full breakfast included in room rate. Queen and twin beds. Open all year. Limited wheelchair access. Many cultural, recreational and historic attractions nearby. No telephone, television, smoking or pets. Two cats in residence. Two-night minimum on weekends. CCs: Visa, MC. Arlene and Jim Moorehead, owners/hosts.

DIRECTIONS: Starting from San Francisco, travel on Hwy. 101 north to Cloverdale, then Rte. 128W and take Hwy. 1 north to Mendocino. Alternate route is to take scenic Hwy. 1 north to Mendocino.

JUGHANDLE BEACH COUNTRY BED & BREAKFAST

Mendocino, California

Su and Jerry Schlecht purchased the Jughandle Beach Country B&B in 1988. "The house answered all our wishes," Su told me as we relaxed on the comfortable wraparound porch, with its view of the glorious Pacific Ocean sunset. "We were looking for a farmhouse in the country with a little land and an ocean view." In the Schlechts' careers as salespersons, their sales area had included northern California, and they grew to love the Mendocino/Fort Bragg area best.

I had arrived on the northern California coast hoping to stay in a place just like this. The blue and white farmhouse is five miles north of the artists' community of Mendocino and close to the lumber and fishing town of Fort Bragg, with its Skunk Train excursion railroad and excellent restaurants. Jughandle is just across from the Jughandle State Reserve, with miles of hiking trails and private beaches. During migration season, (January thru March) whale watching is spectacular.

Built by Swedish immigrants in 1883, the Schlechts' farmhouse has been furnished with family antiques and collectibles. Both Su and Jerry paint, and Su's miniature clay sculptures decorate the living room.

Guestrooms are comfortable, decorated with chenille bedspreads, hand-made quilts and lace curtains. All have private baths, in-room coffee, tea, chocolates and radios.

Breakfast includes fresh-squeezed orange juice, homemade shortbread, gooey baked apples with cheese flowers, feathered eggs, waffles with blackberry or blueberry syrup, and the Jughandle blend of Thanksgiving coffee or tea.

Jughandle Beach Country B&B is a relaxing, comfortable, unpretentious inn where you are treated with warmth. It is centrally located between Mendocino and Fort Bragg and within a short drive from the lovely and unusual coastal Botanical Gardens, with its collection of native plants and rhododendron groves.

JUGHANDLE BEACH COUNTRY BED AND BREAKFAST, 32980 Gibney Lane, Mendocino, CA 95437; 707-964-1415.

A four-guestroom (private baths) country farm house located within walking distance of the beach. Queen, double and twin beds. Breakfast included. One cat in residence. No CCs. Su and Jerry Schlecht, owners/hosts.

DIRECTIONS: From San Francisco, take Hwy. 101 to Hwy. 1, or stay on Hwy. 101 to Cloverdale, then 128 to Hwy. 1. Located five mi. north of village of Mendocino.

MENDOCINO FARMHOUSE
Mendocino, California

Close your eyes and picture the perfect farmhouse: two stories with a peaked roof, tan with white trim, a front porch swing for lazy evenings, and a white picket fence covered here and there with climbing roses—nestled in a clearing surrounded by redwoods and firs. Open your eyes. You've arrived at the Mendocino Farmhouse.

Marge and Bud Kamb had this same vision when they built their home in 1975. "We wanted high ceilings, paned windows and a swing on the porch," said Marge. The Kambs turned their home into a bed and breakfast four years ago when the last of their children left. Recently they converted the barn into two guestrooms, both with private baths, stone fireplaces and separate sitting areas.

The other three rooms are in the main house and are named after the Kamb's children. Each room is homey and comfortable. An antique white iron-and-brass bed is featured in Karen's Room, and John's Room is dominated by a sturdy seaman's chest. Most of the rooms have cozy window seats and

views to the English garden below, or, as in Jim's Room, to the fish pond and its visiting wildlife.

The common rooms are decorated with antiques. A large fireplace, a variety of books and a piano invite guests into the living room. Marge serves a full country breakfast where fresh berries from her garden may appear when in season. She also uses other garden ingredients in her special eggs. Homemade popovers become even more scrumptious with last summer's blackberry jam.

I was lucky to visit in the early summer, when Marge's garden handiwork was in full bloom. Her interest in floral designing has prompted her to grow her own materials. She gave me a tour, accompanied by Sidney, the golden retriever, and the feline contingent, Bonnie, Sadie and Una.

After the tour, I decided to drive the two miles to the village of Mendocino where the famous Mendocino Art Center was having an afternoon jazz concert. Big River beach, canoe rentals and Russian Gulch State park are all nearby.

MENDOCINO FARMHOUSE, 43410 Comptche-Ukiah Rd., Box 247, Mendocino, CA 95460; 707-937-0241.

A five-guestroom (private baths) farmhouse inn located on the rugged Mendocino coast. King, queen and twin beds. Open all year. Breakfast included. Pets by arrangement. Four cats and one dog in residence. Smoking restricted. No CCs. Marge and Bud Kamb, owners/hosts.

DIRECTIONS: From Hwy. 1, turn onto Comptche-Ukiah Rd., just south of Mendocino. Go 1-1/2 mi. to Olson Ln. Turn left. House is at end on right.

INN EVENTS: DECEMBER 1–6—Christmas Open House

PUDDING CREEK INN
Fort Bragg, California

Rumor has it that there might be jewels buried on the grounds around Pudding Creek Inn! Could be, as the inn—actually two homes connected by an enclosed garden court—was built in 1884 by a Russian count, who is said to have fled his homeland with riches that were not his own. Pudding Creek Inn was opened in 1980 as a Bed and Breakfast, and the new owners are trying hard to continue its fine reputation.

Pudding Creek Inn has ten guestrooms, all with private baths, and two have original working fireplaces. The rooms, cozy and comfortable, are attractively decorated in a victorian style and have the native wood lumbered in this area.

A full breakfast, consisting of fresh fruit, juice, Carol's delicious homemade

coffee cakes, main egg dish, and coffee and teas, is served from 8:00-10:00 A.M. The enclosed garden area, separating one house from the other, has a fountain and an abundance of fuchsias, ferns, impatiens and begonias. In the early evening it's an ideal place to relax and meet the other inn guests and enjoy a quiet social hour. Complimentary beverages are served throughout the day in the TV recreation room.

Pudding Creek is in a convenient location on Main Street in the north part of Fort Bragg. The ocean, the famous Skunk Train Depot, shops and restaurants are within easy walking distance of the inn. And the city has much to brag about when it comes to nearby scenic excursions and recreational activities. There is boating, diving, tennis, whale watching and bicycling. And don't forget, if you feel lucky and adventurous, you could strike it rich by uncovering the count's hidden treasure!

PUDDING CREEK INN, 700 North Main St., Fort Bragg, CA 95437; 707-964-9529.

A 10-guestroom (private baths) inn on Ft. Bragg's main street. All size beds. Full breakfast included. Television & rec. room. Open all year. Restaurants nearby. Skunk Railroad, and all the diversions offered by a seaside town nearby. No telephones, no televisions. No pets. Garry & Carole Anloff & Jacques Woltman owners/hosts.

DIRECTIONS: Driving from the south, take Hwy. 101 to Cloverdale then, Rte. 128 west to Hwy. 1, and continue north to Fort Bragg. Inn is located at the north end of the city.

RACHEL'S INN
Mendocino, California

Rachel Binah leads a dedicated life: dedicated to her lovely two-story Victorian bed-and-breakfast inn plus barn; dedicated to making her guests' stay

memorable and enjoyable; and dedicated to preserving a way of life that sustains and supports environmental treasures.

Several years ago, Rachel purchased the dilapidated, unoccupied structure "as is." "It was like putting a collage back together," she told me as we stood at the front door framed by geraniums and daisies. The sign on the door directly announces her commitment to preservation of the picturesque Pacific coastline that is just a few blocks away—"This business is opposed to oil drilling and exploration on our coast." Rachel has taken her political beliefs from conversation around the breakfast table to action as a delegate to the 1988 Democratic Convention.

Rachel chose to focus her attention not only on decor at her new inn, but also on personal attention to her guests. "If you want to be anonymous, you go to a hotel. But at a bed and breakfast, you expect personal attention."

Rachel designed the inn in a very simple way, with the downstairs open, "like a blank canvas. It's the guests who create the picture," she told me. The rooms are furnished with a combination of antiques and contemporary pieces, and the atmosphere is simple and uncluttered. The dining room/parlor has an ocean view and piano.

The four guestrooms are all unique. Three bedrooms on the second floor share a small sitting area, where sherry and fruit or short bread are served. The Grey Room looks south down the rugged coast. All rooms have private baths and include extra towels and fresh flowers.

A few feet away is the barn consisting of a central sitting area with fireplace, two full suites with fireplaces, wet bars and decks overlooking deer meadows, plus two guestrooms (one fully wheelchair-accessible).

Rachel's is known for spectacular and generous breakfasts (which I dare anyone to finish), accompanied by stimulating conversation. She frequently serves "exotic fare."

The artistic village of Mendocino, with galleries and unusual shops, is only a two-mile drive away, and the inn is located right next to Van Damme State Park, an eighty-four acre parcel of coastal parkland where you can walk through woods and fields that finally lead to the ocean. As Rachel tells her guests, "There's a path through the meadows outside; follow it past the pines and keep going until you get to the bluff overlooking the ocean. Spend a half-hour there and then tell me you wouldn't become active in preserving the coast if you were in my place."

RACHEL'S INN, P.O. Box 134, Mendocino, CA 95460; 707-937-0088.

A eight-guestroom (private baths) Victorian near the ocean. Queen and twin beds. Open all year. Breakfast included. Children and smoking permitted. No pets. No credit cards. Rachel Binah, owner/host.

DIRECTIONS: North of Hwy. 1 past Cloverdale. Left on Hwy. 128 to Hwy. 1 (45 mi.). Continue north on Hwy. 1 to Little River. Rachel's is the second left after Van Damme State Park.

STANFORD INN BY THE SEA

Mendocino, California

This section of the northern California coast is one of the most satisfying travel experiences in North America, and a particular treat is an evening walk in the sharp, clean air on the Mendocino headlands, while the dazzling sunset highlights the rugged coastline. Mendocino itself is now designated as a historic site, and the restoration and architecture conform to the general feeling of the 1800s. Wandering through the town is like an expedition into the past.

It was a particular pleasure to visit Joan and Jeff Stanford at the Inn. I had heard many good things about them from the time they were the innkeepers at a bed-and-breakfast inn in Carmel to the present, where they keep upgrading their unusually attractive bed-and-breakfast hostelry. Here is a perfect example of what vision and dreams can do to an ordinary architectural elongated rectangular so-so motel.

The situation certainly provides a great advantage, because there is a beautiful view of the sea and some of the town of Mendocino. Each of the guestrooms opens onto a deck that is lined with all varieties of flowers. All have chairs and a table so that guests can enjoy the splendid view, particularly of the sunsets. You will also see Stanford's organic farm, Big River Nurseries, and

their llamas, the first, an anniversary present to Joan. One of the inn's green-houses is home to the inn's new swimming pool, spa and sauna.

The guestrooms have wood-burning fireplaces, books, plants, secretaries, local art and many interesting paintings. There are four-poster and sleigh beds with down comforters and attractive tablecloths, antiques, and antique repro-ductions.

Joan and Jeff will make dinner reservations and advise guests on galleries and sights to be seen. They have walked all of the walks, and at the Stanford's Catch A Canoe & Bicycle, their livery and shop, guests can acquire canoes for exploring Big River Estuary or borrow mountain bicycles.

STANFORD INN BY THE SEA, P.O. Box 487, Mendocino, CA 95460; 707-937-5615.

A 26-guestroom (private baths) elegantly rustic lodge, just a couple of minutes from the center of Mendocino, with ocean and village views and woodburning fire-places. Continental breakfast. King and queen beds. Dogs, cats and llamas abound. Open every day in the year. Wheelchair access. Centrally located to enjoy all of the historic, scenic and artistic attractions of the Mendocino-Fort Bragg coast. CCs: Visa, MC, AE, CB, ER, DI. Joan and Jeff Stanford, owners/hosts.

DIRECTIONS: From San Francisco, follow coastal Hwy. 1 north to Mendocino, or follow Hwy. 101 to Cloverdale; 128 to coastal Hwy. 1 and then north. Two mi. north of Little River (just to the south of Big River) turn east on Comptche-Ukiah Rd. and look for the Big River Lodge sign.

WHALE WATCH INN BY THE SEA

Gualala, California

"About as close to perfect as you can get," raved one enthusiastic couple about the Whale Watch Inn. To be sure, everything about this splendid and idyllic inn—the location, the furnishings and amenities, the staff, the sweeping ocean views, even the sounds of the surf and the barking sea lions—seems to have been orchestrated to provide guests with an experience in relaxation.

Perched on a bluff just ninety feet above the Pacific, each of the eighteen guestrooms offers dramatic vistas of the coast and ocean beyond. The contemporary inn was built in stages from 1974 through 1985 and now consists of five buildings in a landscaped setting. Wood-burning fireplaces provide warmth and romantic ambiance in nearly all the rooms, while most also have large two-person spas with whirlpools. The Bath Suite, a perennial favorite, features a spiral staircase leading to a second-story whirlpool bath with a skylight and a 270-degree view of the coast. Several of the rooms are furnished with complete kitchens. Each room is individually decorated in a comtemporary style.

Guests may wander at their leisure through the gardens and natural woodlands that comprise much of the two-acre site. At the edge of the bluff, a private stairway leads to the secluded beach below. From November to May, migrating California gray whales are a frequent sight. By "sight" I don't mean the whole animal; only their backs and the water spouting from their blowholes are visible. But even that is enough for quite a thrill. The inn has a large

common area with floor-to-ceiling windows and an expansive deck that provides an excellent lookout. Here you will also find a large telescope and a library with an emphasis on books about natural history and marine life.

Owners Jim and Kazuko Popplewell and family spare no effort in meeting their guests' every need. Breakfast is delivered to your room. Don't be surprised to find Belgian waffles, mushroom-crusted quiche or crepes filled with fresh fruit in a cream sauce.

The town of Gualala is nearby. This historic community has a colorful past: Pomo Indians, Russian trappers, Mexican land owners, German settlers and Chinese cooks have all made their homes here. However, I just stayed on the deck and watched the entertainment of the waves.

WHALE WATCH INN BY THE SEA, 35100 Hwy. 1, Gualala, CA 95445; 707-884-3667. 1-800-whale 42

An 18-guestroom (private baths) contemporary small inn on rock cliffs over the Pacific Ocean about three hrs. north of San Francisco, in northern California. Queen beds. Full breakfast. Open all year. Whale watching in winter and early spring. Smoking on decks only. Beach and driftwood exploring. CCs: Visa, MC, AE. Jim and Kazuko Popplewell, owners/hosts.

DIRECTIONS: Take Hwy. 101 to the Washington Blvd. exit in Petaluma, go west through Two Rock and Valley Ford to Bodega Bay. Follow Hwy. 1 north to the Whale Watch at Anchor Bay, five miles north of Gualala. Or take Hwy. 101 to the River Road exit four miles north of Santa Rosa. Go west through Guerneville to Jenner. Follow Hwy. 1 north to the Inn.

WHITEGATE INN
Mendocino, CA

The Whitegate Inn reflects the Victorian charm of a century ago and is a historical highlight of Mendocino village. Described in an 1887 news article as "one of the most elegant and best appointed residents in town", the Inn's beauty and character endure. Stateley bay windows, steep gabled roof, uniquely patterned fish-scale shingles and original redwood siding attest to the timeless craftsmanship.

In June of 1992, the owners Carol and George Bechtloff moved from Southern California to Northern California and bought the already existing Bed and Breakfast. They also brought Carol's five years' experience in interior designing and George's 22 years as a contractor.

They kept the lovely original wallpaper and the sparkling crystal chandeliers and added a historic piano. Guests gather here for complimentary wine and to play with Siena, the fluffy Himalayan cat.

Adjacent to the parlor is the dining room with its large and inviting table. Breakfast may consist of egg souffle or candied apple french toast, scones, fresh fruit and juice. Amidst the splendor of the room a carved European armoire displays a large collection of American cut glass and French doors open to a spacious redwood deck and romantic gazebo.

There are six guestrooms, all with private baths, five in the house and one across the garden. The cottage features its own secluded deck, king-size bed and armoire, clawfoot tub and shower, and cable TV and refrigerator. The French rose room, a special-occasion favorite, offers a Victorian settee along with a matching armoire and bedstead, TV, refrigerator, fireplace, and ocean views. The other rooms have queen-size antique or brass beds, and most have a fireplace and/or ocean views.

Try to persuade Carol to reveal her secrets of French cooking or have George explain the Civil War mementos in the foyer or hall.

The Whitegate is a block from the best restaurant in town as well as a block from the shops.

WHITEGATE INN, 499 Howard St. or P.O. Box 150, Mendocino, CA 95460l; 707-937-4892, 1-800-531-7282. Fax: 707-937-1131.

A six-guestroom (private Bath) Victorian inn in the heart of Mendocino Village. King and queen beds. Full breakfast, no pets, two cats in residence. Carol and George Bechtloff, owners/hosts.

DIRECTIONS: From the south, turn left into the village, go two blocks, turn right onto Howard Street and go two blocks. Inn is on your right.

Mother Lode North

In the foothills of the High Sierras lies the Mother Lode, a rich vein of gold that laces the western slopes of the Sierra Nevada for 120 miles. Approximately 550 towns sprung up throughout the Mother Lode in the early 1850s, the height of California's famous Gold Rush. Two of these were Grass Valley, the richest gold mining town in the state, and Nevada City. The area code for the numbers listed below is 916.

EVENTS

FEBRUARY	Musical Theatre
FEBRUARY	Valentine's Soiree Musicale (info: 265-6124)
MARCH	Impressions of John Muir (info: 265-5040)
MARCH	Music in the Mountains (info: 265-6124)
APRIL	Antique show (info: 265-5520)
APRIL	Teddy Bear Convention (info: 265-5804)
APRIL–MAY	Living History Days (info: 273-8522)
MAY	Annual Antique Show (info: 265-6161)
JUNE	Bluegrass Festival (info: 265-2740)
JUNE	Bicycle Classic (info: 265-2692)
JULY 4	Parade and Celebration
JULY	Living History Days (info: 273-8522)
JULY	3-day Sierra Storytelling Festival (info: 265-2826)
SEPTEMBER	Constitution Day Parade (info: 265-2692)
SEPTEMBER	Living History Days (info: 273-8522)
SEPTEMBER	Theatre
OCTOBER	Designs for Living House Tour (info: 265-6124)
NOVEMBER	Antique Show & Sale (info: 265-5520)
DECEMBER	Artists' Christmas Fair (info: 265-2692)

SIGHTS

Downieville—historic town
Firehouse Museum
Yuba River—fishing and sightseeing

MURPHY'S INN
Grass Valley, California

Eureka! A word shouted by many a gold miner in early California history to express a triumph on a discovery. So "Eureka," I said when I first discovered Murphy's Inn. Built in 1866 as the personal estate of a mother lode gold baron, Murphy's Inn still retains the splendor and beauty of the Victorian era.

A showplace of the area, the inn looks much as it does in century-old etchings. The white columns of the spacious veranda are completely twined with manicured ivy, a signature of the inn. Owner Marc Murphy comes from a line of innkeepers. His great-grandmother welcomed guests to her Russian River establishment back in 1902. Marc and his wife, Rose, continue the Murphy heritage of hospitality.

Entering the inn, you will find two lovely sitting rooms with marble-tiled fireplaces, period antiques and original gas-burning chandeliers. A rich burgundy carpet enhances the dark wood.

The eight cheerful bedrooms are done in shades of mauve, burgundy and white. Floral wall papers, lace curtains and antiques complete the Victorian mood. Four have fireplaces and all have private baths.

Guests can luxuriate in an outdoor swimming spa, nestled beneath a stately Sequoia, or sunbathe on the surrounding deck. Watch the water for flecks of gold; you just might get lucky!

Breakfast is substantial enough to satisfy a miner, but much more elegant than his hardpan biscuits and thick black coffee. Marc rises early and begins preparing buttermilk Belgian waffles topped with fresh strawberries. A half grapefruit seasoned with brown sugar and raspberry brandy, choice of link or Polish kielbasa sausage, *real* maple syrup, orange juice, and freshly ground New Orleans coffee round out the meal.

Murphy's Inn is in the heart of Grass Valley's historic district and within walking distance of fine restaurants, saloons and historic landmarks. Nevada City is just minutes away. Marc and Rose are happy to share their knowledge about activities in the area. While I didn't come away with a pocket full of gold, I did feel as if I'd discovered a gold mine—Murphy's Inn.

MURPHY'S INN, 318 Neal St., Grass Valley, CA 95945; 916-273-6873.

An eight-guestroom (private baths) Victorian home in the California Gold Country. King and queen beds. Open all year. Full breakfast included. Walking distance to restaurants and historic landmarks. No smoking or pets. CCs: Visa, MC, AE. Rose and Marc Murphy, owners/hosts.

DIRECTIONS: I-80 from San Francisco and Sacramento, north. Exit on Hwy. 49 to Grass Valley. Past junction of Hwy. 20, exit on Neal St.

THE RED CASTLE INN
Nevada City, California

From its forested hillside perch overlooking the gold rush community of Nevada City, the Red Castle Inn holds stately court. Built before the Civil War and carefully restored by its present owners, noted architect Conley Weaver and his interior decorator wife, Mary Louise, the four-story mansion exudes romance. With its whimsical white icicle trim, the genuine Gothic Revival brick home is one of only two on the West Coast.

Mary Louise's volunteer work at the Oakland Museum and the Camron Stanford House Victorian Museum well prepared her for her role as innkeeper. "It gave me practice in setting the stage and serving people's needs," she told me as we looked over her collection of Victoriana.

The Weavers have combined their talents to furnish the inn with family heirlooms, antiques and a unique collection of 20th-century California art, including Buffano sculptures and Partridge etchings. Each of the four floors offers a comfortable sitting area. The light-suffused grand parlor, with its 1880s Storey and Clark pump organ, has many French doors opening onto the wide veranda which encircles the building and provides a perfect view of the Historic District. Just beyond, terraced gardens and a fountained pool provide

tranquility for strolling on warm summer evenings. I spent my afternoon tea time in the third floor reading area while Buster, the inn's popular Siamese cat (Mary Louise says he gets his own fan mail), purred in my lap.

The seven guestrooms are quite lovely. Some have balconies overlooking the treetops, where you occasionally may hear town noises. Art and antiques are again tastefully used to create individual moods. Each room has its own story to tell of the history of the imposing landmark which was called "the castle" even as it was being built in 1857-60.

Morning brings a full breakfast buffet served in the main parlor, or you may stock a tray and take it away to tables on the verandas or gardens. More romantic guests may choose to dine "a deux" in their room.

The Red Castle is only two blocks from the center of town, where antiquing, quaint shops, musicians and good restaurants await. On weekends there are live theater choices and on Saturdays guests can step back into history and take a horse-drawn carriage on a leisurely drive through the Nevada City Historic District.

THE RED CASTLE INN, 109 Prospect St., Nevada City, CA 94610; 916-265-5135.

A seven-guestroom (private bath) romantic brick Gothic Revival mansion in the historic gold rush town of Nevada City. Queen and double beds. Open all year. Close to winter and summer sports. Full breakfast included. One cat in residence. CCs: Visa, MC. Mary Louise and Conley Weaver, owners/hosts.

DIRECTIONS: From the north, take Hwy. 80 to 20, then the Coyote St. exit left to end. Go left over overpass to end, then right to crest of hill, then take a hard left onto Prospect. From the south, take Hwy. 80 to 49, then the Sacramento St. exit. Go past the Chevron Station, right up the hill, then left at fork to end of Prospect.

Mother Lode
Central

As you wander through this area, you'll find ghost towns and abandoned mining camps, as well as towns named according to the temperament of the Gold Rush days: Volcano, Rough And Ready, Savage Digging. Wonderful characters—Mark Twain, Black Bart, Horatio Alger, Lola Montez—visited the hills in those days. SR 49 runs the length of the Mother Lode Country, passing trails of the fortune hunters. I-80 and US 50 are the major east-west routes. The area code for the numbers listed below is 209.

EVENTS

FEBRUARY	Toy & Doll Show, Sutter Creek (267-0529)
MARCH	Dandelion Days Outdoor Fair, Jackson (223-0608)
MARCH	Daffodil Hill Blooms (info: 223-0608)
APRIL	Sutter Creek Duck Race (info: 267-5319)
APRIL	Arts and Crafts Show (info: 295-7791)
APRIL	Annual Home Tour & Tea (223-HOME)
MAY	Run for Gold, antique car show (223-0350)
MAY	Music at the Wineries (info: 223-6368)
MAY	Amador Country Art Show, Ione (223-1026)
MAY	Sierra Showcase of Wines, Fairgrounds
MAY–OCTOBER	Claypipers melodrama
JUNE	Italian Picnic & Parade, Sutter Hill
JUNE–JULY	Theater (info: 223-0587)
JUNE	Wine Festival (info: 245-6314)
JULY	County Fair (info: 245-6921)
SEPTEMBER	Gold Country Jubilee (info: 223-0350)
SEPTEMBER	Chaw'se Indian Pow Wow, Volcano (296-7188)
DECEMBER	Festival of Lights
DECEMBER	Sutter Creek Courrier & Ives Christmas open house
DECEMBER, 1ST WEEK	Christmas Tour

SIGHTS

Amador County Museum
Indian Grinding Rock State Park
Kennedy Mine Remains
Wineries

COURT STREET INN

Jackson, California

I always have a wonderful time when I wander through California's "Mother Lode" country, and Jackson is one of my favorite haunts. Recently I spent a weekend at the Court Street Inn and, besides having a thoroughly relaxing mini-vacation, learned some interesting historical information about the area and the inn itself.

The yellow Victorian was built in 1870 by Edward Muldoon, a jack-of-all-trades who owned a mine, operated a saloon, and ran cattle on land where he eventually discovered gold. The old home was purchased by the Blair family, who oversaw the local Wells Fargo Express Line. The Blairs' silver service is still displayed today in the dining room.

The Blairs' daughter, Grace, gathered an impressive collection of the area's Indian artifacts and housed them in her private museum, the brick structure (now called the Indian House) which is adjacent to the inn. Later, her collection was donated to the University of California at Berkeley's Lowie Museum of Anthropology.

I don't know if Grace would have approved of her museum being transformed into a two-bedroom suite, but I certainly did. The bedrooms are filled with antiques, and the pine- and redwood-beamed living room is cozy and comfortable. Original bricks surround the fireplace. The Indian House is just a few steps from the inn's hot tub/spa, and a certified massage therapist is available to soothe any muscle crinks you might be experiencing.

The main house has five guestrooms, each with some special feature like a fireplace, a romantic sitting room or a small private terrace. The rooms are tastefully decorated with antiques—if possible, take a look at the intricately woven wicker of the Victorian cradle in the Muldoon Room. All rooms have cable television.

All right, now let's get down to the important thing in life—food. While breakfast is tasty, afternoon hors d'oeuvres, including hot dips made from crab and artichoke hearts, juicy stuffed mushrooms, and Brie en croute, were superlative. Local wines are available to accompany these treats.

Gold panning and area theater groups offer entertainment if you need it, but I always seem to find enough to do just by strolling around town enjoying the shops and local atmosphere.

COURT STREET INN, 215 Court St., Jackson, CA 95642; 209-223-0416.

A seven-guestroom (five private baths) inn located in California's historic "Mother Lode" region. Queen and double beds. Full breakfast and hors d'oeuvres. Open all year. Shopping, galleries and Amador County Museum within walking distance. No pets; smoking restricted to porches. CCs: Visa, MC. Lee and Janet Hammond, owners; Scott and Gia Anderson, managers.

DIRECTIONS: Once in Jackson, go up the hill from Main St. to Court St.

THE FOXES

Sutter Creek, California

The little town of Sutter Creek is a historical gem, eagerly visited by Californians as an authentic reminder of the gold country and the Forty-Niners. Its architecture is affectionately termed "mother lode" style and is reminiscent of old Western movie sets with second stories and porches overhanging store fronts, and rough sidewalks, where careful steps are advised.

In the center of town is The Foxes, lovingly watched over by its owners,

Min and Pete Fox. The 1857 home reflects the New England origins of the builders. A second floor was added by raising the ground floor when the house suffered a fire many years ago. Three new guestrooms have been added to the rear, with car parking underneath.

Min operated an antique shop before opening the inn, so the furniture in each guestroom is most admirable. A beamed cathedral-type ceiling with chandeliers and a huge armoire grace the front Anniversary Suite, the Honeymoon Suite has a living area with a cozy fireplace, and the Victorian Suite is equally impressive, with a nine-foot-tall Victorian headboard and matching dresser.

Each guestroom boasts a queen-sized bed and its own breakfast table, set with linen tablecloths, lovely china, and gleaming silver, where a full breakfast is served each morning. A restaurant-type kitchen offers the Foxes an opportunity to show off their culinary skills. Late-afternoon refreshments revive their guests while the innkeepers make suggestions as to the various local restaurants where dinner may be taken.

There is much of historical interest to be investigated in and around Sutter Creek, along with the many antiques and crafts shops, art galleries, wineries, and old gold mines. Outdoor activities are possible on the nearby lakes and in El Dorado National Forest. Or sitting in the garden gazebo, admiring all the flowers, might be just what the doctor ordered.

THE FOXES, Box 159, 77 Main St., Sutter Creek, CA 95685; 209-267-5882.
A six-guestroom (private baths) mid-19th-century B&B in the center of a historic gold rush town. Queen beds. Complimentary full breakfast and afternoon refreshment. Open year-round. Minimum of two nights on weekends. TV in three rooms. City walking tour, antiquing, wineries, exploring gold mines, along with recreational outdoor activities, all within easy walks or drives. No pets. No smoking. Pete and Min Fox, owners/hosts.
DIRECTIONS: On State Hwy. 49, follow Main St. into town.

GATE HOUSE INN
Jackson, California

Not only miners rushed to the mother lode country of California's Sierras when gold was first discovered; merchants and traders came along to meet the needs of those miners. One such family was the Chichizolas, who established a general store in Jackson, offering supplies, clothing, food, hardware and whatever else was needed. The success of this family's efforts was later evidenced by the construction in the early 1900s of the largest and most pretentious Victorian home in the area.

Beverly and Stanley Smith purchased the Gate House in July 1988 and have added various antique furnishings to upgrade the quality of the visual surroundings. They have also fenced in the swimming pool for more privacy.

All rooms in the inn are beautifully furnished and decorated, some with original Early American wallpaper in floral designs still in perfect condition. Light fixtures are Italian imports, installed when the house was constructed, as is the marble in the living room fireplace. Marble-topped chiffoniers and sinks are prominent in the bedrooms.

A unique and separate accommodation is in the "Summerhouse," originally the caretaker's quarters and later the summerhouse for the private residence.

A full breakfast with eggs, meat, fresh fruit and juices, accompanied by an assortment of muffins, is served in the morning.

GATE HOUSE INN, 1330 Jackson Gate Rd., Jackson, CA 95642; 209-223-3500.

A five-guestroom turn-of-the-century bed-and-breakfast inn, including a separate cottage (all private baths) 45 mi. southeast of Sacramento and two mi. from Amador County Airport. Queen-size beds. A full breakfast is served, and two restaurants are within walking distance. Open all year. More than 20 excellent Amador County wineries are nearby, featuring fine chardonnay, zinfandel and Johannesberg Riesling. Also old and historic mining towns, museums, antique stores, gold-panning, golf, skiing, and water sports nearby. No pets. No smoking. CCs: Visa, MC, DI. Beverly and Stanley Smith, owners/hosts.

DIRECTIONS: From either north or south on Hwy. 49, turn off on Jackson Gate Rd. just north of its intersection with Hwy. 88 from Stockton to the west.

THE HANFORD HOUSE

Sutter Creek, California

This modern inn is an unexpected find in a very historic California town in the gold country. The original site supported an old Spanish bungalow, to which extensive additions were made in recent years. The result is reminiscent of an old San Francisco brick warehouse. The inn is decorated with lovely antiques that create a warm and comfortable atmosphere. Floors have been completely covered with slate gray carpeting so unobtrusive yet complimentary that every flower arrangement and piece of furniture is highlighted.

Guests are greeted in an attractive lounge with a cathedral-type ceiling, which opens into a dining area immediately beyond. One receives an instant impression of orderliness without a feeling of formality.

There are four guestrooms in the main house and five in a wing. Headboards for the beds are often old Spanish doors, or even barn doors turned sideways, making great conversation pieces. An old prayer bench may serve as a plant stand, while full, tilting mirrors, armoires and wicker furniture are found elsewhere, as well as teddy bears everywhere.

An expanded continental breakfast consisting of a large buffet of fruits, cheeses, juice, muffins and sweet rolls is served in the dining room. In late afternoon, a soft drink, tea or coffee may be enjoyed on the large deck overlooking the countryside or on the shaded patio. Many good restaurants are nearby.

THE HANFORD HOUSE, Box 1450, 61 Hanford St., Sutter Creek, CA 95685; 209-267-0747.
   A nine-guestroom (private baths) contemporary inn in a historic gold rush town in northern California. Queen beds. Complimentary breakfast and afternoon refreshments. Open year-round. Handicapped-accessible. Panning for gold, wineries,

antiques and specialty shops, city walking tour among Western movie-type buildings. All kinds of recreational activities. No pets. One dog in residence. Smoking on patio and deck only. CCs: Visa, MC, DI. Jim and Lucille Jacobus, owners/hosts.

DIRECTIONS: At the corner of Hanford and Main St., both being Hwy. 49 in town.

THE HEIRLOOM
Ione, California

Slightly west of the famous California towns of Jackson and Sutter Creek lies the country village of Ione. Down a country lane to a romantic English garden, surrounded by century-old trees, is a brick antebellum mansion with classic columns and wisteria-entwined porticos. Built in 1863 by a Virginian, the windows are deep-set in Southern style, a fan transom covers the front entrance, and the living room is all in off-white paneling. A Colonial staircase and mantel complete the background for the antique furnishings in this charming home. Fireplaces in the living room, dining room and winter room add warmth and ambiance to fall and winter visits.

The four seasons provide themes for the decor of the guestrooms. Innkeepers Patricia Cross and Melisande Hubbs have used jonquil yellow in the Springtime room, seafoam and dusty rose for Summer, maple-leaf colors for Autumn, and Winter shades of burgundy and blue. Three of the rooms have balconies. A handcrafted adobe cottage, with wood-burning stoves and skylights, contains the Early American Room and the Early California Room.

The Heirloom Circa 1863

Usually attired in period dress, Patricia and Melisande serve their guests a full breakfast. A typical meal will offer fresh orange juice, home-baked breads or popovers, an entrée of crêpes, soufflés, quiche, or eggs Benedict, and the very best of coffees. Breakfast may be enjoyed in bed or on the balcony, in the garden, or in the fireside dining room.

On arrival in late afternoon, guests are served refreshments. Guests will find fresh flowers, fruit and candy in their rooms.

THE HEIRLOOM, 214 Shakeley Lane, P.O. Box 322, Ione, CA 95640; 209-274-4468.

A six-guestroom (four private baths) historic bed-and-breakfast inn (circa 1863) in the heart of the gold rush country in the foothills of the Sierra Nevadas, west of Jackson and Sutter Creek. King, queen and double beds. Open year-round. Croquet, hammocks and a glider & Gazebo add to outdoor enjoyment. Historic sites, antiquing, wineries nearby. No pets. Walking distance to championship golf course. No CCs. Patricia Cross and Melisande Hubbs, owners/hosts.

DIRECTIONS: From Hwy. 88 or 16 take Hwy. 124 to Ione. Watch for the Heirloom sign on left. A short lane leads to the inn.

THE WEDGEWOOD INN
Jackson, California

Rain pelted against my windshield as I drove down the wooded private drive to the Wedgewood Inn. With great relief I pulled up in front of what I thought would be a modern B&B, having been told that the inn was built in 1987. But the charming two-story building seemed to successfully recreate the Victorian era—through the sheets of rain I could see a wrap-around porch, bay windows and lots of gingerbread trim.

While I struggled from my car, innkeeper Vic Beltz gallantly braved the downpour and came to my rescue with an umbrella and a helping hand. As I shed my dripping coat in the entryway, the rest of the greeting party, Jeannine Beltz and their sloe-eyed cocker spaniel Lacey, warmly welcomed me. "What a storm!" Jeannine exclaimed. "How about something hot to drink and a bit of cheese? Come on in—we're all in the parlor."

The other guests were gathered around the toasty wood stove. A carved pecan Austrian parlor grand piano, a rich Oriental carpet and Victorian lamp shades, made by Jeannine, complimented the warm atmosphere.

After a pleasant hour of relaxing conversation, Vic showed me to my room on the second floor. On our way up the stairs I commented on the impressive stained glass and oak entrance door. "Oh, I'm responsible for that," he told me. I found out later that Vic is not only a craftsman, but is also adept at old car restoration.

My room was comfortably furnished with lovely antiques which Vic and Jeannine have gathered over their lifetimes. Family heirlooms, including unusual collectibles and antique children's toys, add special touches. The rooms are romantic and spacious, with private baths. The Carriage House contains a two-room suite with a separate entrance and private patio.

Jeannine takes great pride and well she should in the elaborate garden. Over one acre of terraced garden park, hammocks, water fountains, a spectacular gazebo, croquet and horseshoes are frequently used by the guests.

Early-morning risers can enjoy coffee at 7:00 A.M. Breakfast is served at 9:00 A.M. and features specialties such as Eggs a la Wedgewood, along with homebaked breads. The elegant dining room displays German, Belgian, and Italian tapestries and a classic German crystal chandelier.

Tucked on five secluded acres of oaks and pines, the inn is only ten minutes from Jackson and central to the the historic gold country. Museums, wine tasting and antique shopping can be found throughout the area.

THE WEDGEWOOD INN B&B, 11941 Narcissus Rd., Jackson, CA 95642; 209-296-4300 or (for reservations) 800-933-4393.

A six-guestroom (private baths) Victorian replica located in the Sierra gold country. Queen beds. Open all year. Full breakfast. No pets. One dog in residence. Smoking restricted. CCs: Visa, MC, DI. Jeannine and Vic Beltz, owners/hosts.

DIRECTIONS: 10 min. from Jackson. Take Hwy. 88 east of Jackson 6-1/2 mi. to Irishtown-Clinton exit sign. Turn right at 2,000 ft. elev. sign. Immediately turn right on Clinton Rd. and go 6/10 of a mi. Turn left on Narcissus.

Mother Lode South

Continuing your quest for mining towns, Sonora became one of the largest and wealthiest mining towns of the Mother Lode. Today it has some of the best-kept Victorian homes in the area. For visitor information regarding the events listed below call 1-800-225-3764.

EVENTS

JANUARY	On Snow Wine Tasting, Bear Valley
MARCH	St. Patrick's Day Dinner, Dance and Line Painting, Murphy
MAY	Frog Jumping Fair and Jubilee, Angels Camp
MAY	Memorial Day, Arnold Arts & Crafts Fair
JUNE	Annual Quit Faire, Arnold
JUNE	Country Western Festival, Bear Valley
JUNE	Classic Cars, Bear Valley
JULY 4	Mark Twain Days, Angels Camp
JULY 4	Parade, Moke Hill, Angels Camp, Balley Springs, Arnold
JULY	Murphy's Homecoming
JULY–AUGUST	Bear Valley Music Events
SEPTEMBER	Labor Day, Black Bart Days, San Andreas
SEPTEMBER	Zucchini Festival, Angels Camp
OCTOBER	Lumberjack Days, West Point
OCTOBER	Oktoberfest, Murphys
NOVEMBER	Quilt Faire, Arnold
DECEMBER, 1ST WEEK	Old Fashioned Christmas, Murphy

SIGHTS

California Caverns—Cave City
Big Trees State Park—Arnold

CHATEAU DU SUREAU

Oakhurst, California

Once upon a time, there was a gentleman who became enchanted while wandering though California's Sierra foothills on a summer day. He met a fellow traveler along the road.

"Let us sit in the cool shade of this oak tree and share tales of our travels," the stranger invited. Since the day was warm, and the man lonely, he accepted.

They sat, sipping a bottle of wine and exchanging tales, until the late afternoon sun shafted light through the oaks's low hanging limbs.

"Oh, my goodness, look at the time!!" the gentleman exclaimed. "Thank you for the wine and conversation, but I must find lodging for the night and do not know of an inn nearby."

The stranger smiled, eyes sparkling, "Ah, but I have the perfect place, and only a short distance." Swirling the last liquid in his glass, he said, "In fact, this sweet nectar was a gift from the innkeeper."

After drawing a map on a well-worn strip of paper bag, the stranger made off down the road turning back just before he rounded the bend.

"Remember, Chateau du Sureau is magical—a romantic mirage—you may never wish to leave!" Punctuating the last word with a poke of his walking stick in the air, he vanished down the road.

Some time later, the gentleman stood in the evening twilight peering through four-hundred year old wrought iron gates to a luxurious hillside country estate.

Surrounded by sugar pines, manzanita and mature elderberry bushes, the terra-cotta tile roofed inn could have been nestled in the terrain of France instead of California.

Two taps with one of the lion-headed brass knockers on the heavy mahogany doors brought immediate response.

"Welcome, traveler. I am Kathryn, Directrice of the Chateau."

As the gentleman was escorted into the high-ceilinged foyer, he glanced up at the expansive cathedral windows. Bouquets of fresh Sierra wildflowers mirrored the colors of the handwoven rugs.

"Shall I check in?" he inquired, seeing no front desk.

"Oh, we never bother our guests with those details when they arrive," Kathryn said, as they made their way across the polished hardwood floors past walls hung in medieval tapestries.

The man noticed a grand salon through a wide archway. A fire in the floor-to-ceiling brick fireplace warmed other guests as they sat reading or conversing while sipping port or cognacs. Oriental rugs and French furnishings created a European ambiance. A piano melody tinkled down from the music tower.

"I have given you the Elderberry Room," Kathryn smiled. "I know you must be hungry from your journey." She turned down the goosedown comforter on the king-sized canopy bed and plumped the pillows, while he set his bags on the floor. "Enjoy your basket of goodies and tea."

Tired as he was, the man marveled at his surroundings. He allowed himself to sink into a comfortable antique chair near the crackling fire and bit into a thick sandwich. The firelight danced on the walls decorated with original artwork.

As his eyes grew heavy, he rose to wash the road dust from his bones. A luxurious, oversized marble tub, accented with French tiles, awaited him. After a long soak, wrapped in a plush terry robe, he stood on his private balcony gazing over the treetops to the starry sky.

Daylight brought new discoveries. A before-breakfast stroll over a 500-year-old paver tile walkway led to the Chateau's herb garden, around the spring-fed swimming pool, to an outdoor chess court and back to the Chateau's sunny, lace-curtained breakfast room where a full European breakfast was laid out.

"Would you prefer breakfast on the terrace?" a charming, dark-haired woman asked. "I saw you enjoying the gardens earlier."

The gentleman took his breakfast of rich espresso, fruit and German dark bread with a platter of pates, cheeses and meats to the terrace. The dark-haired woman joined him.

"I am Erna, the innkeeper," she said.

"Ah, so you are the magician," he responded. "I have sampled your elder-berry wine."

Erna, a native Austrian, sat with the gentleman and shared the secrets of the evening's menu which he discovered changes daily to use the region's finest delicacies.

"Tonight," she said, "we'll begin with shrimp and scallop sausage, followed by a carrot soup with oranges. Roasted medallions of lamb in a mild garlic sauce accompanied by tomato chutney and the freshest of vegetables will follow. Oh, and my favorite," she went on, with a delightful clap of her hands, "chocolate mocha torte for dessert!"

As she scurried off to check on the kitchen, the man called after her, "Is there more of the wine?"

"On the patio this afternoon, near the garden fountain," she responded, "Champagne and elderberry aperitif!"

He leaned back into his chair, and thought, *I must call my good friend, the travel writer. He should write in his book of this magical place.*

CHATEAU DE SUREAU, 48688 Victoria Lane, P.O. Box 577, Oakhurst, CA 93644; 209-683-6890.

A nine-guestroom French-country estate and restaurant on seven wooded acres in the Sierra foothills. King and queen beds. Elegant, private baths. Fireplaces, balconies, CD stereo system in rooms. Full European breakfast included. Lunch offered Wednesday, Thursday and Friday. Six-course prix fixe dinner nightly except Tuesday. Smoking restricted. Two blocks to town, 20 miles to Yosemite National Park, and 10 miles to Bass Lake. Nearby hiking, swimming, croquet and skiing available. Boris, the cat, roams outside. No pets allowed. CCs: V, MC. Erna Kubin-Clanin, owner; Kathryn Kincannon, Directrice (manager).

DIRECTIONS: Forty miles north of Fresno on Hwy.41. Just before Oakhurst, turn through the entry gates at Victoria Lane.

DUNBAR HOUSE 1880
Murphys, California

Somehow I wasn't surprised to see the horse-drawn carriage pull up in front of Bob and Barbara Costa's inn. It just seemed to fit. Here I was in the California gold country, history and nature surrounding me. Why not ride into town in a horse and carriage too?

It was the historic authenticity of the small town of Murphys that attracted them in the first place.

"I always wanted a big, old house. Plus I love to entertain, cook and garden, so what better way?" Barbara explained, obviously just as much in love with the idea as she was in 1987, when they purchased the 1880 Italianate Victorian. "Bob is still a pilot for the San Francisco Fire Dept., so I pretty much handle this place during the day."

At breakfast, I discovered where Barbara's mother's real talents lie, as I helped myself from a huge platter of homemade scones, bread and muffins, still warm from baking. I was careful to save room for a special crab souffle just coming out of the oven. The large dining room was furnished in oak, the cabinet buffets are filled with crystal and silver, with lace curtains over the windows. The wood stove and hutches filled with knick-knacks just added to the warm, cozy feeling. If you are feeling the need for privacy, just request that breakfast be delivered to your door. In the warm months, the garden becomes the favorite spot to dine.

Even though Dunbar has exceeded the century mark, I found it to be updated in just the right ways. Central heating and air conditioning are throughout the house. TVs and VCRs exist in each of the four guestrooms, as well as a personal refrigerator stocked with a complimentary bottle of wine. My room was on the garden level (first floor) and named the Cedar Room.

The queen bed, complete with spread and pillows of deep teal and rose floral print, faced the wood stove. Some hand-crocheted pieces done by Barbara's grandmother were on display. A private sun porch that extended out into the gardens became my own reading retreat. There are only two guestrooms on the first floor and two, with views overlooking the garden, on the second floor. Each has its own unique features, but none offered the luxury of a whirlpool bath as mine did.

In the late afternoon we nibbled from an appetizer buffet set up in the parlor. One of the guest with musical inclinations played some requests on the old piano. The weather had warmed a bit since breakfast, so a huge basket of flowers sat behind the screen of the tile fireplace. As I stood conversing with another guest, my fingers trailed the carved out grooves on the mantel, handcrafted by Bob.

"Would you like me to make dinner reservations at any particular restaurant in town?" Barbara interrupted. Cody, their cocker spaniel, was at her heels, eying us curiously. "There are several I can recommend, and only a short walk away. If you leave a little early, the shops and galleries may still be open. Or stop for some tasting at the wineries. They supply us with the wine in your rooms."

As it states in the inn brochure, "your visit feels like a stay at a friend's house."

DUNBAR HOUSE 1880, 271 Jones St., P.O. Box 1375, Murphys, CA 95247; 209-728-2897 or 800-225-3746 x321.

Intimate four-guestroom bed and breakfast of Italianate Victorian design. Queen-size beds, private baths. Enjoy the included home-cooked breakfast, afternoon appetizers and complimentary bottle of wine in your room. Open year-round, two-night weekend minimum stay. Smoking restricted to outdoors. Not suitable for children under 10. Only a two-block stroll to downtown Murphys. Bear Valley Ski Resort and Big Trees State Park within an hour's drive. Cody, the owner's cocker spaniel, resides here. No pets. CCs: Visa, MC. Bob and Barbara Costa, owners/hosts.

DIRECTIONS: From Highway 49 in Angels Camp to Highway 4 east. Then take the Murphys exit.

SERENITY
Sonora, California

As I heard the history of Serenity, I was reminded of the pioneer quilters and how they poured the frustrations and grief into each square of the quilt. Owners Fred and Charlotte Hoover did much the same after a fire in 1988 turned Serenity into a large pile of ashes. Charlotte's 85-year-old mother began hook-

ing a new rug that very day, igniting the "pioneer spirit" for rebuilding the inn. Fred dug a set of the original plans out of storage and immediately called a contractor.

"Time was most important now, so we didn't have the luxury of doing the construction ourselves," Fred relayed. "I worked alongside, though, and did a lot of the finished work like these Victorian moldings and the bookshelves," pointing towards the wall of the library in which we were standing.

Charlotte joined us, "And we really liked the original design." She was referring to the two-story Colonial-style white clapboard offset with black window shutters. Though new, it seems as though it's been here forever. "The size (4,000 sq.ft.) was just right, as well as the number of rooms (just four). I always liked having two stories. It gives the guests even more of a feel of privacy, don't you think? Why try to improve on something that works so well?"

I nodded my agreement to both questions, although they seem not to be strangers to practicality and common sense. Fred is a retired Navy man and Charlotte was an elementary school teacher. This is probably not the first challenge they have ever faced!

I was allowed a quick peek into each of the two upstairs guestrooms. The Lilac Room sported a quilted comforter handmade by Charlotte and wallpaper with lavender sprigs of lilac. The walls of the Violet Room were unusually sponge-painted!

Mai Ling, the house Siamese, joined us as we wandered down the stair to the comfortable parlor. An antique Empire sofa was centered in the room and—I couldn't believe it—an old Victrola plus a collection of records! Fred chuckled at my surprise. "Let's visit the dining room next." A large Sheridan-style table accommodates the early risers that come to enjoy a delicious home-cooked breakfast as the sun comes up. "This is some of my work, too," Fred informed me, touching the wrap-around spice cabinet in the adjoining kitchen. "Charlotte was once a part-time caterer, and she likes convenience when she cooks."

"I plan to whip up a double banana cake for tomorrow morning, to go with the eggs Florentine," Charlotte tempted.

As we walked on, the door to the Daffodil Room was closed, ensuring the privacy of its occupants. Charlotte concurred it lives up to its name with splashes of bright yellow, green and white. Bringing the outdoors inside, it would seem. I was sleeping in the more peaceful Rose Room, muted with soft shades of rose, dark green and cream.

We parted company at this point while they tended to innkeeping, leaving me to explore the six wooded acres that surround the inn. Phoenix Lake, with it water recreation, is not far. The town of Sonora is only six miles away, and a little over an hour's drive takes you to Yosemite. I spent the afternoon in the woods, capturing the secrets of. . . Serenity.

———————————

SERENITY, A Bed & Breakfast Inn, 15305 Bear Cub Drive, Sonora, Ca. 95370; 209-533-1441 or 800-426-1441.

Peaceful and serene best describes this four-guestroom bed and breakfast on six private acres. (Breakfast included, of course.) Private baths and varied bed sizes. Some holiday minimums, but conveniently open all year. Wine and cheese served in the late afternoon. In the summer, swim in nearby Phoenix Lake or hike through the pines. Ski nearby slopes in the winter snow. Yosemite National Park is within comfortable driving distance. Sonora is only six short miles away. Smoking permitted on the outdoor veranda only. Siamese cat in residence. No pets. Fred and Charlotte Hoover, owners/hosts.

DIRECTIONS: East of Sonora on Hwy. 108 to Phoenix Lake Rd. Turn left, and continue three miles to Bear Cub Dr. Turn right, and watch for inn (second drive on the right).

Sacramento

The major supply center for the northern and central Mother Lode country, this city is now the capital of California and the marketing center for the great central valley's abundant agricultural goods. Old Sacramento is a four-block renovated section containing museums, restaurants and shops that preserve the city's historical character. The area code for the numbers listed below is 707.

EVENTS

MARCH	Camellia Festival (info: 442-7673)
MAY	Dixieland Jubilee (info: 372-5277)
JUNE	Country Bluegrass Picnic (info: 447-2343)
JULY	Courtland Pear Fair (info: 775-1053)
JULY	Music Circus (info: 441-3163)
AUGUST	Bicycle Classic (info: 443-8653)
AUGUST	California State Fair (info: 942-2000)
SEPTEMBER	Blues Festival (info: 482-2215)
SEPTEMBER	Hot Air Balloon Festival (info: 486-1288)
NOVEMBER–DECEMBER	Dickens Christmas Fair (info: 800-52-FAIRE)

AMBER HOUSE
Sacramento, California

Sacramento, the capital city of one of America's largest states, has many fine inns. Among the best is the air-conditioned Amber House, a completely restored California Craftsman.

Only a few blocks east of the capitol, the house sits on a street lined with towering elm trees, distinguished by its clinker brick front, shiny redwood porch, tan awnings and handsome brass nameplate.

The colorful stained-glass creations sparkle in every room, and classical music lilts through the house. There are original oil paintings, Oriental rugs and fresh flowers. A working fireplace and a boxed beam ceiling dominate the impressive living room, where complimentary wine is served in the late afternoon.

There are eight rooms, all with private baths, all handsomely and individually furnished. The light and airy Emily Dickinson Room is lined with windows on three sides and features an antique white iron bed. The Longfellow room's private bath boasts a 70-year-old porcelain tub with brass and ivory fixtures. Four of the rooms have marble baths and Jacuzzi tubs for two.

A full and varied breakfast, consisting of seasonal fresh fruits, homemade muffins, gourmet omelets or quiche, potatoes, and house-blend coffee, is served in the formal dining room or guest's room on fine china, with silver and crystal accessories.

Sightseeing in the city includes the completely restored state capitol, the Railroad Museum and the Old Town.

AMBER HOUSE, 1315 22nd St., Sacramento, CA 95816; 916-444-8085 or 1-800-755-6526.

An eight-guestroom (private baths) handsomely restored bed-and-breakfast inn seven blocks from the state capitol. Open year-round. Direct-dial telephones; TV & VCR available. City sightseeing: Railroad Museum, Old Town. Amador County wine and gold country 45 min. away. No pets. No smoking. Off-street parking; also local train station pick-up service available. CCs: Visa, MC, AE, DI, CB. Michael and Jane Richardson, owners/hosts.

DIRECTIONS: From I-5 take J St. exit and continue to 22nd St. Turn right to inn. From I-80 Business Loop, westbound, exit at J St. onto 29th, go three blocks, turn right on Capitol, left on 22nd, and go 1/2 block. From I-80 Business Loop, eastbound, take N St. exit onto 30th St., go one block, turn left on Capitol, left on 22nd, and go 1/2 block to inn.

ABIGAIL'S BED & BREAKFAST

Sacramento, California

Remember how much you dreaded a visit to see your great-aunt Lottie? There was never anything fun to do, and you always got stuck sitting on uncomfortable furniture in a stuffy front parlor. Well, a visit to Abigail's will make you wish your grandma's brother had met Abigail before he married Lottie.

Located in California's state capitol of Sacramento, Abigail's Bed and Breakfast is truly a home away from home. Owners/hosts Susanne and Ken Ventura stayed at the 1912 Colonial Revival mansion as guests the year before they purchased it. "It was such a wonderful old house," said Susanne. "I just had to have it!" Ken currently works for the Board of Corrections inspecting jails.

The white and teal blue mansion is situated in an older neighborhood of stately homes and majestic tree-lined streets. Past the wrought-iron gate, the walkway leads you between pillars to the huge front door crowned by a unique fantail beveled-glass transom. Pillars again appear in the entryway to the living room. Oriental rugs and comfortable upholstered chairs pick up the creamy yellow and dusty rose tones of the room, while a fireplace provides warmth. The sitting room is stocked with games and a piano for entertainment.

Named after Susanne and Ken's relatives, the guestrooms are furnished in mostly Edwardian antiques. Every room is decorated to suit its name: Uncle Albert has a walnut bed; a romantic brass bed awaits in Aunt Rose; Anne is elegant, with antique white and wedgewood blue tones and a Victorian armoire; and Margaret, with its large clawfoot tub, overlooks the garden.

After a full breakfast, including the house specialty of french toast stuffed with boysenberry jam, you can enjoy morning coffee in the sunny garden. Hot tub located in secluded garden area.

Abigail's is only a five-minute drive to the recently refurbished State Capitol building, Old Town Sacramento and the Railroad Museum. Fine restaurants, Sutter's Fort, Almond Plaza and the Crocker Art Museum are within walking distance.

ABIGAIL'S BED AND BREAKFAST, 2120 "G" St., Sacramento, CA 95816; 916-441-5007, 1-800-858-1568.

A five-guestroom (private bath) historic mansion in the heart of Northern California. King and queen beds. Centrally located to all cultural offerings and shopping. Breakfast included. No pets. Two cats in residence. Smoking limited to outside. Radios in rooms, TV and phone available. CCs: Visa, MC, DC, DI. Susanne and Ken Ventura, owners/hosts.

DIRECTIONS: From business loop 80 toward Reno, take H St. or E St. exit to G St. (one-way). Just past 22nd St. on left side. From I-5, take Downtown—J St. exit to 22nd St., left on 22nd, left on G St.

Sonoma Valley

The Sonoma Valley can be divided into three wonderful tourist areas: the Coast, Redwood Country and Wine Country. The coast's rugged panoramic views are simply spectacular. The redwoods grow slightly inland; this world-famous forest reaches northward almost as far as Eureka and includes the towns of Cloverdale, Geyersville, Guerneville and Occidental. The entire area, also known as Russian River for the beautiful river that meanders through it to the coast, is renowned for the apples and other fruits that are grown here. The Wine Country towns of Healdsburg, Santa Rosa, and Sonoma cherish what remains of their original Spanish heritage. They are surrounded by great wineries, large and small. The area code for the numbers listed below is 707.

EVENTS

MARCH	Barrel Tasting, Alexander Valley Wineries (info: 433-6782)
MARCH	Annual Russian River Wine Road Barrel Tasting
APRIL	Annual Fitch Mt. 10K/3K Footrace & Walk, Healdsburg
APRIL	Dry Creek Valley Passport Weekend: food and wine pairing (info: 857-3531)
APRIL	Pick of the Vine (info: 1-800-648-9922)
MAY	Healdsburg Wine Festival (info: 433-6935)
MAY, THIRD WEEKEND	Russian River Wine Festival (info: 433-6782)
MAY THROUGH OCTOBER	Downtown Santa Rosa on Thursday nights, magicians, storytellers, jugglers.
JUNE	Cotati Jazz Festival (info: 795-5451)
JUNE	Late-Ox roast, Sonoma Plaza
JUNE	Sonoma Country Arts Festival in Santa Rosa
JULY	Living History Day, Fort Ross (info: 847-3286)
JULY, LATE	Annual Harvest Century Bike Tour, 40 miles (1-800-648-9922)
AUGUST 6–9	Sonoma County Showcase & Wine Auction(info: 579-0577)
SEPTEMBER 4–7 (LABOR DAY WEEKEND)	Scottish Games
SEPTEMBER 12–13	Jazz Festival (info: 1-800-253-8800)
OCTOBER 2–4	Sonoma Harvest Fair (info: 545-4203)
OCTOBER 30–31	Geyserville Fall Color Tour (info: 857-3745)

SIGHTS

Armstrong State Redwood Reserve
Geysers
Ice Arena and Snoopy's Gallery
Jack London's Beauth Ranch
Luther Burbank House & Garden, Santa Rosa

SIGHTS *(continued)*

Fort Ross (restored Russian settlement)
Korbel Gardens (April–October)
Sonoma Coast
Sonoma County Farm Trails
Wineries

APPLEWOOD
Guerneville, California

In 1922, a wealthy and flamboyant banker created a Mission Revival mansion as the centerpiece for a life of elegance and refinement. Located on six wooded acres just a half-mile from the resort town of Guerneville, the magnificent home has been lovingly restored by Darryl Notter and Jim Caron. The estate is now deemed a Sonoma County historical landmark.

I was immediately impressed by the heavily beamed ceilings and massive river-rock fireplaces of the solarium and living room. The solarium, with three walls of glass and a huge window looking out on majestic redwoods, is a lovely spot to enjoy an afternoon nap or a glass of wine before dinner in the estate's dining room. For the guests' amusement, a selection of games and a radio and compact-disc player with a full stock of tapes are provided.

Furnishings throughout the common rooms are a tasteful combination of antiques and contemporary pieces. All guest and common rooms have original paintings or prints, some by local artists. A first-floor library contains a wide selection of books available to guests.

While the heated pool and spa overlooking the Inn's hillside Vineyard tempted me, I could hardly leave my exquisite room, the Master's Suite. Charcoal gray carpet softly draws together a decorator's dream. A deep-red duvet spread on the queen-sized bed, with down pillows, enhances the red brick wall behind. The remaining walls, which curve to form a large sitting bay, are a soft moss green.

A massive corbeled beam separates the bedroom from the sitting area where a wicker settee, green velvet club chairs and mahogany tables center around a wine-red Persian carpet. An original painting by Darryl and a Victorian print of Japanese theater sets add finishing touches. In the bath I felt pampered with complimentary toiletries in a Revere bowl, imported cut glass drinking glasses, and large, soft towels.

All guestrooms have remote-control color television and direct-dial phones. For a final indulgence, your bed will be turned down in the evening.

APPLEWOOD, 13555 Highway 116, Guerneville, CA 95446; 707-869-9093.
A classic 10-guestroom (private baths) country estate B&B. Queen beds. Open year-round. Full breakfast included, dinner available. Close to Russian River resort, redwoods, wineries and Pacific Ocean. Smoking restricted. No pets. Two dogs in residence. CCs: Visa, MC, AE. Darryl Notter and Jim Carron, owners/hosts.
DIRECTIONS: From San Francisco, take Hwy. 101 north past Santa Rosa. Take River Rd./Guerneville exit, 14 mi. west on River Rd. to Guerneville. Left onto Hwy. 116. Cross bridge, 1/2 mi. to the Applewood.

CAMPBELL RANCH INN
Geyserville, California

100 -145

While old Victorians are often the style among bed-and-breakfast inns, it is sometimes refreshing to enjoy the atmosphere of a warm and friendly home, especially one with a view of the verdant Sonoma valley with its thousands of acres of fruit trees and vineyards, as well as the distant mountains that separate it from the better-publicized Napa Valley.

Such a place is the home of Mary Jane and Jerry Campbell, as pleasant and accommodating a couple as ever hosted a B&B. Not content with opening their extremely comfortable split-level ranch-style home with its spectacular view, its gardens, large swimming pool, hot tub spa and professional tennis

court, they ply their guests with sumptuous breakfasts, poolside lemonade or iced tea, homemade pie or cake, evening dessert, fruit, and fresh flowers. Breakfast choices are made from a menu with over twelve items.

Perched on a hilltop high above the Pedroncelli vineyard, one of California's premium winemakers, Campbell Ranch commands literally miles of scenery. One could sit all day and gaze at this view from the balcony off the three upstairs light and airy guestrooms. All of the rooms are fully carpeted and furnished in a contemporary style with king-sized beds. One room has a piano. A rustic room has been added in the cottage with an extra bed to accommodate a family group.

The soaring beamed ceiling of the living room, the floor-to-ceiling used-brick wall with its "see-through" fireplace, and the open kitchen-breakfast-lounge area with windows all around provide a most pleasant feeling of spaciousness.

CAMPBELL RANCH INN, 1475 Canyon Rd., Geyserville, CA 95441; 707-857-3476.
A four-guestroom (private baths) split-level home on a hilltop with a magnificent view in the Sonoma County section of northern California plus a cottage with two bedrooms and fireplace. King beds. Complimentary full breakfast and refreshments. Open year-round; two-day minimum stay on weekends. On-premise diversions include swimming, tennis, spa, bicycles, horseshoes, table tennis, other indoor games, TV, VCR. Hiking nearby. Good restaurants within a few miles. No pets. No smoking. CCs: Visa, MC. Mary Jane and Jerry Campbell, owners/hosts.

DIRECTIONS: Take Geyserville off-ramp of Hwy. 101 and proceed immediately westward on Canyon Rd., 1.6 mi. Watch for Campbell Ranch sign on left.

GRAPE LEAF INN
Healdsburg, California

90 -145

Healdsburg, Geyserville and Cloverdale are just a few moments apart on / 101, which leads to upper northern California.

In Healdsburg, the Grape Leaf Inn, at one time a private home, is located on a rather quiet residential street. Proprietor Terry Sweet has furnished this restored 91-year-old home to reflect the turn of the century.

The first thing that impressed me upon walking into the entry hall was the parlor and dining-living room with its very comfortable couch, love seat, fireplace, swag lamp and lots of flowers.

The seven comfortably furnished bedrooms, all with private baths (including whirlpool tub/showers for two), are named after the wines of the Alexander Valley. The new rooms upstairs have skylight roof windows and air conditioning.

Within a 20-minute drive of the inn there are over 60 wineries that are still family-owned. During the wintertime especially, you can go right into the

wineries and talk to the winemakers. There is also a canoe company nearby where rental canoes are available for day trips on the Russian River, which runs through Healdsburg.

The full breakfast, served by Karen Sweet, includes freshly ground coffee that is roasted nearby, fresh orange juice, fresh fruit, eggs prepared in a variety of ways, and home-baked muffins or coffee cake. In addition, in the afternoon, Karen pours red and white local wines to be enjoyed with Sonoma County cheeses.

GRAPE LEAF INN, 539 Johnson St., Healdsburg, CA 95448; 707-433-8140.

A seven-guestroom (private baths) bed-and-breakfast home in the northern Sonoma wine country. Five rooms have whirlpool tub-showers for two. King and queen beds. Open year-round. Full breakfast. Conveniently located to visit all of the cultural and historic attractions and wineries. Night tennis, bicycles, canoe trips and other recreation nearby. CCs: Visa, MC. Terry and Karen Sweet, owners/hosts.

DIRECTIONS: From San Francisco, follow Hwy. 101 north, exiting at Central Healdsburg Ave., and continue in the same direction for four traffic lights. Turn right at Grant St., go two blocks to Johnson St. and turn right. Grape Leaf is on the right with a small, unobtrusive sign.

HAYDON HOUSE
Healdsburg, California

The ancient pump organ in the Haydon House is the only reminder of its former life as a convent. The owners have banished all traces of austere convent surroundings from their cheerful, homey, light and airy 1912 Victorian house.

From the rose-entwined white picket fence to the vintage ball-and-claw-footed tubs, the atmosphere is one of friendly warmth and hospitality.

The house boasts many interesting architectural details in the picture moldings, chair railings, baseboards and stenciling. The pine floors are polished to a fare-thee-well, and the antique furnishings, Laura Ashley prints and other designer wallpapers and handmade rugs create an altogether delightful environment.

Custom-made down comforters, lace curtains, baskets of thick towels and flowers—dried, silk and fresh—decorate the guestrooms on the second floor. A special room under the eaves is the Attic Room (very popular with honeymooners), which has a sitting room, skylights and a step-down bedroom. There are washstands set in old-fashioned dressers, and several of the aforementioned claw-footed tubs reside right in the guestrooms.

A detached Victorian Gothic cottage has two separate units each with a

large room with cathedral ceilings and two-person whirlpool baths. In one room a Ralph Lauren natural wicker queen-size bed beckons the guests. Colors in shades of rose and green with black accents provide a visual feast in the Victorian room. In contrast the Shaker room is a white-on-white fantasy with an inviting white pine pencil four-poster and battenburg lace canopy.

Breakfast in the dining room sparkles with silver service sets, lace linens and French tableware. The sideboard is laden with fresh coffee, juice, fruit, quiches, muffins and, on most Sundays, a special treat of Keri's Estonian pancakes. After breakfast you can relax in the common room, large front porch or garden.

This is a place where guests return often, and even the nuns from the convent drop in to see their former home. I wonder if they sit down to play the organ.

HAYDON HOUSE, 321 Haydon St., Healdsburg, CA 95448; 707-433-5228.

An eight-guestroom (four private baths) Queen Anne Victorian inn on a quiet residential street in the Sonoma wine country of northern California. Queen, double and twin beds. Full breakfast. Open year-round. Russian River, wineries, antiques, museums, restaurants, and shopping nearby. No pets or smoking. CCs: Visa, MC. Keiu and Tom Woodburn, owners/hosts.

DIRECTIONS: From the south on Hwy. 101, take 2nd Healdsburg exit to Healdsburg Ave. Turn right at the Plaza onto Matheson and right at Fitch to Haydon. Turn left at Haydon. From the north on Hwy. 101, take the Dry Creek exit going left under the freeway to Healdsburg Ave. Turn left onto Matheson and follow above directions.

HEART'S DESIRE INN
Occidental, California

Waking in the morning under a fluffy goose-down comforter and snuggling back on your large, European-style pillows, you may think you've been transported to Germany. You haven't. But Justina Selinger brought the European ambiance from her native Germany when she and her husband, Howard, opened Heart's Desire Inn.

Dating back to 1867, the inn is one of the oldest buildings in Occidental. Located on a wooded hillside, the white-on-bone three-story Victorian has large covered porches with wicker furnishings and a lovely courtyard garden. The Selingers opened the inn in 1988 after a total renovation. They now have a full-time innkeeper, chef, and resident manager.

All the rooms are light and airy. The common rooms feature English pine antiques, with a warm brick fireplace in the country parlor where you can enjoy a complimentary afternoon sherry while nosing through a book from the library.

Guestrooms have four-poster beds and are also furnished in antiques. With its stone fireplace and private deck, the honeymoon suite offers a perfect setting for romance. All rooms have private baths.

I rose early and took my steaming mug of coffee out on the porch. A full breakfast is served in the dining room or on the garden terrace between 8:00 and 10:00 A.M.

Occidental is located near the Point Reyes National Seashore and the

Russian River. An easy drive will take you to the rugged Sonoma coast, or you can bicycle through the peaceful surrounding hills.

After a day of hiking, I returned to my room, muscle-sore but not that tired to try the inn's new restaurent. Then back to my room and off to sleep listening to the doves and the fountain splashing in the garden below.

HEART'S DESIRE INN, 3657 Church St., Occidental, CA 95465-0857; 707-894-1047.

An eight-guestroom (private baths) Victorian inn and restaurant in a quaint Sonoma valley town. Queen, double and twin beds. Open all year. Breakfast included. Near Pt. Reyes National Seashore, Russian River, antique and craft shops, art galleries, and Occidental's famous Italian restaurants. No pets. Smoking restricted. Wheelchair access. CCs: Visa, MC, AE, Dis. Justina and Howard Selinger, owners.

DIRECTIONS: From San Francisco, 101 north to Sebastopol via Hwy. 116. West on Bodega Hwy., to town of Freestone. Right on Bohemian Hwy. to Occidental. Right at the only stop sign.

HOPE-MERRILL HOUSE
Geyserville, California

The Hope-Merrill House is one of the most impressive renovations and restorations I have seen. Earlier "modernizations" had installed new windows

and lowered ceilings that covered up the original Gothic arches over the bay
windows throughout the house—all of which had to be torn out and the moldings retrimmed. Turn-of-the-century wainscoting is a highlight of the interior—it is known as Lincrusta-Walton and is the same wainscoting that has
been restored in the state capitol. Even the original silk-screened wallpapers
are custom-designed.

This loving effort extends to the very elegant guestrooms that are decorated with Victorian carved headboards, a wicker chaise longue, a free-stand-
ing mirror, a marble-top dresser, and nice old sepia and tinted prints. The
bathrooms are equally elegant with lots of pictures on the walls, and three
have whirpool tubs.

Favorite spots for relaxation and conversation are the heated swimming
pool, latticed gazebo and large grape arbor.

Bob and Rosalie Hope also own the Hope-Bosworth House, located immediately across Geyserville Avenue, so if one house is filled, there is a good
chance you can be accommodated in the other one. The Hope-Bosworth
House has four guestrooms and a very pleasant atmosphere.

Rosalie and her daughter, Kim, offer a scrumptious picnic lunch by
advance reservation.

HOPE-MERRILL HOUSE, 21253 Geyserville Ave. (P.O. Box 42), Geyserville, CA
95441; 707-857-3356.
A seven-guestroom (private baths) restored Victorian home. Queen and double
beds. Reservations can also be made for the Hope-Bosworth House, across the street,
with five guestrooms (two shared baths) and a very pleasant atmosphere. Wheelchair
access. Swimming pool on grounds. Conveniently located to enjoy all of the wine
country scenic and historical attractions. No pets. CCs: Visa, MC. Bob and Rosalie
Hope, owners/hosts.
DIRECTIONS: From San Francisco, take Hwy. 101 north 80 mi. to the Geyserville
exit, drive east one block to Old Redwood Hwy., turn left on Geyserville Ave. (Old
Redwood Hwy.), and go one mi. north. The two houses are across the road from each
other.

MADRONA MANOR
Healdsburg, California

135-210

Many Easterners visiting northern California for the first time are struck with
the unusual number of Victorian homes and buildings. I was reminded of this
once again during a short drive around downtown Healdsburg on my way to
Madrona Manor. I turned in at the impressive archway, flanked by a rainbow
mass of flowers, and drove up the long winding drive to the three-story man-

sion. From the rambling front porch, I turned to look over the grounds and noticed that Madrona Manor sits on top of a knoll with flower gardens, sculptured hedges, numerous varieties of trees and bushes, and acres and acres of lawn.

I heard a step behind me and realized that the couple coming out the front door were the innkeepers of Madrona Manor, John and Carol Muir. "Oh, I see you are enjoying our view," John said.

Madrona Manor is furnished with beautiful Victorian antiques. There is a 100-year-old square piano in the music room, and throughout the house are massive pieces of carved walnut and mahogany furniture and Oriental carpets. "Five of our rooms have the antique furniture of the original owner, John Paxton, who was a San Francisco financier," Carol told me. "He built this house and also the Carriage House in 1881."

One of the guestrooms has a 10-foot-high canopied bed and a huge armoire. The others have carved headboards, chaise longues, dressing tables with beveled mirrors, original light fixtures and period wallpapers. There are fourteen-foot-high ceilings and many fireplaces with brightly painted tiles.

"I love fireplaces," I told John. "How many of your guestrooms have them?" He thought for a moment. "We have eighteen rooms with fireplaces, including the four we added in the third-floor rooms, which were originally servants' quarters. These rooms have antique-reproduction furniture.

John, a former engineer, converted the Carriage House into more guest-rooms, and has used vast amounts of carved rosewood for lamps and tables, as well as door trim and paneling. My favorite suite is in this house as one can sit in a Jacuzzi and watch the fire in the fireplace. There is also a Garden Suite surrounded by lawn and flowers and another building with a very private country bedroom and suite. Madrona Manor is listed on the National Register of Historic Places as a historic district.

However, I think the big story at Madrona Manor is the food. Their big, efficient kitchen is a delight to behold, and includes a wood-burning oven, a mesquite grill and a separate smokehouse. The Muir's son, Todd, is in command. The Muirs are obviously very proud of his talents as chef. "Todd's cooking has attracted the attention of *Gourmet* magazine, and we have guests who drive all the way from San Francisco just for dinner," John told me. I'd certainly be happy to make the trip for the dinner I had, which included a wonderful crusty goat-cheese soufflé seasoned with rosemary and garlic, a perfect green salad, and mesquite-grilled monkfish that was absolutely delicious. I couldn't resist trying the Mexican flan with rose petals (delightful). There is a prix-fixe menu and an à la carte menu. Everything is given special and interesting treatment and served with great aplomb.

Later that night as I stood on the balcony of my room, looking out over the beautiful view, with Mount Saint Helena to the east, I thought a stay here in the Sonoma wine country at this beautiful inn is a very special experience.

MADRONA MANOR, 1001 Westside Rd., Box 818, Healdsburg, CA 95448; 707-433-4231; 1-800-258-4003: Fax: 707-433-0703.

An 18-guestroom, three-suite (private baths) Victorian mansion in the heart of Sonoma County wine country, 65 mi. north of San Francisco. All-size beds. Breakfast included in room rate. Dinner served daily; reservations recommended. Open year-round. Wheelchair access. Swimming pool on grounds. Golf, tennis, hiking, canoeing, fishing, winery tours nearby. Children and pets welcome by prearrangement. CCs: All major cards. John and Carol Muir, owners/hosts.

DIRECTIONS: From San Francisco, follow Hwy. 101 north to the central Healdsburg exit. Continue north and turn left at Mill St. (first stoplight), which becomes Westside Rd.

TIMBERHILL RANCH
Cazadero, California

Standing in a clearing beneath spicy-scented, majestic redwoods, a thousand feet above the Pacific Ocean's coastal fog and wind, I could see why, in the 1800s, the Pomo Indians had chosen this sheltered bit of Northern California coast for their winter home. The serenity is a balm. Apparently the owners of Timberhill Ranch, Barbara Farrell, Frank Watson, Tarran McDaid and

Michael Riordan, felt the same way when they left hectic corporate positions in San Francisco and purchased Timberhill.

Formerly a working ranch, and then the location of an alternative school, the main ranch house and 10 cottages sit on 15 secluded acres. The ranch's other 70 acres are covered by meadows peppered with wild iris, bluebells and forget-me-nots. Groves of blood red madrone and oak and fir neighbor stately redwoods. The ranch is surrounded by the 317-acre Kruse Rhododendron Reserve and the 6,000-acre Salt Point State Park. Miles of hiking trails traverse the park and meander to the sea.

As I hefted my bags, the shadow of a red-tailed hawk crossed over me. Watching this graceful bird ride an updraft, I hoped my grandfather had been right when he told me that it was a good omen.

The shake cedar exterior of the main ranch house may look rustic, but the interior will immediately dispel any worries about "roughing it." A cozy, cushion-strewn sofa beckons guests to sink in front of the large stone fireplace. Smaller grouped seating areas encourage conversation. And books, magazines, puzzles, cards and games offer entertainment after the last bit of daylight steals the spectacular views.

Fresh flowers appear in abundance in the cottages as well as the main lodge. The cottages are also rustic cedar, and are comfortable and romantic.

Each has a wood-burning fireplace, with wood already cut and stacked, mini-bar, coffee maker, reading lamps and armchairs, and luxury amenities like fluffy robes and hair dryers. Colorful quilts, hand-made by local artisans, adorn the beds. Private decks look onto views of the surrounding natural landscape, not on other cottages or the two world-class tennis courts or heated swimming pool and hot tub.

Should you choose to become somewhat of a hermit, you can easily stay at your cottage until dinner, since breakfast is delivered to your door. Lunch can be arranged and the staff will make up a picnic basket if you decide to do some hiking.

At dinnertime, a wonderful six-course meal is served in the intimate can-dlelit dining room. The meal begins with a selection of appetizers and pro-gresses leisurely through soup, salad, a palate-cleansing sorbet, an entree and dessert. The menu changes nightly as the chef uses only the freshest of ingredi-ents, and can include such specialties as roast Petaluma duckling with sun-dried figs or grilled Pacific salmon with tomatillo coulis. All breads, pastries and desserts are homemade, and a good selection of California wines is available.

On Sunday afternoon I decided that my hedonistic behavior needed to be tempered, so I grabbed my tennis racket for a bit of lobbing on the courts. Just as I bounced my first ball, two of the ranch's ducks, Mutt and Jeff, hurriedly waddled down, hoping to beg a treat. After greeting them, I turned back to my bucket of balls and, again, was crossed by the shadow of the redtail. This time I knew my grandfather had been right. It was a good omen. My stay at Timber-hill Ranch had been nothing less than exceptional.

TIMBERHILL RANCH, 35755 Hauser Bridge Rd., Cazadero, CA 95421; 707-847-3258.

A 15-cottage (private baths) secluded ranch resort 1100 ft. above the spectacular north-ern Sonoma County coast. Open all year. Queen beds; twins available. Modified American plan. Handicapped and non-smoking cottages provided. Tennis courts, heated pool and hiking trails on property. Close to beaches, whale-watching, golf and art galleries. One Aus-tralian shepherd in residence. Barbara Farrell, Frank Watson, Tarran McDaid and Michael Riordan, owners/hosts.

DIRECTIONS: Take Hwy. 101 north from San Francisco to the Washington St. exit in Petaluma. Go west through Bodega Bay and continue north on Hwy. 1; five mi. past Jenner, turn right on Meyers Grade Rd. Stay on paved road for 13.6 mi. The inn is on the right.

VICTORIAN GARDEN INN
Sonoma, California

The Victorian Garden Inn is a lovely bit of Old California settled in Sonoma, the heart of the picturesque Valley of the Moon wine country. A Greek

Revival farmhouse with an Italian-Swiss influence, the home was built in 1880. The old tank house is still standing. Owner Donna Lewis welcomed me on the front walkway. As we stood admiring the spacious wraparound veranda, with its summery wicker furniture, I asked her how she had come upon the place. "As a designer, I came up the front walk to look at an historical house to renovate and said to myself, 'This looks like a B&B.' So be it!"

Well-ordered Victorian gardens surround the house and provide fragment scents as you walk along brick paths. A swimming pool is secluded in the back of the property, nestled among patios and walkways. I sat in the sun for a moment and enjoyed the rushing sound of Nathanson Creek, which runs alongside the property, before going in.

The inn's interior is comfortable, with a parlor for relaxing and conversation. Cozy seating areas surround the fireplace, and a variety of books and games are available for entertainment.

Guestrooms offer a multitude of moods. The Woodcutter's Cottage, for example, is a cozy retreat decorated in hunter green and redwood and comes complete with a fireplace, extra-large clawfoot tub and country-style antiques. All rooms are tastefully appointed, fresh and airy.

A large breakfast of seasonal fresh fruit, baked goods, local cherry or unfiltered apple juice, cheeses, and gourmet coffees and teas is served family style in the dining room overlooking the gardens, in your room or on the patio or poolside.

Sonoma has much to offer sightseers. The Sonoma Mission, founded in 1823, the Sebastiani Winery, and historic Sonoma Plaza are only a half-block stroll from the inn. Jack London's home and the fascinating home of General Vallejo are within a short drive. Fine restaurants and unique shops are nearby.

VICTORIAN GARDEN INN, 316 E. Napa St., Sonoma, CA 95476; 707-996-5339.

A four-guestroom (three private baths) Greek Revival home in the quaint village of Sonoma. Queen and double beds. Open all year. Breakfast included. Near historic points of interest; in the heart of the wine country. No pets. CCs: Visa, MC, AE, Optima, ER. Donna Lewis, owner/hostess.

DIRECTIONS: From Hwy. 101, north. Follow Hwy. 12 south into Sonoma Plaza. At the Plaza, go east on East Napa St. Two blocks to Old Schoolhouse (now Community Center). Inn is three doors past Center.

VINTNERS INN

Santa Rosa, California

At the hub of the northern California wine country, Vintners Inn offers the ambiance of a village in the south of France, right down to its house wine made from grapes grown on the property. Owner John Duffy, an ex-nuclear physicist, set out to recreate the French Mediterranean feeling when he began thinking about a design for their inn. He traveled to Europe and searched the

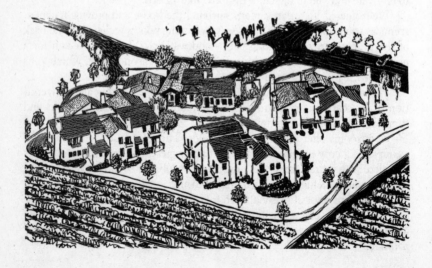

regions surrounding Provence, photographing historical buildings and hamlets to garner information and inspiration.

The units are joined by matching tiled walkways and surround a central plaza with a tranquil fountain. Arched windows, wrought-iron railings and patios create a relaxed atmosphere. Antique European pine furnishings have been restored and refinished to compliment the charming country-print fabrics and floral-patterned wall-papers. The rooms offer beamed ceilings, wood-burning fireplaces, wet bars and views of the lush 45 acres of Pinot Blanc, French Colombard and Sauvignon Blanc vineyards. All rooms have private baths with luxurious oversized oval bathtubs.

The lobby sports an enormous wine basket, and along with old antique farm equipment decorating the walls, creates an old-world feeling. Plan to enjoy a glass of Vinters Inn Chardonnay as you relax in the outdoor sundeck Jacuzzi and watch the colorful hot-air balloons as they drift overhead. There is also a VCR with a good movie library available for guests.

Breakfast is served in the sunlit dining room overlooking the courtyard. You'll enjoy a sumptuous buffet of fresh fruit and juices, cereals, homemade breads, and croissants along with teas and rich fresh-ground coffee and/or a luscious waffle.

When John designed the inn, he also provided a building to house the acclaimed restaurant John Ash & Co. Executive-chef John Ash focuses on local foods. He carefully selects produce from nearby farms, oysters from the Tomales Bay, chicken and game birds grown on Sonoma ranches, and the county's famous cheeses. The freshest of seafood is purchased from northern California and Oregon.

I had a wonderful dinner that began with a salad of fresh Oregon scallops sprinkled with coriander. A flaky California sea bass, grilled with fresh herbs and served on a bed of flavorful eggplant came next, followed by a palate-cleansing sorbet of mandarin oranges. My entree of boned quail stuffed with a forcemeat of veal, walnuts and leeks, served on top of fresh spinach, was done to perfection.

To finish, I sampled local goat cheeses, with baby greens and roasted walnuts. Elegant desserts will certainly tempt you, but I just couldn't eat another bite. The restaurant's wine list is excellent.

The concierge is happy to help you plan tours of the area and will make recommendations on wineries, restaurants, points of interest and picnic areas. Guest privileges can be arranged at nearby clubs for tennis, swimming, golf and racquetball.

The Sonoma County wine country is in one of the most beautiful valleys in northern California. As I stood on my balcony overlooking the lovely manicured vineyards, I could see why John chose this very special spot for the inn.

VINTNERS INN, 4350 Barnes Rd., Santa Rosa, CA 95403; 707-575-7350 or 800-421-2584. A 44-guestroom (private baths) inn complex nestled in the center of a vineyard in the heart of the Sonoma wine country in northern California. Open year-round. Queen beds. Breakfast included. Dinner at John Ash & Co. Accommodations for handicapped guests. Children welcome. CCs: All major cards. John Duffy, owner/host; Cindy Young, manager.

DIRECTIONS: From Hwy. 101 about three mi. north of Santa Rosa, take River Rd. turnoff west. First left turn is Barnes Rd.

YE OLDE' SHELFORD HOUSE
Cloverdale, California

$5-110

Ye Olde' Shelford House is a country Victorian farmhouse nestled amidst acres of lush vineyards. The home, now completely restored and beautifully decorated, was built in 1885 by Eurastus M. Shelford. The property was originally a part of the Rancho Musalacon.

Innkeepers Ina and Al Sauder have taken great care in maintaining the authenticity of decor when restoring the inn. The parlor and common rooms are all furnished with family antiques and are completely wallpapered, including the ceilings. A game room is available for fun and entertainment, and a wide, wraparound porch, complete with swing, is a relaxing place to curl up with a good book.

The six guestrooms are split between the main house and the newly completed carriage house. Rooms are cozy, with window seats from which you have sweeping views of the vineyards. Ina loves needlecrafts, and she quilts and embroiders the colorful quilts that cover comfortable beds. Plants and fresh flowers from the inn's garden help create a cheerful atmosphere. As Ina says in the inn's brochure, "Crisp and clean—light and airy," a motto with which I heartily agree.

A full country breakfast is served and includes fresh-squeezed orange juice, fresh fruit, an egg dish and fresh-baked muffins. Beverages are available at all times, and raids on the kitchen cookie jar are encouraged.

Ye Olde' Shelford House is centrally located near a multitude of activities, but the most unusual and entertaining is offered right at the inn. Ina and Al hitch up Brandy, a strawberry roan Belgian draft horse, and Casey, a quarter horse, to their turn-of-the-century surrey for a spin through the scenic back roads of Cloverdale for wine tasting. Ina calls these rides "Surrey and Sip" excursions. Or, if you feel like a little more active involvement, you can coast off on the bicycle built for two and pedal at your own rate through the vineyards. Another fun event is the "Antique Car Wine Tour," with a picnic included.

When you return, you can take a relaxing swim in the inn's pool or soak in the hot tub under the clear, starry sky.

Al and Ina are a gracious host and hostess who make every effort to make your stay exceptional.

YE OLDE' SHELFORD HOUSE, 29955 River Rd., Cloverdale, CA 95425; 707-894-5956; 1-800-833-6479.

A six-guestroom (four private baths) Victorian farmhouse. King and queen beds. Open all year. Breakfast included. Near wineries and the Russian River resort area. No pets or smoking. CCs: Visa, MC, DC. Ina and Al Sauder, owners/hosts.

DIRECTIONS: From San Francisco, go 85 mi. north on Hwy. 101 to Cloverdale. At signal light, turn right on First St. Go one mile. Inn on righthand side.

INN EVENTS: Surrey & Sip rides
Antique car wine tours

Napa Valley

Internationally known for its award-winning wines, Napa is a small but beautiful valley, just 28 miles long and three miles wide. Quaint homes, hot springs, the Petrified Forest, and of course the vineyards and wineries are among its many attractions.

EVENTS

MARCH	Marathon
JUNE	Napa Valley International Wine Auction (1-800-458-8080)
SUMMER	Mondavi Jazz Festival
SUMMER	Concerts in the Caves

SIGHTS

Calistoga Mud Baths and Hot Springs
Lake Berryessa
Robert Louis Stevenson State Park
Sharpsteen Museum
Silverado Museum
Wineries

BEAZLEY HOUSE
Napa, California

110-105

Built in 1902 as the residence of a prominent Napa surgeon and opened by the Beazleys in 1981 as the first bed-and-breakfast in Napa, Beazley House is situated on a busy street in a residential neighborhood. It was recently added to the list of historic houses.

The large, comfortable living room with its antiques is the setting for afternoon sherry and tea in front of the fireplace. The unusual "light" windows with eighteen tiny panes make it a sunny and inviting place for guests to visit or play games. The formal dining room, its attractive redwood paneling stained to look like mahogany, is the scene for the full "California" breakfast, featuring fresh fruits, fruit juice, oatmeal with cinnamon and raisins, quiche, homemade muffins, jams, and fresh coffee or tea.

A staircase with a window seat and half-round stained-glass window leads to five attractive upstairs guestrooms. The Sherry Room has a splendid 125-year-old cherrywood bedroom set, set against dark blue wallpaper. The Burgundy Room, done in various rose shades, has two beds. The Master Bedroom has a fireplace and a brass bed. The Wedgwood is the soft blue of its namesake with pink curtains and a garden view. Sonja's Room is cozy with a double bed and a pedestal sink at its foot.

The Carriage House, completed in 1983, offers an additional five bedrooms, each with its own entrance; one offers wheelchair access. Special features in these open-beam-ceiling rooms include fireplaces, double-paned windows, private cedar-lined bathrooms, double bathtubs complete with

Jacuzzis and iron and brass queen- and king-sized beds with bright, handmade quilts. Those wanting a quieter room should stay here.

The Beazleys offer an extensive selection of Napa Valley wine.

BEAZLEY HOUSE, 1910 First St., Napa, CA 94559; 707-257-1649, 800-559-1649.

An 11-guestroom (private baths) bed-and-breakfast inn in the heart of the wine country. King, queen and twin beds. Open year-round. Wheelchair access. Many recreational activities in the area. No pets. One cat in residence. No smoking. CCs: Visa, MC. Carol and Jim Beazley, owners/hosts.

DIRECTIONS: Take Rte. 29 into Napa; then the Calistoga fork to the Central Napa— First Street exit. Turn left on Second Street for 0.3 mi., and turn left on Warren and left onto First Street. The inn is at the corner of First and Warren. Ample parking.

FOOTHILL HOUSE
Calistoga, California

125 - 250

From the early summer days of newly budded vines until the final grape press in the fall, the Napa Valley with its many wineries has a constant stream of visitors. Most of this activity can be avoided by continuing north on busy Highway 29 for some 20 miles to Calistoga, where tourists infrequently venture.

In a lovely country setting surrounded by trees and mountains, innkeepers Gus & Doris Beckert offer their guests a very special brand of hospitality with three guest suites.

Colorful handmade quilts were the beginning, and each room was then decorated to blend in with their colors. Aided by indirect and concealed lighting, a guest steps into a literal fairyland. There are four-poster queen-sized beds, separate outside entrances, small refrigerators and wood-burning fireplaces. In the private baths, towels are thick and rich, and replaced as they are soiled.

Upon your return in the evening from any one of the fine nearby restaurants, your bed will be turned down, soft lights will glow, and a miniature cookie jar filled with homemade cookies and a decanter of sherry will be on your bedside table. Possibly, also, a personal note from your innkeeper wishing you pleasant dreams.

A full gourmet breakfast is served in the morning in the sunroom or on the patio, shaded by a huge tree whose base is a flower bed and a fountain. If you prefer privacy, a breakfast basket will be brought to your room. Doris is a past student of the California Culinary Academy. This experience with the many years of entertaining (as many as 30 guests at her previous Russian River home) has been her training ground for what she hopes will be adding a gourmet kitchen and a larger dining room to serve dinners.

The grounds contain many 100-year-old trees, as well as private patios, and provide a great view of Mt. Helena on the eastern side of the valley.

FOOTHILL HOUSE, 3037 Foothill Blvd., Calistoga, CA 94515; 707-942-6933: 1-800-942-6933.

A three-room (private baths) remodeled country farmhouse nestled in the foothills on the northern edge of Napa Valley. King, queen and twin beds. Breakfast and afternoon refreshments included. Open year-round. Famous Calistoga healing waters and mud baths, winery visits, ballooning. Sharpsteen Museum and Robert Louis Stevenson State Park nearby. Hiking, biking, swimming, antiquing. No pets. Three cats in residence. No smoking. CCs: Visa, MC, AE. Gus & Doris Beckert, owners/hosts.

DIRECTIONS: Hwy. 29 north to Calistoga. Take Hwy. 128 for 1-1/2 mi. to Foothill House. Follow to 3037.

LARKMEAD COUNTRY INN
Calistoga, California
125

Passing through the old fieldstone gates, I approached the loggia of the inn. The turn-of-the-century Italianate sat regally amidst vineyards on the floor of the famous Napa Valley. Joan Garbarino cordially welcomed me back into the intimacy of the three-guestroom house.

Larkmead was my first bed and breakfast experience when the Garbarinos purchased it in 1979, and my wife and I have revisited many times. Rich Persian rugs carpet the floors. The Garbarinos' art collection of oils and prints is displayed on many walls. A fine array of antiques completes the furnishings.

Gene accompanied me to my room, which overlooked lush green vines. The fresh cut flowers on a small table emitted a subtle, sweet fragrance.

"Here is some fine wine from one of the local wineries for you to sample," said Gene, indicating a decanter and glasses. "But we'd love to have you join us on one of the porches downstairs. Joan is setting out cheeses and wine right now. I'd better go see if she needs any help." I promised him I'd be down shortly. I quickly unpacked my bags, then strolled out onto the private porch off my room, taking a moment of solitude in the late afternoon shadows cast by surrounding magnolia and cypress trees. The beauty of this quiet spot was breath-taking.

Downstairs, tasting the cheeses and wines, I questioned Joan about their backgrounds. Gene had been a dentist, and she, a school teacher. They had travelled extensively in Europe for many years, staying at many inns and auberges. Joan had long dreamed of owning an inn, and the purchase of Larkmead was the culmination of that dream. They were drawn by the tranquil setting and the beautiful architecture of the old house, which was the family home of the founders of Larkmead Winery. I chatted with some of the guests, and later followed Gene's directions to a restaurant in nearby St. Helena for a tasty evening meal.

The following morning was a little overcast and chilly, so breakfast was served in the dining room rather than out on the porches. A colorful fruit platter offered a variety of citrus selections. This was followed by baskets of warmed brioche and French rolls with preserves and butter.

Downing a final cup of coffee, I grabbed a map and headed out to do some local wine touring and sightseeing. The Hanns Kornell Winery, maker of the famous champagnes, is right next door. Many more wineries are within easy driving distance, so I had to be selective. Two nearby state parks have hiking trails in the foothills that provide panoramic views over the valley. The best view of all, however, was provided on the final morning of my short stay, when I rose at dawn and saw the sun rise over the valley from the lofty heights while taking a hot air balloon ride.

LARKMEAD COUNTRY INN, 1103 Larkmead Lane, Calistoga, CA 94515; 707-942-5360.

Intimate three-guestroom inn, surrounded by the tranquil beauty of Napa Valley vineyards. King and queen beds. Continental breakfast included. Afternoon wine and cheese served. Closed Dec. and Jan. Two-night minimum on weekends. Smoking allowed. Tour the wineries, hike the hills or shop in nearby towns. No pets. Gene and Joan Garbarino, owners/hosts.

DIRECTIONS: Four miles north of St. Helena on Hwy. 29. Larkmead Lane connects Hwy. 29 with Silverado Trail.

MEADOWOOD RESORT HOTEL
St. Helena, California

It was harvest time in the heart of the wine country. My car slowly trailed a truck and grape-ladened gondola as I headed north along Silverado Trail in the Napa Valley. Gazing westward, I could see expanses of vineyards with traces of autumn colors extending up into the opposing foothills. Oak groves and manzanita shrubs created natural borders. My irritation at the traffic hindrance became a peaceful serenity. Eager as I was to get to my destination, Meadowood Resort Hotel, I could lose myself in this picture for awhile.

Soon enough I turned onto the entrance road to the resort's 250 pic-

turesque wooded acres. A few die-hard golfers were enjoying their last few holes before the sun set on the resort's nine-hole golf course. I was unprepared for the magnificence of the buildings, which had been rebuilt after a fire in 1974 to resemble early 1900s New England design. Wrap-around porches and dormered wooden windows were abundant, trimmed neatly in white upon a seaboard gray surface.

There are two main lodges. The Croquet Lodge, appropriately enough, fronts several English croquet courts, making Meadowood home of the annual Domaine Mumm Napa Croquet Classic. (Traditional white clothing is required on the courts.) Fieldstone dividing walls separate the private balconies and patios extending from each guestroom, most of which have accompanying fieldstone fireplaces. The Fairway Lodge houses the resort's two restaurants, a full-service bar, and two levels of outdoor seating overlooking the golf course.

As I was checking in, my eyes wandered around the room. The tile-floored reception area with high cathedral ceilings appeared very spacious. Separated into intimate seating clusters were soft cushioned sofas and leather wing-backed chairs. The massive stone fireplace along one wall, unlit now, would provide cozy warmth during the cooler late autumn and winter months.

I followed the directions to my Lakeview Terrace room. Homey touches included a basket of fresh apples, a thick terrycloth robe, a small refrigerator, a wet bar, a coffee maker and a toaster. The chintz-covered bed had stacks of matching pillows along the headboard, and a down comforter hung over a wooden stand nearby. There was a small reading area with a chair and footstool. French doors opened onto a balcony with white patio furniture, a perfect spot to enjoy morning coffee.

Donning a suit, I strolled back to the formal atmosphere of the Starmont Restaurant, elegantly furnished and decorated in pastels of pink and green. Sipping a glass of famous Napa Valley Cabernet Sauvignon, I perused the menu, selecting the roasted Maine lobster with Thai herbs and mixed Chinese greens. It was delicious. I enjoyed a nightcap on the patio, gazing at the starlit sky.

The next morning found me at the breakfast buffet in the Fairway Grill, choosing from fresh muffins, croissants, dried fruits, French toast with marzipan, omelets made to order and spicy apple sausage. This casual restaurant also serves lunches and, during the summer months, offers an informal supper menu. I attempted, without much success, to eat lightly as I was scheduled for a tennis match that morning on one of the six championship courts which dot the wooded hillside.

The rest of the day would be devoted to relaxation, sunning by the pool with an occasional swim, and perhaps a leisurely hike in the hills before dinner. Tomorrow would be soon enough to visit the wineries and investigate local sights, I decided. The short length of the Valley makes it conveniently possible to travel to the larger city of Napa to the south, which has a unique restored Wine Train that makes lunch and dinner runs up the valley. Vintage 1870 in Yountville provides a variety of shops. St. Helena has some of the oldest wineries of the area. At the northern tip in Calistoga, home of natural hot springs, I experienced my first hot mud bath.

MEADOWOOD RESORT HOTEL, 900 Meadowood Lane, St. Helena, CA 94574; 707-963-3646, 800-458-8080.

An 82-guestroom (private baths), informally luxurious resort tucked in the heart of famous wine country at St. Helena. Mostly king and queen beds. Some suites. Fireplaces. Private patios. Smoking allowed in all areas. Open all year. Two-night minimum on weekends; no charge for children under 12. Two restaurants. Swimming pools, tennis and croquet courts, nine-hole golf course. Wine tasting and shopping within easy driving distance. No pets. Bill Harlan and John Montgomery, owners; Maurice Nayrolles, manager.

DIRECTIONS: North on Hwy. 29, turn right onto Zinfandel Lane. Follow for two miles, turn left on Silverado Trail. Head north two miles, turn right on Howell Mountain Rd. Follow Meadowood signs and turn left on Meadowood Lane.

THE OLD WORLD INN
Napa, California

I must give my wife credit for finding the Old World Inn. . . although I wish I could take claim.

About two months before our anniversary I found, tucked under my coffee cup, an Old World Inn brochure with a little note; "How about celebrating our anniversary at one of 'The Best Places to Kiss in Northern California'?" Well, I was definitely intrigued.

When I phoned innkeeper Diane Dumaine to make reservations, she was ebullient. "Oh, great. . . wonderful! You're just in time for my midweek 'Romancing the Vine' package. I designed it specifically for romantic couples!" (I actually think Diane and my wife were in cahoots on this.)

Diane was watering begonias on the inn's wide, shady front porch when we arrived. "This inn is a real mix of styles," she told me. "Craftsman, Colonial Revival and Queen Anne. The builder, E.W. Doughty, used this private residence to showcase his skills." The eclectic mix of wood shingles, bevelled and leaded glass, and clinker brick work well together to create a structure of historic charm.

The inn's interior color scheme was inspired by Swedish artist Carl Larsson. Mint green, apricot and other pastels create a soft, airy atmosphere.

Chintz-covered love seats snuggle into Dhurrie carpets in the living room. Woodwork of curly redwood accents the downstairs rooms. Stencilled artwork and homilies adorn the walls.

Diane ushered us to our room, Stockholm, where complimentary wine awaited. Stockholm's decor mirrored the air of romance and whimsy in all the guestrooms. Decorative stencilling in shades of peach and French blue repeat the colors of floral fabrics and painted antiques. Stepping into our private sun-room, we found fluffy robes draped over a wicker chair beside the sunken spa tub. An outdoor spa surrounded by a lovely garden is also available to guests. The inn is located on a main street and traffic noise is noticeable.

Don't plan to limit your calories when you pay this place a visit! From morning to late evening, there is a generous assortment of food. Breakfast on croissants, coffee cakes, crepes or frittatas along with juicy, fresh fruit. Tea time brings Scottish shortbread and sugar and spice cookies. Wine-tasting hour is celebrated with sampling of Napa Valley wines, gourmet cheeses, garlic toast, French bread and pates. After an evening out, satisfy your sweet-tooth with a scrumptious slice of Chocolate Box Cake made with pistachios, Grand Marnier and crushed cookies.

While most of Napa Valley's tourist literature focuses on the wineries, be sure to explore downtown Napa, which is within walking distance from the inn. You'll discover a variety or restaurants, coffee houses, the summer Farmer's Market and outdoor concerts in a park by the Napa River.

Was the Old World Inn one of "The Best Places to Kiss in Northern California?" I'll never tell. You'll have to find out for yourself.

OLD WORLD INN, 1301 Jefferson Street, Napa, CA 94558; 707-257-0112.

An eight-room turn-of-the-century Victorian near downtown. Open all year. Two-night weekend minimum stay April-November. King and queen beds. Breakfast, afternoon tea, wine and cheese social, and dessert buffet included. Midweek and off-season packages offered. Walk to shops and restaurants. Ride the Napa Valley Wine Train. Go aloft in a hot air balloon. Or tour the many wineries. No pets. Not suitable for children. No smoking. Kenya and Peanut, resident cats, will greet you outside. CCs: Visa, MC, AE, DISC. Diane Dumain, owner/host.

DIRECTIONS: From San Francisco go north on Hwy. 101. Exit on Highway 37 to Napa. Turn left on Hwy. 121, then left on Hwy. 29. Take the Lincoln Avenue Exit east. Turn right onto Jefferson Street. Watch for inn on the right.

SCOTT COURTYARD AND LODGING

Calistoga, California

100 -135

I occasionally visit an inn which has unique style; Scott Courtyard and Lodging is such an inn. Located on a quiet corner of tree-lined streets, it is just a few blocks from historic Calistoga's world famous spas with natural mineral springs and mud baths. The California bungalow-style inn offers the serenity of a Mediterranean resort.

Once you walk into the white-trellised courtyard toward the soft peach and white main house and cottages (all rooms are suites with private entrances), you feel as though you've entered a hideaway. A pathway wanders past gardens and an effervescent fountain, leading to a gated pool and hot tub.

The cottage, updated for comfort, has tropical Art Deco and polished hardwood floors adorned with Oriental rugs. Comfortable queen-sized beds are draped with collectible Chenille bedspreads. While the ambiance of the suites

U.S. $125

is casual, the attention to creating a relaxing and informal atmosphere shows an artistic sensitivity to detail. All the rooms have private sitting areas and their own baths.

Art Deco also dominates the large social room where a floor-to-ceiling fireplace warms the somewhat chilly wine country evenings. Art and books are a focal point along with tiled floors and Oriental rugs.

Here, also, a full family-style buffet breakfast is served, highlighted by blueberry pancakes, locally made Thai-chicken sausage, soft-boiled eggs, fresh fruits and cereals. The inn's aviary of active finches and canaries provide visual entertainment.

If the pampering of the nearby spas and mud baths seem a bit too public, spend an afternoon soaking in the inn's hot tub, swim in the pool or work out in the privacy of the recently installed exercise room. For a more robust work-out, borrow a bike to explore the countryside or head out for a breath-taking glider plane ride.

Calistoga is a small town at the north end of the famous Napa Valley wine country and has superb gourmet restaurants, unusual shops, and a great book store. Winery tours are always a highlight—particularly a visit to the lime-stone caves at the Greystone Cellars, a winery in nearby St. Helena. Innkeep-ers, Joe and Lauren Scott, are delighted to help you with arrangements for any of these excursions.

SCOTT COURTYARD AND LODGING, 1443 2nd Street, Calistoga, CA 94515; 707-942-0948. An intimate inn with six private-entry Art Deco suites in historic Calistoga at the north end of the famous wine country of Napa Valley. Well-known for its min-eral spring spas and mud baths. Queen beds. Complimentary full breakfast. Closed in January; two-night minimum on weekends May-October. Smoking restricted. No pets. Hot tub, pool and exercise room on premises. Two blocks to spa, shops, gourmet restaurants and bicycle rentals. Short drive for winery tours, glider plane rides, bal-loon rides or golf courses. Resident pooch named Spike, a Maltese, greets all guests. Joe and Lauren Scott, owners/hosts.

DIRECTIONS: Hwy. 29 north to Calistoga. Turn right into downtown Calistoga (becomes Lincoln Street). Travel approximately three blocks and make a left on Fair-way. Go two blocks to 2nd Street. Inn is on the corner.

SILVER ROSE INN
Calistoga, California

The town of Calistoga has long been dedicated to the comfort and relaxation of those who visit. Located just two miles from town, the Silver Rose Inn is also dedicated to the comfort of those who visit.

Perhaps owner/host J-Paul Dumont needed some of the tranquility of this sylvan spot. J-Paul, an investment banker, and his wife, Sally, decided to purchase the inn in 1985. "Our hobbies are food and wine," said J-Paul as we strolled around the beautifully landscaped property. "We both just fell in love with this area, and the Silver Rose, when we visited." Sunning by the large swimming pool, carved out of the natural rock hillside, with its adjoining Jacuzzi, I could see why they had been charmed. A gentle waterfall feeds the pool, and the scent of hundreds of rose bushes permeates the air.

The Gathering Room is a cozy place to enjoy an expanded continental breakfast around tables set with colorful linen. Or take your coffee and sit by the waterfall. Every afternoon at 4:00, Sally arranges a tray of cheeses and crackers for guests to enjoy along with their complimentary bottle of Silver Rose Cellars Napa Valley Chardonnay.

Each of the nine guestrooms is unique. The Oriental Suite, the largest room, is simple elegance, with its shoji-screen-covered windows and matching light fixtures. Rustic beamed ceilings, hardwood floors covered by Oriental rugs, rattan furniture, and a Japanese lacquered-wood headboard complete the tone. A large private balcony overlooking the rose gardens and a bath with a Jacuzzi will certainly create a state of serenity.

Bears In Burgundy offers a bit of whimsy, with its profusion of teddy bears to keep you company. Peach Delight is delightful; Country Blue is restful in shades of blue; and Turn of the Century, with its small, private balcony, is decorated with old-time touches such as sepia photographs, period dolls, and a clawfoot tub.

Four newly constructed rooms have the themes of Carousel, Western, Garden and Safari. Although I haven't yet stayed in the Safari room I assume by the name that they let you sleep with their tiger. Two of the rooms have whirlpool tubs.

Leaving the next day, I felt sufficiently restored to attempt a day of serious wine tasting.

SILVER ROSE INN, 351 Rosedale Rd., Calistoga, CA 94515; 707-942-9581; 800-995-9381, fax: 707-942-0841.

A nine-guestroom (private baths) B&B in the beautiful Napa Valley wine country. Queen beds. Continental breakfast. Open year-round. No smoking or pets. Two-night minimum when Saturday night is included. Near spas, glider rides, hot air ballooning, wineries. CCs: Visa, AE, MC. Sally and J-Paul Dumont, owners/hosts.

DIRECTIONS: From San Francisco, north on Hwy. 101 over Golden Gate Bridge to east 37, then north 29 to Calistoga. Turn right on Lincoln to Silverado Trail. Turn right 1/4 mi. to 351 Rosedale.

INN EVENTS: BLIND WINE TASTINGS—Each guest purchases a bottle of wine or brings one from their cellar of a prearranged varietal and year and owner challenges with same varietal and year from private cellar. Offered all year.

Barbeque dinners are also available.

THE WINE COUNTRY INN
St. Helena, California

It was a wonderful day in March. There were new leaves on the trees, the spring flowers were blooming in profusion, wild geese were flying, and the small vineyards in the little valley just below the inn were starting to perk up. The natural wild mustard, lupines, poppies, and live oak trees blended with plantings of oleanders, petunias, and Chinese pistachios. This inn, which I saw

almost the first day it was opened, has now taken on the patina that comes as buildings put on additional years.

The guestrooms are furnished almost entirely in antiques; some have intimate balconies and some have patios leading to the lawn. Many of the rooms have fireplaces, canopied beds, tufted bedspreads and handmade quilts, along with a generous supply of magazines and books and big, comfortable, fluffy pillows.

Visitors to the Napa Valley enjoy visits to the many wineries, as well as to mineral baths, balloon rides and great restaurants. There are also a number of antique shops in the area. Dotted with century-old stone bridges, pump houses, barns and stone buildings, all of which are a delight to both painter and photographer, the manicured agricultural beauty of the valley contrasts with the rugged, tree-covered hills surrounding it.

Patience and constant attention to details and maintenance have allowed the building, the trees, shrubs and flowers to take on a real character of their own. It's hard to realize that it was actually built in 1975 as an inn. The architecture is batten board with a center section of stone and a mansard roof that is quite in keeping with the other winery architecture of this part of California.

I think other innkeepers in California are fortunate to have such a model inn after which to fashion themselves. The care and consideration that have gone into the designing, and the result, prove that a country inn doesn't have to be old to be legendary.

It's the spirit that matters.

THE WINE COUNTRY INN, 1152 Lodi Lane, St. Helena, CA 94574; 707-963-7077.

A 24-room (private baths) country inn in the Napa wine valley of California, about 70 mi. from San Francisco. Queen, double and twin beds available. Continental breakfast served to houseguests; no other meals served. Restaurants within walking distance. Open daily except the week before and including Christmas. This inn is within driving distance of a great many wineries and also the Robert Louis Stevenson Museum. Swimming pool and spa on grounds. Golf and tennis nearby. No children. No pets. Jim Smith, innkeeper.

DIRECTIONS: From San Francisco take the Oakland Bay Bridge to Hwy. 80. Travel north to the Napa cutoff. Stay on Hwy. 29 through the town of St. Helena, for 1-3/4 mi. north to Lodi Lane, then turn east 1/4 mi. to inn.

ZINFANDEL INN
St. Helena, California

As I drove north on Highway 29 through the famed Napa Wine Country, I passed acre upon acre of gnarled vines with the early green of new leaves accented against the almost fluorescent yellow of the wild mustard that grows

between the rows. I turned west on Zinfandel Lane, and the Zinfandel Inn
appeared on my left. Surrounded by the vineyards of the Raymond Winery
and Sutter Home Winery, the English Tudor home is magnificent. The stone
craftsmanship is reminiscent of a European castle.

Innkeepers Terry and Diane Payton purchased the inn in 1988 after having managed it. Diane and Jerry enjoy serving people, as innkeepers and also
in their other professions. Terry is a claims adjuster and Diane an insurance
agent. "We've really tried to create an intimate atmosphere here," Diane told
me as she finished arranging a crystal vase of purple irises. "Guests can use
most of the inn, including the kitchen and family room. We like them to feel
right at home."

The three guestrooms are appropriately named for wine varietals: Zinfandel, Chardonnay and Petite Sirah. The Zinfandel Suite, decorated in restful
blues, has an elegant tile Jacuzzi surrounded by stained glass and plants, fireplace, and a private deck. A large stone fireplace warms the first-floor
Chardonnay Suite, with its king-sized brass bed and private entrance. The
Petite Sirah is furnished in original French Victorian furniture and features a
feather bed. All have cozy love seats and private baths.

You may decide to bring your complimentary wine from your room outside
to enjoy it in the garden gazebo or while strolling around the fish pond. Or
perhaps to visit with Terry as he works on one of the antique autos he loves to
restore.

A full breakfast is served during the week. I enjoyed the eggs benedict. On weekends they have Belgium waffles with strawberries.

After my final cup of tea, I set out for an enjoyable day of sightseeing. The Zinfandel Inn is centrally located, only two miles from the town of St. Helena, and close to hot-air balloon rides, glider rides, the Calistoga mineral hot springs and mud baths, and of course, wine tasting.

ZINFANDEL INN, 800 Zinfandel Lane, St. Helena, CA 94574; 707-963-3512.

A three-guestroom (private baths) English Tudor country home in the Napa Valley. King and double beds. Open all year. Full breakfast. No pets. No smoking. CCs: Visa, MC, AE, Optima. Terry & Diane Payton owners/hosts.

DIRECTIONS: Hwy. 29 north toward St. Helena to Zinfandel Lane. Turn right, inn is on left.

Marin County Coast

Noted especially for its beautiful beaches and headlands, Marin County also boasts Muir Woods, a 550-acre tract of redwoods that reach up to 250 feet in height.

EVENTS

AUGUST–SEPTEMBER	Renaissance Pleasure Faire
SEPTEMBER	Film Festival
SEPTEMBER	Art Festival, Mill Valley.

SIGHTS

Johnson's Oyster Farm
Point Reyes National Seashore
Mt. Tamalpias State Park
Tomales Bay State Park

CASA DEL MAR
Stinson Beach, California

"I fell in love with the natural beauty of Stinson Beach and the gardens surrounding the house, so I created Casa del Mar. It allows me to pursue a lifestyle that fits my nature," said Rick Klein, who spent part of his career on a fishing boat and is now the proud owner of this bed and breakfast. Rick and I were wandering through the terraced gardens that have existed here in all their botanical glory since 1930. They were even used in the 1970s by the School of Landscape Architecture of the University of California as a teaching garden.

"I never tire of walking through here," said Rick, "even with the trails on Mt. Tamalpias so available." We walked in reverent silence for a while to sounds of the distant surf. Pausing by a plot overflowing with fragrant pineapple sage, Rick told me that the original house had been built in the early 1900s as a family lodge. It remained in that family over 80 years. He purchased it in 1987 and rebuilt it as a Mediterranean-style two-story, with a pale peach stucco exterior and a heavy tile roof. With Mt. Tamalpias nearby, the inn sits atop a knoll with broad views of the Pacific Ocean.

"Hors d'oeuvres will be served late this afternoon; be sure to join us," Rick reminded me with a wave as I began the short trek to the beach. Shops, restaurants and beaches are all within easy walking distance in this small community. Mt. Tamalpias State Park is just across the street from the inn.

The fog had crept in and a damp chill was in the air by the time I

returned. A fire had been lit in the living room fireplace and the hors d'oeuvres trays were already set out. I settled on the rattan sofa and admired the
individually illuminated works of Marin County artists hanging on the walls.
The firelight cast shadows across the Mexican floor tiles, colorful throw rugs
and soft pastel hues of the room.

Tired from my long walk, I opted to settle in my room for the evening.
Named the Shell Room, it had white stucco walls and a brilliant blue down
comforter on the bed. Natural matchstick shades hung over the windows. The
bathroom had an unusual shell-shaped sink. French doors opened onto a private balcony.

Appetizing scents led me to the sunny dining room the following morning.
If the views of the ocean and "Mt. Tam" weren't satisfying enough, I was further treated to blueberry-poppy seed coffee cake, a Mexican egg-sausage casse-
role dripping with hot salsa and fresh strawberries. The fruit was garnished
with flowers from the gardens. Rick's culinary talents compete with those of
his friend Nancy Sullivan, who often assists him. They are always on the lookout for new recipes.

CASA DEL MAR, 37 Belvedere Ave., P.O. Box 238, Stinson Beach, CA 94970; 415-
868-2124, 800-331-3761.

Five-guestroom (private baths) Mediterranean-style B&B overlooking the Pacific
Ocean. Queen beds. Breakfast included. Afternoon hors d'oeuvres. Open all year.
Two-day minimum on weekends. Hike in Mt. Tamalpias State Park. Short walk to
beach, shops and restaurants. No smoking indoors. No pets. Two outside cats in residence. CCs: Visa, MC. Rick Klein, owner/host.

DIRECTIONS: From Hwy. 101 take Stinson Beach/Hwy. 1 exit. Follow Hwy. 1 to
Stinson Beach. Turn right at small firehouse onto Belvedere Ave. Watch for Casa del
Mar on left side.

ROUNDSTONE FARM

Olema, California

"The B&B was completed May 1987, the same year I turned 69!" stated Inger
Fisher, owner of Roundstone Farm. Not exactly how she intended to spend her
"golden years," and quite different from the retirement dream she and her husband shared of raising Connamara and Arabian horses on the 14 acres.

"When my husband died in 1981, I was left with a house that was awk-
ward, 14 acres of land, and six horses. I did not want to sell the land. This is
where I felt I belonged. To stay and maintain the status quo meant I had to
develop the land myself. My profession as an interior designer didn't quite pre-

pare me for the local bureaucracy and bankers! But once those hurdles were cleared, the fun began. I knew I wanted to create a very special environment. Roundstone is a passive solar house of five levels, designed to fit the hillside."

I shared with her that I felt she had accomplished her creation with the design. But I, however, was mesmerized by the magnificent views of horses nuzzling in rolling, green pastures, the lulling motion of wind on the pond creating the slightest of waves, swaying of hillside grasses and, in the far distance, Tomales Bay sending just a subtle smell of salt air.

Each morning after a hearty home-cooked breakfast consisting of various egg and vegetable casseroles and fresh, warm muffins, I would leave to wander in the hills. Late afternoon, the thought of a warm cup of tea in the cedar-walled living room would bring me back to what rapidly felt like home. I would settle into a comfortable chair in the living room, alternately reading, gazing from picture windows, and visiting with other guests. With a total of only five guestrooms, an intimate feeling is a natural progression. I discovered that, although each room has its own scheme, all have fireplaces, European armoires and custom wooden headboards carved by a local craftsman. White goose down comforters are welcome on those cold, coastal nights.

Visitors have labeled this place "an island in time." I am counting on that to hold true for my next visit.

ROUNDSTONE FARM, 9940 Sir Francis Drake, Olema, CA 94950; 415-663-1020. Five-guestroom elegant farmhouse. Queen and twin beds. Breakfast included. Open all year, with a two-night minimum on weekends and holidays. Accommodations not suited for children. Smoking permitted outside only. No pets. Hike the surrounding hills of the Golden Gate Recreation Area. Ride horses or bicycle the trails. Stroll the Tomales Beach, just a short four miles away. Abundant in nature and wildlife. Mittens, the house cat, will welcome you at the door. CCs: Visa, MC. Inger Fisher, owner/host.

DIRECTIONS: 10 mi. north of the Golden Gate Bridge. Then west 20 mi. on Sir Francis Drake Highway.

TEN INVERNESS WAY
Inverness, California

"Remember to show hospitality. There are some who, by so doing, have entertained angels without knowing it." This quote is part of innkeeper Mary
Davies' "Innkeeper's Creed." And while all guests may not be angels, Mary
Davies certainly treats them as if they are. As co-author of *So You Want to Be
an Innkeeper* she keeps working to make the inn better for the guests. "We've
just added a suite," she said, "a sort of private cottage in the inn, with its own
french doors leading out to its own private patio and a complete kitchen. But
you don't have to cook! We deliver breakfast in bed, our famous Banana Buttermilk Buckwheat pancakes, for example. It's the perfect spot for romance,
and also works great if you want to bring a baby."

Ten Inverness Way is a rustic 1904 redwood-shingled inn located in the
coastal village of Inverness. A writer, Mary came to Inverness to join the
active community of writers and artists. "Also, my small family couldn't eat all
the jam I made!" she laughed. We were standing under the wisteria-covered
arbor, chatting. A profusion of flowers flank the flagstone path up to the inn.

The living room is very large, with all the comforts of home, right down to
a popcorn popper to accompany rainy-day Monopoly marathons. Floors and
walls are of the original Douglas fir. A stone fireplace, Oriental rugs, cozy armchairs and couches, overflowing bookcases, and good brass reading lamps
inspire some serious lounging. A guitar and player piano are provided for the
musically inclined. Tea is available anytime.

Guestrooms are intimate and romantic. All have queen-sized beds, hand-
made quilts and individual heaters. All have private baths and lovely views of

Tomales Bay, Inverness Ridge or the colorful garden. A private hot tub/spa in its own redwood cottage is available for guest use.

Mary is crazy about hiking, and says she and her assistant innkeepers can easily map out four full days of different hikes at Point Reyes. Ask her about the Twelve-Mile Little Bit of Everything hike, her current favorite.

A statement Mary Davies made in an article she wrote sums up her philosophy of innkeeping. "Inns are personal, so they're different. . . I run my inn so it's fun for me, and my guests seem to like it that way." I certainly did.

TEN INVERNESS WAY BED AND BREAKFAST, P.O. Box 63, Inverness, CA 94937; 415-669-1648.

A four-guestroom (private baths) rustic redwood inn near Point Reyes National Seashore, Tomales Bay State Park, beaches, redwoods and Johnson's Oyster Farm. Queen beds. Breakfast included. Open all year. Weekend two-night minimum. No smoking or pets. One garden cat. CCs: Visa, MC. Mary Davies, owner/host.

DIRECTIONS: From San Francisco, take Hwy. 101 north to San Anselmo-Sir Francis Drake Blvd. exit. Sir Francis Drake will take you to Olema (1/2 hour). Turn right on Hwy. 1, left at road to National Seashore Visitor's Center. Go three mi. to stop sign. Turn left, continue to Inverness. Left at Inverness Restaurant. Inn on right.

San Francisco and the Bay Area

It has been called the most beautiful city in the world, resting on 40 hills surrounded by the Pacific Ocean and the San Francisco Bay. The inhabitants of the city have come here from all parts of the globe, settling in ethnic enclaves that make for wonderful touring experiences: Chinatown, North Beach (wherein a veritable renaissance of Italian restaurants, bakeries and cafes is happening as you read), Fisherman's Wharf, the Latin American section south of Market, Japantown, the Russian accent of the Richmond District and many more. The incredible diversity has bred a spirit of tolerance and sophistication that no other city has.

Only seven miles by seven miles in area, there is enough to do in San Francisco to keep you busy for a week. Remember to bring warm clothes during the summer, as that is the foggy season. But September and October are filled with sunny and warm days. My own list of special Bay Area places includes Alcatraz, Chinatown, Fisherman's Wharf, North Beach, Ghirardelli Square, Union Street and Cliff House

---

EVENTS

JANUARY–APRIL	Ballet Season
FEBRUARY–MARCH	Chinese New Year Celebration
MARCH	St. Patrick's Day Parade
APRIL	Cherry Blossom Festival Parade
APRIL–MAY	International Film Festival
MAY, 1ST SUNDAY	Cinco De Maya Parade
MAY	Bay to Breakers Race
MAY	Black & White Ball
JUNE	Lesbian-Gay Freedom Day Parade
SUMMER	Shakespeare Festival in Park
SEPTEMBER	Cajun Festival in Park
SEPTEMBER	Annual West Coast Stunt Kite Championship
SEPTEMBER	Annual Blues Festival
SEPTEMBER–DECEMBER	Opera Season

ALAMO SQUARE INN

85-175

San Francisco, California

Even the famed San Francisco earthquake of 1906 couldn't shake the Victorian gentility of the magnificent Alamo Square Inn. Located in San Francisco's largest historic district, the elegant Alamo Square Inn occupies a complex of two Victorian-era mansions—an 1896 English Tudor and a Queen Anne that was constructed for Eliza Baum in 1895, who had been inspired by the Midwinter Fair of 1894. Innkeepers Wayne Corn and Klaus May have kept Eliza's vision before them during their detailed restoration.

I was served afternoon tea in the drawing room after I arrived and stepped back into an era when wood was polished lovingly and the utmost care was given to the harmony of design. Rich oak floors, warm wood paneling, exquisite wall coverings and the glow of a stained-glass skylight over the curved staircase merge to create a mood of restful elegance.

Joined by a conservatory atrium complex that overlooks English-style gardens, the guestrooms offer unique variety, with access to a large, shared deck. The Alamo Suite, with its sitting room, fireplace and two bedrooms, has luxury and privacy. And what could be more relaxing than a soak in the sunken Jacuzzi of the art deco Sunrise Suite and its panoramic city views?

The morning room provides a comfortable atmosphere for a full breakfast amid European furnishings and Oriental rugs.

Wayne, a former university administrator, and Klaus, a professional chef, and their staff will happily share their wealth of information about the Bay Area. Alamo Square Inn is only minutes from San Francisco's attractions. Private parking is available, and necessary; taxi service is prompt. As I drove off, I felt as if I were taking a souvenir of San Francisco's grandest era with me.

ALAMO SQUARE INN, 719 Scott Street, San Francisco, CA 94117; 415-922-2055, 800-345-8055.

An elegant 13-guestroom (private baths) Victorian mansion with views of San Francisco's skyline. King, queen and double beds. Open year-round. Full breakfast. Centrally located to all cultural offerings, shopping and Golden Gate Park. Telephones in all rooms. No pets. Restricted smoking. CCs: Visa, MC, AE. Wayne Corn and Klaus May, owners/hosts.

DIRECTIONS: From the north, take Golden Gate Bridge to Park Presidio exit and continue south. Turn right at Cabrillo, immediate left onto 14th Ave., left at Fulton, right on Scott St. From east and south, Bay Bridge/I-80 and Airport/U.S. 101 merge. Follow signs for the Golden Gate Bridge. Take Fell St. exit, go west approx. 10 blocks. Right on Scott St.

ARCHBISHOPS MANSION INN
San Francisco, California

The romance of the 19th century reigns at the Archbishops Mansion Inn. At first glance the opulence of this "grand lady" commands an almost reverent response. The hand-painted ceilings, Oriental carpets and glowing redwood interior are truly a sight to behold. Built in 1904 as a residence for the Arch-

bishop of San Francisco, the Second French Empire style inn is decorated in Belle Epoque fashion. When Jonathan Shannon and Jeffery Ross purchased the inn in 1980, the grand old girl had survived the San Francisco earthquake, served as a refugee center during the fire, and weathered 35 years as a boys' school and medical clinic.

No amateurs at renovation and restoration, having already saved the famous Spreckles mansion, Jonathan and Jeffery spent two years refurbishing and scouring Europe and the United States for furnishings and decorations before they opened Archbishops.

Their attention to detail is evident from the moment you enter. A three-story grand staircase with hand-carved mahogany columns sweeps upwards, illuminated by a 16-foot stained-glass dome. The parlor, dining room, English salon and many guestrooms have carved mantelpieces and floor-to-ceiling fire-places. Crystal chandeliers, gilded mirrors and the parlor's hand-painted ceiling create a lavish atmosphere. Of the many elegant period furnishings, Noel Coward's 1904 Bechstein grand piano is a prized piece.

The guestrooms are romantic and luxurious. Named after 19th-century operas, every room contains an exquisitely carved bed. One of the most unusual resides in Don Giovanni. From a castle in southern France, the early 18th-century canopied bed is patterned after a 400-year-old bed and is carved with life-size angels. Other treasures include a tall gilt mirror once in Mary Lincoln's family and a huge crystal chandelier used in "Gone With the Wind." All rooms are supplied with French soaps, down comforters and fine linens. Most of the rooms have fireplaces, and all have lovely bathrooms, some with double Jacuzzis.

If you choose, you can be served your complimentary breakfast of pastries, boiled eggs, raspberry jam, juice and coffee or tea in your bed. For a romantic treat, order a half-bottle of champagne, snuggle back, and read the Sunday paper.

THE ARCHBISHOPS MANSION, 1000 Fulton St., San Francisco, CA 94117; 415-563-7872. Reservations: 800-543-5820. Fax: 415-885-3193.

A 15-guestroom (private baths) opulent mansion across from a park in a historic landmark district, six blocks from the Opera House, Civic Center and Symphony Hall. King and queen beds. Breakfast included. Open all year. Limited off-street parking. No pets. Restricted smoking. CCs: Visa, MC, AE. Jonathan Shannon and Jeffrey Ross, owners/hosts; Kathleen Austin, innkeeper.

DIRECTIONS: From airport, take Hwy. 101 north to Fell St., five blocks to Steiner St., turn right, two blocks to Fulton St., turn left, on corner.

THE INN AT UNION SQUARE

San Francisco, California

There are probably few inns in America that deliberately strive to be inconspicuous in their outward appearance. Yet, at a very select location in San Francisco, directly across from the Post Street entrance of the Westin St. Francis Hotel on Union Square, amidst fine shops, international airline ticket offices and some 50 steps from the cable cars, is the Inn at Union Square.

Only a neat awning and brass plate identify the inn, formerly a sixty-room hotel that Norm and Nan Rosenblatt (she, an interior decorator by profession) completely remodeled into a very comfortable 30-room inn, all with Georgian furniture, colorful fabrics, private facilities, direct-dial telephones and TVs concealed within stylish armoires.

For guest convenience, each of the five floors has its own common room with fireplaces, icemakers and refrigerators. It is here or in the guest's room that a continental breakfast of fresh fruits and juices, scones, croissants and hot drinks is served in the morning, with the latest news and financial papers.

As security is paramount in any centrally located, metropolitan inn, 24-hour desk and concierge service is provided. Access to upper floors is by a keyed elevator.

Most of the well-furnished guestrooms are above adjacent buildings and face east, so natural lighting, while brightest in the morning hours, continues throughout the day. Turndown bed service is provided in the evenings and shoes will be given a gratis shine if placed in the hallway upon retiring.

The inn staff assures constant attention to guests. Earliest possible reservations are necessary.

THE INN AT UNION SQUARE, 440 Post St., San Francisco, CA 94102; 415-397-3510.

A 30-guestroom (private baths) bed-and-breakfast inn in the very heart of San

Francisco's fine shops, hotels and theaters. All size beds. All rooms with private baths, concealed TVs and direct-dial telephones. Continental breakfast. Open year-round. Wheelchair access. Cable cars a few steps away. Valet parking if desired. Minimal accommodations for children; inquire in advance. No pets. Norm and Nan Rosenblatt, owners/hosts; Brooks Bayly, manager.

DIRECTIONS: At the Union Square corner of Post and Powell, across from Post St. entrance to St. Francis Hotel.

THE INN SAN FRANCISCO

San Francisco, California

75-175

The first thing Martin Neely and Connie Wu did when they purchased the Inn in 1990 was to hire a famous "colorist" and paint the Inn. The Inn now is in the famous *"Painted Ladies"* book. They then completed the rooms in the Garden Cottage thereby bringing the total of the rooms to 22. Five have Jacuzzis, one a redwood hot-tub, and four have fireplaces. Antiques and paintings were added throughout.

The double parlors are elegant. Massive wooden pediments frame etched parlor doors. Large gilt-edged mirrors reflect flickering candles on marble mantles, and the perfume of roses, along with soft classical music, create a romantic atmosphere. Forest-green walls enhance the Oriental carpets and antique furnishings.

The house was built by Charles I. Havens, who was the San Francisco "City Architect" for 12 years. The interior decor is authentic to the period.

The inn also has a roof-top sundeck where you can bask during the day or view the twinkling city lights at night.

Outside there is a lovely and peaceful English garden, with a redwood hot-tub in a tropical gazebo. There are many avocados each year on the huge avocado tree, zillions of walnuts on the walnut tree, delicious figs on the fig-tree and among several unique plants, there is a large "flowering maple" with year-round beautiful "Japanese Lantern" flowers.

Enjoy breakfast in the parlor, in the shaded garden, on the sun deck or in your room. Connie bakes the breads for breakfast.

The block on which the inn resides was known as "Mansion Row" in horse-and-buggy days. A trip to the symphony hall took two hours then. Now you can whisk off to hear the *The Magic Flute* in just fifteen minutes. The fire that destroyed much of San Francisco after the 1906 disaster burned to within 1 block of the Inn.

THE INN SAN FRANCISCO, 943 South Van Ness Ave., San Francisco, CA 94110; 415-641-0188.

A 22-guestroom (17 private baths) Victorian in the sunny Mission District. Queen and double beds. Open year-round. Two-night minimum July thru Oct. Breakfast included. No pets. Martin Neeley and Connie Wu, owners/hosts.

DIRECTIONS: From Golden Gate Bridge, take Lombard St. exit to Van Ness Ave. Right to South Van Ness Ave. (across Market St). From Bay Bridge, exit toward Hwy. 101 North (Golden Gate Bridge). Exit right onto Mission St. to South Van Ness, right. From Hwy. 101 south, Army St. west exit to South Van Ness, right.

THE MANSION AT LAKEWOOD

Walnut Creek, California

As I walked through the classic white wrought-iron gates of the Mansion at Lakewood, I entered a world of sweeping verandas and lush lawns skirted by colorful displays of flowers; three acres of nature only a quarter mile from downtown Walnut Creek and just 10 miles from crowded Oakland. A heritage hickory nut tree, 100-year-old oaks, magnolias, redwoods and an ancient cactus garden separated me from the hurried world that existed just outside.

Mike and Sharyn McCoy also felt the tranquil charm of the Mansion when they toured the estate in 1986. After two years of hearings, their application for a B&B was approved, and major renovation began. Originally, the 1861 rambling two-story Victorian was part of a Mexican land grant. Sporting the rustic siding and raised verandas of the period, the 8,000-square-foot building still has its glass-etched transom with 34 stars to commemorate the year Kansas became the 34th state.

The Mansion has two parlors, a majestic library with redwood bookshelves and a black marble fireplace, and an elegant dining room. The large drawing room is decorated with wallpaper in shades of teal, mauve and burgundy. You may notice Sharyn's collection of toy bunnies peeking around corners throughout the inn.

All seven guestrooms are decorated with fine antiques and fabrics to create a feeling of country-fresh charm. The summerhouse is most unusual, with hand-painted floors, an original vault now used as a closet, and a clawfoot tub on the enclosed porch. All rooms have private baths and some suites include fireplaces. One suite has a black marble bath with a double Jacuzzi.

After a wonderful breakfast of homebaked croissants, crêpes or quiche, step onto one of the lovely manicured lawns for a game of croquet. Or take a relaxing stroll on a nature path and catch the glint of Koi as they slide among the water lilies. Whatever your mood, the McCoys have created a gracious environment of tasteful elegance where you will feel pampered and completely relaxed.

THE MANSION AT LAKEWOOD, 1056 Hacienda Dr., Walnut Creek, CA 94598; 415-946-9075.

A seven-guestroom (private baths), secluded country Victorian. Breakfast included. Open all year. One-quarter mi. to downtown Walnut Creek, two mi. to Mt. Diablo State Park. No smoking, pets or alcohol. CCs: Visa, MC, DI, AE. Michael and Sharyn McCoy, owners/hosts.

DIRECTIONS: Where Hwy. 24 and 680 cross in Walnut Creek, take Ygnacio Valley Rd. to Homestead Ave., turn right. First left after stop sign is Hacienda.

✗ THE MANSIONS 89-350
San Francisco, California

Unique, elegant and certainly out of the ordinary, The Mansions offer guests a visit they will long remember. Settled in a prestigious neighborhood that includes a number of San Francisco's most splendid homes, the hotel—an artistic joining of two adjacent houses—is only a short walk from the refurbished Fillmore district and Union Street, where some of the city's most unusual and fashionable boutiques, restaurants, and clubs are located.

From the moment you arrive and step into the grand foyer of the original hotel, welcomed by the soft tinkle of crystal chandeliers, there is an aura of excitement. To the strains of Bach's "Invention in C-Major," a large multicolored macaw screeches "hello" from his perch. Inventive murals tell the life story of the original Mansion. Tapestries, artifacts, great paintings and sculptures surround you—treasures of times past.

The main parlor is an impressive example of Art Nouveau and is dominated by a nine-foot turquoise jardiniere. "Sotheby's wanted it shipped to New York," The Mansions' owner, Bob Pritikin, told me. Built in 1887 by Senator

Chambers, the twin-turreted Queen Anne Victorian is one of San Francisco's original Grandes Dames and a designated city landmark. In 1990, the Greek Revival home next door—complete with its own parlor, nine guestrooms, and a lovely breakfast nook—became part of the hotel.

An author, advertising agency owner and entertainer, Bob hosts a nightly Victorian Cabaret Theater that includes a fabulous magic show and a ghostly concert on the grand piano by the Mansions' resident ghost, Claudia. Claudia performs requests until the evening's end, when she completes her concert with a Scott Joplin rag, accompanied by guests who have been supplied with a multitude of rhythm instruments. Billed as America's Foremost Concert Saw Player, Bob often treats guests to a performance of "Moonlight Saw-nata." "I just love to step up to my saw and warble," he laughed. "You know, I've played with Liberace and Johnny Cash!"

The common rooms display more than a million dollars worth of art and antiques, including works by Turner, Reynolds and the famed sculptor Benjamin Buffano. The Mansions' dining room features a breathtaking stained-glass mural, one of the world's largest. The turn-of-the-century masterpiece stretches 32 continuous feet. "I'm not sure if I'm staying in a hotel or an art museum," said fellow guest Mildred Salway.

Murals are a theme throughout the hotel, even in many of the guestrooms. The rooms are furnished with valued antiques and decorated with whimsy and drama. Most rooms have king or queen beds, and all have additional sofa beds and private baths. Special gifts of candy and silk roses await guests, as do fresh flowers.

The full breakfast, which is included with the room rate, is opulent. Eggs any style, fresh-squeezed juice, jumbo "banger" sausages, hot cheese potatoes in mini-crocks, toasted crumpets, cereal, and fresh ground coffee are served in the cheerful West Wing breakfast room. Or, on request, you may have breakfast in bed!

The Mansions offers elegant evening dining. The restaurant is restricted to the pleasures of its guests and may include a menu of fennel soup, filet of elk or roast grouse. A list of fine California and French wines is available, along with a full beer selection, including San Francisco's rare steam beer.

Packing my bags just prior to checkout, I couldn't help but wonder how Claudia had met her demise. When asked, Bob just smiled and glanced toward the soft tinkle of the chandelier. I guess I really don't want to know. The magic and elegance of the Mansions should remain a mystery.

THE MANSIONS, 2220 Sacramento St., San Francisco, CA 94115; 415-929-9444, 800-826-9398.

A 29-guestroom (private baths) Queen Anne Victorian and Greek Revival mansion located in one of San Francisco's most lovely neighborhoods. Open all year. King, queen and double beds. Within walking distance to shops, restaurants and clubs. City bus and taxi curbside; cable car four blocks away. Full breakfast included; dinner Mon.-Sat., by reservation. Telephones in rooms. Children and pets welcome. Bob Pritikin, owner-host; Tracy Pritikin-Pore, manager; Mark Evans, assistant manager.

DIRECTIONS: From Golden Gate Bridge drive to Marina and take a right on Webster St. to Sacramento. From Bay Bridge or from Peninsula take Van Ness Ave. and turn left on Sacramento St.

PETITE AUBERGE

San Francisco, California

"The first time we took the girls to France, we just fell in love," says Sally Post. "It was natural that one of our inns had to be French!" And French it is. Sally is the decorating force behind each of the Four Sisters Inn hotels (for the story of this enterprising family, see the Green Gables Inn), and when you step into the Petite Auberge you could just as well be in the French countryside.

This five-story inn is located between Union Square and Nob Hill, a terrific headquarters for exploring downtown San Francisco. You can pick up a cable car just a block from the inn that will take you to Fisherman's Wharf.

The inn has three types of guestrooms, all decorated in charming French country style with salmon and blue colors used extensively. Oak armoires, carved headboards, lace curtains and fabrics of peach, green, and blue give the rooms a delicate feel. Most of the rooms tend to be on the small size and the smallest, although comfortable, would be too confining for a stay of more than a few days.

The dining room and parlor are located on the first floor. Handpainted walls in the dining room depict a cafe scene with countryside beyond, while the cozy parlor gives guests a place to gather at the end of the day for an afternoon tea that includes such delicious appetizers as hot artichoke dip and filo pizza. Breakfast consists of pancakes, homebaked muffins, fruit and a beverage.

Those sensitive to traffic noise should mention this when making reservations.

PETITE AUBERGE, 863 Bush St., San Francisco, CA 94108; 415-928-6000.
A 26-room (private baths) intimate hotel in the heart of Nob Hill, next to the

White Swan. One king and 25 queen beds. Close to cable car and Union Square. Open all year. No pets. CCs: Visa, MC, AE. Roger & Sally Post, owners; manager on premises.

DIRECTIONS: From Van Ness Ave. go east on Bush. Inn is on the right.

THE SHERMAN HOUSE

San Francisco, California

"Luxury, elegance and tasteful comfort" is the way The Sherman House is described in its brochure. I would add impeccable service and graciousness. The Sherman House is chiefly Italianate in style. The magnificent, asymmetrical white-frame three-story structure is located in the prestigious Pacific Heights area of San Francisco, near famed Union Street with its unique boutiques.

In January 1981, Manouchehr Mobedshahi, an Iranian-born San Franciscan entrepreneur, purchased the Sherman House and began major restoration work. Both the main house and the original Carriage House were lifted so new concrete basements and foundations could be poured. Additionally, new steel beam supports were added to bring the buildings up to seismic code.

Since the home is a Designated Historical Landmark, no torch or chemicals could be used to remove the peeling exterior and interior paint, so it had to be painstakingly stripped by hand. Restoring the Sherman House to its original condition was quite a feat, but the results are spectacular, right down to the recreated plaster ornamentation and entrance posts and handrails. Besides the home's magnificently refinished hardwood floors, the solarium was refloored in black and white marble, and the bathrooms were done in black South American granite.

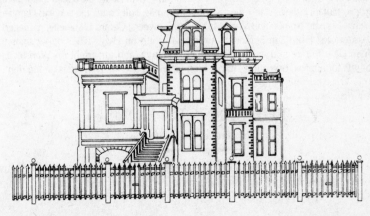

Both the public and individual rooms have been sumptuously decorated in French Second Empire, Austrian Biedermeier and English Jacobean motifs and antiques. I was escorted to my room by the concierge as there is no traditional check-in. If requested, your luggage will be unpacked by the attentive staff, only one of the many services available, including tailoring, securing of opera and symphony tickets, and personalized shopping. If you must work while you travel, special arrangements can be made for stenographic, word-processing, translation, telegram and facsimile services.

The elegant bedrooms have marble wood-burning fireplaces, draped canopy beds and feather-down comforters. Modern features include wet bars, televisions (even in the bathrooms!) and whirlpool baths. There are spectacular views of the Palace of Fine Arts, the Golden Gate, San Francisco Bay and the hills of Marin.

I particularly enjoyed spending time in the hotel's large west wing, which consists of a three-story music and reception room, containing a platform for musicians, and a ceiling glowing with an ornate, leaded-glass skylight. The blue finch in the room's birdcage may cheerfully perform for you as you sit.

The gourmet dinner consisted of a salad of seared prawns, sugar snap peas, and betts in a basil mint vinagrette, napoleon of salmon, artichokes and new potatoes with a lemon chive cream, a sorbet, pepper-roasted duck breast with fennel and caramelized onion compote, duck confit and natural juices and white peach and pistachio cloud with fresh raspberries.

Just before leaving, I spent a few quiet moments in the replicated Victorian greenhouse to steep in the wonderful service and luxury I had experienced.

THE SHERMAN HOUSE, 2160 Green St., San Francisco, CA 94123; 415-563-3600. A 14-guestroom (private baths), intimate, restored Victorian in San Francisco's elegant Pacific Heights district. Open all year. Queen and twin beds. European plan. Near shops, restaurants, theater and most sightseeing areas. Full concierge services. Limited smoking. No pets. Manou and Vesta Mobedshahi, owners; Gerard Lespinette, manager.

DIRECTIONS: From San Francisco Airport, go north on Hwy. 101. Follow signs to Golden Gate Bridge and exit on Fell St. Go 1/2 mile and turn right on Webster St. Continue for approx. two miles , turn left on Green St. Sherman House is on the right.

✕ THE SPENCER HOUSE
San Francisco, California

There is an old saying: "Buy land—they aren't making it anymore." Well, by the same token, be sure to visit the Spencer House, because they aren't mak-

ing homes like this anymore. Built in 1887, the Queen Anne-style mansion features a prominent polygonal tower, Palladian windows, marble staircase entry, triple-arched main entry porch, ten stained-glass windows with faceted crystals and extraordinary exterior Victorian ornamentation. Numerous gables crown the graceful roof. Barbara and Jack Chambers, fortunate owners of the Spencer House, purchased the mansion in 1984 and opened it as a B&B in 1985.

Barbara and Jack worked diligently to restore the home to its original interior and exterior elegance. They added a six-foot iron fence made for around the house and painted it blue-black with a little gold leaf on the spears at the top. Barbara even traveled to England for furnishings, linens and housewares.

Vaulted ceilings, upholstered walls, gilded Lyncrist wallpaper, and bay windows and alcoves are featured in the grand salon and formal dining room on the lower floor. The large front parlor is cozily elegant, with down-filled couches, Persian rugs and antiques.

A grand staircase of hand-carved oak leads to the six upper-floor guestrooms. Heavy, oversized solid wood doors open into enormous, airy rooms with huge bay windows. All the guestrooms have feather mattresses and down comforters and are furnished with antiques. Each room has a glorious view of the park, the gardens or Golden Gate Bridge.

The Chambers' cocker spaniels, Percy and Perry, roused from their nap spot in the sunny breakfast room when I entered, kept me company as I enjoyed a breakfast of poached pears, eggs Benedict and homebaked muffins. The bay window framed the view of the lovely east garden.

The Spencer House is centrally located to all San Francisco attractions. It offers a unique opportunity to live, for a moment, in a style that showed the reverence for and mastery of craftsmanship, a style that "they're just not making anymore."

THE SPENCER HOUSE, 1080 Haight St., San Francisco, CA 94117; 415-626-9205. Fax:626-9208.

A six-guestroom (private baths) Victorian landmark mansion in a quiet residential neighborhood. All size beds. Open all year. Breakfast included. No pets. Two dogs in residence. Near Golden Gate Park and cultural attractions. CCs. Barbara and Jack Chambers, owners/hosts.

DIRECTIONS: From Hwy. 101, take all signs that say Golden Gate Brdg. Exit on Fell/Laguna. Take Fell to Baker, turn left. Inn on left at corner of Haight and Baker.

UNION STREET INN
San Francisco, California

"We are Edwardian, not Victorian."

Helen Stewart and I were having breakfast, seated in the sunny garden at the rear of the Union Street Inn. The fragrance of lilacs, camellias and violets filled the air, and an occasional hummingbird darted from blossom to blossom. Some guests were enjoying breakfast on the spacious deck overlooking the garden, and there was the unmistakable aroma of fresh coffee and croissants. In this quiet retreat it was difficult to realize that we were in the heart of one of San Francisco's most attractive shopping and entertainment areas. "I say Edwardian," Helen continued, "because we're rather proud of the fact that in a city that has so much Victorian, we are a bit different. The Edwardians, already into the 20th century, were less ostentatious than their elders. Their ornamentation was tempered by a new conservatism, and we like to feel that many of our decorations and furnishings are understatements."

Helen is a former San Francisco schoolteacher who found herself involved in a mid-life career change. She restored and remodeled this handsome turn-of-the-century building, using tones and textures that are not only in the period but also increase the feeling of hospitality.

The bedrooms have such intriguing names as Wildrose, Holly, Golden Gate and English Garden.

Two of the bedrooms have queen-sized beds with canopies, two have gleaming brass beds; all have really impressive, carefully chosen antiques. The

brochure of the inn explains the different color schemes for each room. "If reservations are made sufficiently in advance, and the guests can anticipate a mood, these can all be coordinated." Helen made this comment with the faint suggestion of a twinkle.

My room had one of the queen-sized beds with very pleasant dark green wallpaper and matching draperies, which were most helpful in keeping the sun from intruding too early. The walls were adorned with two of the well-known Degas prints of ballet dancers. I thought they were quite appropriate, remembering King Edward's fondness for pretty women.

One end of the room had been turned into an alcove containing a rather elegantly decorated washbasin with mirrors and generous, fluffy towels. A very handsome antique mahogany dressing table had a three-way oval mirror. This is typical of the appointments of the other bedrooms, and I found many welcome living plants in all of the bedrooms.

Helen has converted the old carriage house at the bottom of the garden into a very fetching accommodation, with a large bay window overlooking the garden and its own Jacuzzi. The garden has been remodeled, and a Victorian-looking curved fence with a lovely old-fashioned gate has been added. It truly does resemble an English garden.

A glance at the comments from the guest book told me the story: "Happiness is staying here!" "What a refreshing change from typical hotel stays."

"Like returning to visit an old 'friend.'" "We'll be back for a second honey-moon."

Very fine restaurants are within walking distance.

UNION STREET INN, 2229 Union St., San Francisco, CA 94123; 415-346-0424.

A six-guestroom (private baths) bed-and-breakfast inn. King and queen beds available. Convenient to all of the San Francisco attractions. Breakfast only meal served. Open every day except Christmas and New Year's. No pets. Two dogs in residence. CCs: Visa, MC, AE. Helen Stewart, owner-host.

DIRECTIONS: Take the Van Ness exit from Hwy. 101 to Union St. and turn left. The inn is between Fillmore and Steiner on the left side of the street.

VICTORIAN INN ON THE PARK
San Francisco, California

94-154

Lisa and William Benau are contemporary San Franciscans with a pleasant and easy informality that makes their guests feel very much at home. Lisa, who practiced law for several years, has forsaken that high-pressure world to take

up innkeeping. William, or Willie, as Lisa calls him, is the in-house bread baker & wine collector.

As we sat over a continental breakfast in front of the huge fireplace in the oak-paneled dining room, Willie was explaining the location of the inn to the guests at the next table. "We're across from the east end of Golden Gate Park, and this section is popularly known as 'the Panhandle,' the gathering place for the flower children of the sixties."

I asked Lisa how they found such a perfect example of Victoriana. "My mother rescued it," she said. Shirley Weber, Lisa's mother, made an offer to the owner, "and everything fell into place."

Then the work began. In addition to hiring the restoration experts and craftsmen who preserved original woodworking and decorations, Shirley and Lisa spent hours combing through salvage yards for moldings, matching trims, marble, clawfoot tubs and the like. "There are pictures in the parlor showing all the steps of our restoration. It's been declared a registered historic landmark," Lisa proudly remarked. I thought just walking in the large, beautiful mahogany front door with amber and crystal stained glass was exciting.

A lovely place to sip sherry, the parlor has an 11-foot-high ceiling; four tall, gracefully draped windows on a curved wall; a classic hand-carved maple mantel over a white marble fireplace, and period Queen Anne antiques.

The choicest guestroom is called the Belvedere Room, for the belvedere turret, a balustraded porch. Willie told me there is only one other house with an open belvedere, a signature of the architect, in San Francisco.

All of the guestrooms are decorated with taste and imagination, offering comforters, down pillows and flowers. However, the inn is located on a busy San Francisco street and so the noise can filter through the windows.

The Victorian Inn on the Park will give you an experience of an elegant San Francisco of days gone by.

I enjoyed the cranberry bread for breakfast. "I do different bread every day," Willie said. "Sometimes it's bran muffins, sometimes zucchini bread."

VICTORIAN INN ON THE PARK, 301 Lyon St., San Francisco, CA 94117; 415-931-1830, 800-435-1967.

A 12-guestroom (private baths) Victorian mansion overlooking Golden Gate Park and 1-1/2 mi. from Civic Center. Queen and twin beds. Open year-round, two-night min. on weekends. Close to Golden Gate Park. No pets. CCs: Visa, MC, AE. Lisa and William Benau, owners/hosts.

DIRECTIONS: From Hwy. 101, exit at Fell St. and continue past Divisadero St. to Lyon. The inn is on the right.

WASHINGTON SQUARE INN

San Francisco, California

The hustle and bustle of the colorful North Beach District never ends, I thought, gazing out the window of our room. The brightly lit restaurants and shops below were quite a contrast to the quiet elegance of The Washington Square Inn. Earlier that evening, my wife and I had become part of the side-

walk scene as we ventured out to dine at a fine Italian restaurant in the neighborhood. Being raised in San Francisco during the "beatnik" era, which was closely followed by the age of the "flower children," I was delighted to see the Italian heritage being revived in the neighborhood. There are many more espresso houses, bakeries and good Italian restaurants here now than ever before.

Upon our return, we enjoyed a final glass of wine in the inn's parlor. The fire warmed our feet as we sat quietly on a floral printed loveseat. I slipped off my shoes and buried my toes into the plush green carpet. A mature ficus climbed upward from a large wicker basket and nearly touched the high ceiling, where brass chandeliers were mounted. Under one window, a fresh flowered centerpiece sat on the antique dining room table. I knew that early in the morning the flowers would be replaced with platters of warm, flaky croissants and fresh fruits, followed by late afternoon tea and cookies and, early in the evening, hors d'oeuvres and wine.

Our room overlooked Washington Square Park. Mauve cushions were tucked into the corners of the bay window. Bright pink and yellow flowers on the curtains and duvet brought some gaiety to the beige walls and dark wood of the antique furniture which filled the spacious room. Special touches such as thick terry bathrobes, handmilled soap and down bed pillows added to our comfort. Our host and the manager of the inn, Brooks Bayly, told me upon our arrival that he and his staff strive to provide the services one might find in a small hotel.

The double-storied gray Victorian with brilliant blue trim was rebuilt after the 1906 earthquake which devastated much of the city. The somewhat non-descript exterior does not prepare guests for the beauty that awaits beyond the front door. The current owners, Innkeeper Associates, purchased the inn in 1978 and promptly enlisted interior designer Nan Rosenblatt to completely refurbish the inside. She employed brightly colored French floral prints in the bedrooms which accented the refinished European antique furniture. It has become a tradition of the inn not only to display artwork from local talents on the walls, but to offer it for sale.

Washington Square is conveniently located midway between Fisherman's Wharf and the downtown Financial District. We hopped aboard a cable car and traveled to Union Square for shopping. A short stroll to Chinatown uncovered several restaurant choices. . . no forks allowed!

WASHINGTON SQUARE INN, 1660 Stockton St., San Francisco, CA 94133; 415-981-4220, 800-388-0220.

A 15-guestroom Victorian (some shared baths) in famous North Beach. Complimentary breakfast, afternoon tea and early evening cocktail hour. No smoking. Open year round. No minimum stay. Parking available nearby for a reasonable fee, valet service provided. Centered between the Financial District and Fisherman's Wharf; a cable car or bus can get you to most sight-seeing destinations, once you have exhausted the sights of North Beach. No pets. CCs: Visa, MC, JTB, DI. Innkeeper Associates, owners; Brooks Bayley, manager/host.

DIRECTIONS: Take 4th St. exit off Hwy. 80. Go south on Bryant St. to Market St. (Market turns into Kearny St.). From Kearny, turn left on Columbus St., then right on Stockton St. Inn is between Filbert St. and Union St.

WHITE SWAN
San Francisco, California

"The Petite Auberge was such a success, we decided to open another European inn next door," said Roger Post, which he and his wife transformed into a very English lodging in the middle of a very American city. They did an excellent job. The house was built in 1917 in a baroque style with gray marble facade and detailed trim. (There is an exact copy of the building, but reversed, one block down the street.)

The moment you enter White Swan, you feel as though you've stepped into a small London hotel. The heavy front doors have a swan etched on them and the floor is a lovely granite. Up a few stairs, one of the inn's 30 fireplaces glows next to the registration desk. The common areas are downstairs, away from the busy traffic outside. My favorite room is the cozy library with its book-lined shelves, an overstuffed plaid sofa and, of course, a fireplace. A lovely afternoon tea, though not always English, is served each afternoon in the parlor. On this visit, I tried the hot salmon dip and the pesto cheese torta.

My guestroom had a king-sized bed with tall European-style mattresses, a vanity room and walk-in closet, a bathroom and a separate sitting area with a fireplace. A color television was discreetly tucked away in a mahogany cabinet. The deep rich colors of hunter green and burgundy were contrasted with white chintz curtains and an heirloom bedspread. In the morning the birds were chirping in the trees outside my room; I hardly remembered I was in the heart of the city.

Each morning a newspaper was delivered to my door; the shoes I had left outside it the night before were shined. Valet parking, concierge assistance and one-day laundry service are featured. When I returned to my room after dinner, my bed was turned down and clean towels were in the bath.

For business travelers a fax machine, conference room and corporate guest programs are available.

The breakfast is served buffet-style and is superb. There is always fresh juice, a hot dish of eggs or quiche, and homemade coffee cake and croissants.

Those sensitive to traffic noise should not take a room in front.

WHITE SWAN, 845 Bush Street, San Francisco, CA 94108; 415-775-1755, Fax 415-775-5717.

A 26-guestroom (private baths) intimate small hotel on Nob Hill close to cable car and Union Square, next to Petite Auberge. King and queen beds with one twin. Open year-round. No pets. CCs: Visa, MC, AE. Roger & Sally Post, owners; manager on premises.

DIRECTIONS: From Golden Gate Bridge drive to the Marina. Turn right on Van Ness Ave. to Bush St. and then left to inn, which will be on your right just past Petite Auberge.

Half Moon Bay

Although Half Moon Bay offers many sandy beaches, it's best known as the largest pumpkin-growing region in the state—so if you're visiting in the fall, be prepared for traffic tie-ups. You'll see numerous flower farms in the area as well. The bay is accessible to fishing or whale watching all year round. The area code for the numbers listed below is 415.

EVENTS

MAY	Chamarita Festival
JUNE–SEPTEMBER	Flower Market, third Saturday of each month (info: 726-5202)
JULY	Coastside Country Fair
OCTOBER	Pumpkin Festival (info: 726-5202)
DECEMBER–MARCH	Whale watching (info: 726-7133)
DECEMBER–MARCH	Elephant Seal breeding & Season tours (1-800-444-7275)

SIGHTS

Año Nuevo State Reserve: elelphant seals, November–May (info: 879-0227)

Filoli House & Garden Tour (info: 364-2880)

Pigeon Point Lighthouse Hostel (tour info: 879-0633)

MILL ROSE INN
Half Moon Bay, California

Tucked away just off the road and two blocks from Half Moon Bay's Main Street is Mill Rose Inn, an intimate country retreat with a garden that could compete with any of the loveliest gardens in the English countryside. Bursting with beautiful color all year round, this oasis is the creation of Terry Baldwin, innkeeper, owner and landscape designer. He has tastefully planted hundreds of perennials, annuals and over 200 roses! Inside the inn there is also an abundance of flowers with a fresh-cut bouquet and a bowl of dried flower petals in each guestroom.

Mill Rose Inn has six elegant, spacious and comfortable rooms, all decorated by Terry's wife, Eve, who has an obvious flair for rich colors and soft lighting. The accommodations feature such special amenities as European feather beds, wood-burning fireplaces with hand-painted mantels, bay-window seating, European antiques, claw foot tubs, small refrigerators, VCRs and in-room movies, complimentary wine and sherry, and coffee makers—and each guest will find a Japanese dressing robe in the armoire.

Eve and Terry extend a warm welcome to guests when they arrive by treating them to complimentary refreshments in each room. And in the morning, a full country breakfast with champagne is presented either in one's room or in the dining room.

Another treat for the guests at Mill Rose is the spa, which is tucked inside an enclosed garden gazebo. Here there's room for seven people or it can be reserved for a private escape. Once again the theme of Mill Rose—tranquility and romance—are evident in the lovely surroundings in the spa area, tropical blooms, a charming brick courtyard, fragrant vines and a cascading fountain.

MILL ROSE INN, 615 Mill St., Half Moon Bay, CA 94019; 415-726-9794.

A six-guestroom (private baths) Victorian inn within walking distance of the ocean and center of town. King, queen and double beds. Open year-round. Advance reservations necessary. Many diversions nearby: sandy beaches, wineries, jazz and classical concerts, historic sites, fishing, golf, riding and sailing. Pets are not permitted. One cat and dog in residence. Smoking on decks and garden areas only. CCs: Visa, MC, AE. Eve and Terry Baldwin, owners/hosts.

DIRECTIONS: From San Francisco, travel south on Hwys. 101 or 280 and go west on Hwy. 92 to Half Moon Bay. Turn left on Main St. and right to Mill St.

OLD THYME INN
Half Moon Bay, California

Owners George and Marcia Dempsey bring a varied background to the innkeeping business. Formerly a banker and attorney, George and Marcia, who works part time in advertising, purchased the Inn in 1992 after an exhaustive three-year search for what they consider the perfect bed and breakfast.

You will often find George in the kitchen preparing homemade buttermilk raisin scones or frittatas. A full breakfast can also include blueberry-orange muffins, lemon-thyme pound cake, orange-pecan popovers, lemon-yogurt bread, baked croissants with cheese and turkey or raisin spice coffee cake with vanilla glaze.

The atmosphere of the inn is informal. The lounge is the center of communal activities with complimentary beverages served around the wood-burn-

ing fireplace in the evenings. Furnished in antiques, the lounge is supplied with a variety of magazines and books.

Anyone who has even the tip of a green thumb has admired the English-style garden. Over 50 varieties of herbs and flowers provide a tranquil setting.

The guestrooms, as well as the inn, take their names from herbs: Thyme, Mint, Rosemary, Oregano, Lavender, Camomile and the Garden Suite. All the rooms are unique, with lovely antiques, whimsical stuffed animals, fresh cut flowers and private baths. The garden suites Thyme and Rosemary boast luxurious whirlpool baths while the Suite has its own VCR, selection of tapes and refrigerator stocked with beverages. Mint and Oregano have clawfoot tubs.

Within a short walking distance of the inn are quaint shops, art galleries and restaurants. Or venture off to Año Nuevo State Reserve and view the fascinating and cumbersome elephant seals as they loll in the sun. There's also whale-watching by boat or seaplane, golfing, horseback riding and visiting local farms. The inn is located just a half-mile from the ocean.

OLD THYME INN, 779 Main St., Half Moon Bay, CA 94019; 415-726-1616.

A seven-guestroom (private baths) Victorian on historic Main Street in Half Moon Bay. Queen beds. Open year-round. Full breakfast included. No pets. No smoking. Close to the beach. CCs: Visa, MC. George and Marcia Dempsey owners/hosts.

DIRECTIONS: Four blocks east of Hwy. 1 in Half Moon Bay.

Silicon Valley

Located just south of San Francisco is the valley that developed the personal computer into a common household appliance. Stanford University, the "Harvard of the West," is located in Palo Alto.

EVENTS

JANUARY	Valentine Invitation Exhibition and Silent Auction, San Jose
FEBRUARY	Clam Chowder Cook-off, San Jose
MARCH	San Jose Mercury News 10K Race and 5K Walk
APRIL	Roaring Camp's Amazing Egg Hunt, San Jose
MAY	Blues Festival, San Jose
	Paul Masson Summer Series
JUNE	Great Chili Cook-off, San Jose
JULY	Jumping Frog Contest, San Jose
	Garlic Festival, Gilroy
AUGUST	San Jose Grand Prix
SEPTEMBER	Logger's Festival
	Mexican Independence Day
	Almaden Art & Wine Festival
OCTOBER	Brussels Sprout & Italian Heritage Festival, San Jose
	Octoberfest

SIGHTS

Allied Arts Guild
Coyote Point Museum
Filoli
Lick Observatory
Saso Herb Gardens
Stanford University
Winchester Mystery House

THE HENSLEY HOUSE
San Jose, California

I had heard The Fremont was the most requested guestroom. It certainly was elegant. . . a deep teal motif, massive canopy bed, mahogany armoire, marble sink, sparkling crystal chandelier and faux marble tub. A tea table and antique sofa created an inviting sitting area. The remaining four rooms were all individually named and decorated. The romantic Judge's Chambers has a feather bed, fireplace, plus an over-sized bath with a whirlpool built for two. The Hensley Room features Louis XIV furniture and gilded mirrors on the wine-colored walls. Sunlight streams into the forest green sitting room of the Fallon Suite, tempting one to enjoy breakfast curled up on the day bed. The bath has an old clawfoot tub. The Library, the only guestroom on the first floor, is ideal for the professional traveler. It features a roll-top desk, handcarved sideboard and a unique stained glass window. TV, VCR and phones are in each room, with a movie library in the dining room providing selections for all tastes.

Speaking of tastes, the breakfast frittata was unbeatable, served on lace-covered tables within the elegant surroundings of the dining room. Guests gather for afternoon high tea, complimented with wine and hors d'oeuvres in the Tudor-style parlor/living room. Dinner can be prepared by special arrangement with the staff.

The 1883 Queen Anne Victorian is now on the National Registry of Historic Places. It has taken $500,000 of renovations to transform the neglected relic to its present state. Even though the neighborhood is still undergoing changes, owners Sharon Layne and Bill Priest express confidence in the future. Sharon, a real estate broker, told me that Hensley is only the second B&B in San Jose, but the city officials are very supportive.

"We have to make it extra special, because everyone is watching closely," said Sharon, a real estate broker who is used to close scrutiny. "We are determined to restore her [Hensley's] reputation as a grand lady!"

THE HENSLEY HOUSE, 456 North Third Street, San Jose, CA 95112; 408-298-3537. Five-guestroom Queen Anne Victorian in San Jose's Historic District. Queen beds. Breakfast included. Dinner by special arrangement. Afternoon High Tea or wine and hors d'oeuvres. Open year-round. No pets. No smoking. Walk to restaurants, theaters, nightclubs and shopping. Rail transit nearby. CCs: Visa, MC, AE, Disc, DC. Sharon Layne and Bill Priest, owners/hosts.

DIRECTIONS: Highway 280 to downtown San Jose. Take Guadalupe Expressway North to Julian St. exit. Go east five blocks to Third St. Turn left and travel two blocks to Hensley Avenue.

THE INN AT SARATOGA

Saratoga, California

A very good friend, a designer of those amazingly wild computer games that perplex me beyond belief, recently wrote to me recommending the inn at Saratoga. Apparently he had spent a think-tank weekend there and found it bucolic and charming.

Located in the foothills of the Santa Cruz mountains, the five-story modern hotel blends old-world hospitality with an English country setting. In the center of the quaint town of Saratoga, noted for its Mediterranean-like climate, the inn stands on a historical site that was once the location of a toll gate built in 1850 to transport great redwood logs out of the Santa Cruz mountains.

The English manor-style lobby is decorated in green, peach and mauve, with prominent oak and brass accents. A platter of croissants and muffins is served here each morning, along with juices and huge thermoses filled with coffee and tea. Here, too, afternoon wine and hors d'oeuvres are set out around 4:00 P.M.

All 46 guestrooms are designed for seclusion and privacy and have indoor and outdoor sitting areas that overlook bubbling Saratoga Creek and Wildwood Park. Towering eucalyptus, sycamore and lush elms, some over 200 years old, surround the inn and create a serene setting. Ruby red bougainvillea and heavily scented jasmine line the romantic pathways below.

The rooms have oversize beds, televisions, personal computer capabilities, telephones, built-in hair dryers, luxurious baths and air conditioning. White antiqued armoires and desks, along with comfortable love seats, furnish the sitting areas. Suites are larger and have the addition of whirlpool baths and European-style towel warmers. The executive and parlor suites may be combined for added comfort and convenience. Original California art decorates the walls, and floor-to-ceiling French windows make the rooms bright and airy.

The Inn at Saratoga is part of historical Saratoga Village. The area offers a wide variety of shopping possibilities including unique designer boutiques, quaint shops and fine art and antique galleries. A number of award-winning restaurants featuring international cuisines are just three blocks away. The Inn is at the beginning of a self-guided historic walking tour, and in June the city celebrates its culture with the Blossom Festival.

Curving Highway 17 will take you to the Santa Cruz Beach and Boardwalk's looping roller coaster and give you a chance to watch California's surfers in action. You can stop on the way home for some wine tasting at the valley's best wineries or to have early afternoon tea at the Hakone Japanese Gardens.

I could see why my friend found the tranquility of The Inn at Saratoga conducive to the complex mental gymnastics he must do when designing computer games. Me? I just found my visit extremely refreshing and enjoyable. And that's what really matters.

THE INN AT SARATOGA, 20645 Fourth St., Saratoga, CA 95070; 408-867-5020.

A 46-guestroom (private baths) modern hotel nestled at the foot of the Santa Cruz mountains in the town of Saratoga. Open all year. All size beds. Continental breakfast included with tariff. Close to wineries, boutiques, fine restaurants, Paul Masson Winery summer concerts and theaters. Tennis, swimming, windsurfing, horseback riding, and jogging and walking trails nearby. No pets. Jack Hickling, manager-host.

DIRECTIONS: From Rte. 280 take Rte. 85 (Saratoga/Sunnyvale Rd.) to the intersection with Rte. 9 (Big Basin Way). Turn right on Big Basin and go approx. 1/4 mi. to 4th St., then turn right for 1/2 block. From Hwy. 17, take Rte. 9 exit (Los Gatos/Saratoga) to Saratoga. Turn left on Big Basin Way (Rte. 9) then right onto 4th St. The inn is 1/2 block on the right.

THE VICTORIAN ON LYTTON

Palo Alto, California

Palo Alto has a lot going for it: a gentle climate, fine restaurants, cafes, theaters, museums, art galleries, shops, Stanford University with its beautiful grounds, and now it has its first legal bed-and-breakfast inn, the Victorian on Lytton. Set back off the street in a peaceful residential neighborhood and only one block from the downtown center, it is a stunning Victorian house built in 1895. Susan and Max Hall bought the house in 1985, which by this time had had a number of owners and was in very poor condition. The Halls hoped to open the city's first B&B and found that they literally had to "fight city hall" in order to realize their dream. The years of meeting all of the city codes and the hard work associated with completely restoring the interior have paid off, for now the Victorian on Lytton has been transformed into an elegant, comfortable inn, owned and operated by charming innkeepers.

There are 10 spacious guestrooms, named after Queen Victoria and each of her nine children. They all have a separate sitting parlor and private bath, and most rooms have canopy or four-poster king- or queen-sized beds.

Guests convene each evening in the front room over a glass of sherry or port and discuss the day's events, and in the morning a continental breakfast is served in each room.

The feeling of cordiality that pervades the inn makes it very obvious that the Halls are enthusiastic about their role as innkeepers. And last Christmas

some of the guests were so impressed with Susan's tree ornament creation (a hand-stenciled child's playing block) that she gave them to the guests as presents. Being a guest at Victorian on Lytton is an invitation to take life a little easier in an area that offers so many diversions!

THE VICTORIAN ON LYTTON, 555 Lytton Ave., Palo Alto, CA 94301; 415-322-8555. Fax; 415-322-7141.

A 10-guestroom (five in adjacent building; private baths) Victorian inn located one block from the downtown center. King and queen beds. Open all year. Theater, musical concerts, museums, galleries, fine restaurants, unlimited sports and recreational facilities, Stanford Univ., and Silicon Valley all nearby. No pets. No smoking on the premises. CCs: Visa, MC, AE. Maxwell and Susan Hall, owners/hosts.

DIRECTIONS: From Hwy. 101, take University Ave. (west) exit. Continue on University for two mi. and make right turn on Middlefield and left to Lytton. Parking available at the back of the inn.

Santa Cruz Area

The town of Santa Cruz boasts one of the last of America's boardwalks, full of old-fashioned carnival atmosphere and featuring the Big Dipper rollercoaster. Across Monterey Bay, you can see Monterey and Carmel. Farming communities like Gilroy—known even today as the Garlic Capital of the World—dot the surrounding countryside. The area code for the numbers listed below is 408. Also the number 1-800-833-3494 will provide you with information regarding events in the area.

EVENTS

JANUARY–MARCH	Surfboard Competition
FEBRUARY	Clam Chowder Festival
MAY	Boardwalk opens, Santa Cruz.
MAY	Annual Fly-in, Watsonville
JULY 4	World's Shortest Parade, Aptos (info: 688-2428)
JULY	Wharf-to-Wharf Run (info: 475-6522)
SUMMER	Pro Volleyball Tournament
SUMMER	Friday Night Boardwalk Concerts
SUMMER	Cabrillo Music Festival
SEPTEMBER	Beach Street Revival; Vintage Cars
SEPTEMBER	Begonia Festival (info: 475-6522)
SEPTEMBER	Wine Festival (info: 475-6522)
AUTUMN	Garlic Festival, Gilroy
OCTOBER	Laguna Seca Races
OCTOBER	Brussels Sprouts Festival (info: 423-5590)
OCTOBER–NOVEMBER	Big Bands and Dancing, Coconut Grove (info: 423-5590)

SIGHTS

Beach Boardwalk Amusement Park
Mystery Spot
San Juan Bautista
Surfing Museum

APPLE LANE INN

Aptos, California

The sweet fragrance of apple blossoms hung in the air as I walked up the path
to the Apple Lane Inn. It was springtime, and the day fairly vibrated. Built in
the 1870s by the founding fathers of Aptos, the restored Victorian farmhouse
is nestled on three acres surrounded by orchards, woods and fields.

Doug and Diana Groom chose Apple Lane for their wedding in 1987.
Returning year after year, they fell in love with the peaceful grounds and historic home. They bought it in 1990.

As the afternoon sun shifted overhead, I gathered with some of the other
guests for coffee on the brick patio, shaded by grape and wisteria arbors.
Nearby, a recently completed gazebo had just been given a final coat of paint.

The inn's large, comfortable Victorian parlor has a well-stocked bookcase,
a unique travertine fireplace and a wonderful player piano with 30 working
rolls. Upstairs, a sunny sitting room is a quiet place for reading. If the day is
really warm, retire to the cool wine cellar for a game of darts or, perhaps, a ball
game on television.

The guestrooms are decorated in French country style. Soft shades of
peach, mauve, rose and lavender create a restful mood. Hand-painted stenciling on walls and antique furnishings lend an air of an earlier, more tranquil
age.

A full country breakfast is served in the parlor and includes homemade
cinnamon rolls, ham and eggs, fruit, muffins, and fresh roast coffee and teas.

You may want to visit the barn to see the mares or geldings. Bring along some apples.

APPLE LANE INN, 6265 Soquel Drive, Aptos, CA 95003; 408-475-6868.

A five-guestroom (three private baths) country Victorian farmhouse secluded on three acres of grounds. King and queen beds. Open all year. Close to Santa Cruz; walk to the beach or parks; visit antiques shops; fine restaurants. No pets. One cat in residence. CCs: Visa, MC. Doug and Diana Groom, owners/hosts.

DIRECTIONS: From the north on Hwy. 1, exit at Park Ave./New Brighton Beach. Turn left on Park. Go 1/4 mi. to light. Turn right. This is Soquel Dr. Go 1/2 mi. Look for inn's sign on left. Go to end of traffic island, U-turn, come back to drive.

THE BABBLING BROOK INN
Santa Cruz, California

The name of this inn is not irrelevant, since there is indeed a lovely babbling brook (with the historic water wheel)—actually Laurel Creek—that meanders through the terraced gardens surrounding the four chalet-type shingle buildings of the inn. Beside the cascading waterfall lies the ancient Ohlone Indian burial ground. The property was host to an 18th-century grist mill operated by the Mission Fathers and then a tannery until the log cabin, which today is the heart of the inn, was built on the original foundation in 1909. Silent films were made on the property until it became a restaurant. In 1981 the inn opened as the first and largest B&B in Santa Cruz County.

As you climb the wooden staircase and cross the brook, redwoods tower overhead and the sound of the waterfall greets each guest.

All of the 12 rooms have private entrances, baths, telephones, TVs tucked away in closets and fireplaces; several have deep-soaking jet bathtubs. Most have decks overlooking the garden with rocking chairs to enjoy the afternoon sunshine.

Breakfast is served buffet style over a two-hour time period in the main building, and large wooden trays are provided so that guests can enjoy the meal in the dining room by the cozy fire, or on the outside deck or in the privacy of their rooms. The complete breakfast always includes fresh orange juice, fresh ground coffee, two or three kinds of fruit, granola, an egg dish, fresh baked croissants, and some kind of muffin or bread.

The inn is made inviting by innkeeper Helen King, a mother of six. She welcomes her guests as she would her family—with kindness, warmth and happiness. Guests are invited to join her for wine or sherry in the late afternoon. Tea and coffee and Helen's delicious cookies are always on the tea cart for your enjoyment.

Although the setting is very romantic, it is next to a very travelled street.

THE BABBLING BROOK INN, 1025 Laurel St., Santa Cruz, CA 95060; 800-866-1131, 408-427-2437, fax 408-427-2457.

A 12-guestroom (private baths) relaxed and comfortable inn built around a winding stream located about two hrs. south of San Francisco on Monterey Bay. King and queen beds. Breakfast included. Open year-round. Wheelchair access. Nearby beach, shopping, tennis and many excellent restaurants featuring ocean catch. No pets. Two cats in residence. CCs: Visa, AE, MC, DI, CB. Helen King, owner/host.

DIRECTIONS: At the Laurel St. signal turn south from Hwy. 1 and continue towards the ocean 1-1/2 blocks down the hill on the right. The brick pillars and large redwood sign are at the parking lot entrance.

CHATEAU VICTORIAN
Santa Cruz, California

Waking to the timeless sound of the ocean waves crashing on the beach, I knew I had chosen a perfect B&B in which to unwind after a busy travel schedule. The Chateau Victorian is only a block from a wide beach that stretches nearly a mile from the mouth of the San Lorenzo River. An 1880s Victorian, the inn was converted from an apartment house to a charming inn by Alice-June and Franz Benjamin in June 1983. "We decided to spend the later part of our lives in a relaxed and fun way," Franz told me. I was surprised

to find out that part of Franz's relaxation comes from the rather unnerving sports of flying and auto racing!

The inn is picturesque, painted plum with black cherry and cream trim. Common rooms are decorated in comfortable Victorian furnishings. Large overstuffed chairs invite conversation or reading around the living room fireplace. In the late afternoon, complimentary wine and cheese are served in the lounge. Socks, the house cat, may choose this time to greet guests as he watches hopefully for a smidgen of cheese to fall his way.

Calming colors of beige, off-white and mauve are picked up in the patterned wallpaper of the guestrooms. Each room has a private tiled bath, a fireplace, carpeting and a queen-size bed. Each has controlled heating systems, and four of the rooms have Victorian armoires. The Benjamins have made every effort to create a quiet, peaceful atmosphere. No televisions, radios, phones or clocks are in any of the guestrooms.

Breakfast is served buffet style and includes fresh fruit, juice, coffees and teas, fresh croissants, muffins, preserves, whipped unsalted butter, and cream cheese. You may take your plate to the lounge dining area, the secluded side deck or the large front deck.

Santa Cruz is a casual beach town with exceptional restaurants. After a morning beachcombing, you may want to visit the Municipal Pier with its interesting souvenir shops and resident seals forever begging for a treat. Evening can be spent at the famous Casino and Boardwalk.

CHATEAU VICTORIAN, 118 First St., Santa Cruz, CA 95060; 408-458-9458.

A seven-guestroom (private baths) seaside Victorian in the resort town of Santa Cruz. Queen beds. Open all year. Breakfast included. Near fine restaurants and shops; one block to the beach. No pets or smoking. One cat in residence. CCs: Visa, MC, AE. Alice-June and Franz Benjamin, owners/hosts.

DIRECTIONS: Highway 1 north or south becomes Mission St. Turn off on Bay St. towards the Bay. At end turn left onto West Cliff Dr, then take right fork (Beach St.). At second stop sign turn left onto Cliff St. then drive one block and turn left on First St. Inn on right, parking across street.

INN EVENTS: JULY—Pre-Wharf-to-Wharf Race Spaghetti Feed
NOVEMBER—Annual Thanksgiving Dinner
DECEMBER—Annual In-house New Year's Eve Party

CLIFF CREST BED AND BREAKFAST INN

Santa Cruz, California

Cliff Crest is a historic Queen Anne Victorian nestled in the Beach Hill area of Santa Cruz. William Jeter, Lieutenant Governor of California from 1895 to 1899, built the beautiful landmark home in 1887. Jeter's interest in ecology is evident in the inn's spacious gardens. John McLaren, Jeter's friend and the designer of the famous Golden Gate Park, planned the grounds on the elegant estate that Bruce and Sharon Taylor purchased two years ago.

Furnished in antiques, the common rooms are warm and comfortable. Handcrafted woodwork, Oriental carpets and unique, jewel-toned stained-glass insets above the parlor windows speak of a time when craftsmanship flourished. Originally used as the dining room, the parlor has a cozy fireplace surrounded by built-in china cabinets, now filled with books and games. The soft shades of blue and cream create an airy atmosphere.

All five guestrooms have been decorated with an eye to romance. I stayed in the second-story Rose Room with its views to the mountains and Monterey Bay. The spacious room has a queen-sized Eastlake Victorian bed with a canopy over it and a sitting area furnished with a pale pink love seat and chair. The deep rose of the ceiling sets off the walls, papered in white with tiny blue flowers. Bruce's mother donated an heirloom *Gone With the Wind* lamp which sits beside the bed. The Empire room has been redecorated with pale muted rose and deep forest green in a bordered ceiling. The Pineapple room has a Bradbury & Bradury frieze at the ceiling. The guestrooms all have private baths.

Sharon's career as manager of Carnation Company's test kitchens in Los Angeles certainly prepared her for the task of designing a creative breakfast menu. A breakfast of juice and fresh fruit, an egg dish plus coffee cakes or french toast with bacon or sausage is served in the garden solarium or outside on the sunny terrace. You may also have breakfast in bed!

The Santa Cruz area has a wealth of activities to keep you entertained. Cliff Crest is only 2-1/2 blocks from the beach, and the Boardwalk with its dizzying rollercoaster is within walking distance. Cultural events and festivals abound, and hiking through the redwoods is always a spectacular experience.

CLIFF CREST BED AND BREAKFAST INN, 407 Cliff Street, Santa Cruz, CA 95060; 408-427-2609.

A five-guestroom (private baths) Victorian close to the beach. King and queen beds. Breakfast included. Near excellent restaurants and shopping. No pets. Two dogs in residence. Bruce and Sharon Taylor, owners/hosts.

DIRECTIONS: Take Hwy. 17 to Santa Cruz. Take Ocean Ave. to the end and turn right; go two blocks. At traffic signal turn left and cross the bridge. Turn right on 3rd St. Proceed up hill to Cliff and turn left.

COUNTRY ROSE INN
BED AND BREAKFAST
Gilroy, California

"It was a romantic idea. I tried to create an intimate setting, a place where people can relax and feel nurtured," explained Rose Hernandez, owner of the inn. Rose's elderly mother sat in a nearby rocker, the soft smile on her face offering nonverbal approval of her daughter's ideas.

I felt as though I had just dropped in to visit a neighbor. We were in the parlor. Dancing flames were visible behind the glass doors of the fireplace. Marmalade and Spunky, the resident cats, were curled up close-by enjoying the warmth. Rose and I were seated on a comfortable sofa covered with a rose bouquet print. The room, like the rest of the inn, had a country, farmhouse feel. Rose labeled it "understated decor" consisting of very pale pink walls, wood-beamed ceilings, and a plush carpet of deep rose.

"As you can see, I have an affinity to roses," she said. "Maybe because of

my name. Anyway, they somehow ended up in every room by the time we completed furnishing the inn."

Rose told me that she had spent her childhood in this area. After ending a fourteen-year teaching career in Palo Alto in 1988, she returned and purchased the 1920 Dutch Colonial. Reminiscent of a bygone era, the stately old farmhouse, surrounded by giant oaks, sits on five acres at the end of a country lane. About midway between Morgan Hill and Gilroy, location of the famous Garlic Festival, the site offers peaceful views of the Gabilan Mountain Range.

We ended our comfortable conversation so that Rose could assemble fruit and cheese trays which would accompany afternoon tea, served in the Music Room with its baby grand piano and guitar leaning against the wall. I left Rose's mother, still rocking by the fire, and went back to my room.

I was staying in the Garden Room, which offers a picturesque window view over beds of perennials. This spacious room has hardwood floors and an antique bed with a comforter patterned in tiny spring bouquets. Square matching pillows were stacked on the wicker settee, which sits in front of the fireplace. Small family heirlooms on the walls and tables add an old-fashioned touch to the decor.

The next morning I was among the first guests seated in the dining room to enjoy Rose's "favorite meal." Granola and juice preceded an entree of warm potato custard and fresh fruit. Her breakfasts are not considered complete without dessert. I devoured the delicious strawberry shortcake.

Tourist attractions such as Gilroy's fine vineyards, the historical town of San Juan Bautista with its sights and shopping, and the more metropolitan atmosphere of San Jose are all within easy driving distance.

Provided you share her love of roses, you will enjoy the ambiance of Rose Hernandez's Country Rose Inn.

COUNTRY ROSE INN BED AND BREAKFAST, 455 Fitzgerald Ave. #E, San Martin, CA 95046; mailing address: P.O. Box 1804, Gilroy, CA 95021-1804; 408-842-0441.

A quaint five-guestroom Dutch Colonial farmhouse on five secluded acres in the Silicon Valley. Bountiful breakfast included. King, queen and double beds. Open all year. Some weekend minimum stays. No smoking. Restaurants and sight-seeing in nearby Gilroy, San Martin and Morgan Hill. Two house cats. Please leave pets home. Rose Hernandez, owner/host.

DIRECTIONS: Off Hwy. 101, take the Master Ave. exit and go west. Cross Monterey Rd. Street name changes to Fitzgerald. Take Fitzgerald .04 mi. to first set of mailboxes. Turn right onto private lane.

INN AT DEPOT HILL
Capitola-by-the-Sea, California

Imagine you are aboard a train: the clank-clank of metal wheels on the tracks, the scenery a slow moving picture past your window, the constant gentle rocking motion lulling you into a dreamy state.

"Next stop...The Inn At Depot Hill!" calls the conductor of imagination. "All those getting off at Sissinghurst, Paris, Delft, Portofino! Next stop!" The hooting whistle heralds your approach into the station.

My dream state ends, replaced by the reality of my approach by car to the newly refurbished Inn at Depot Hill, on the bluffs above the Monterey Bay. Trains still pass by the Southern Pacific Depot several times a week. They do not stop, however, for the Depot was transformed into Capitola's first bed and breakfast in 1990 by Suzie Lankes, a onetime insurance adjuster, and Dan Floyd, a Silicon Valley entrepreneur. Suzie's great-grandfather was an architect for Southern Pacific Railroad, leaving her no stranger to depot blueprints. The inn became her inspiration.

The simple design of the old depot station, dating back to 1901, still retains much of its original style. Doric columns, some original and some hand-milled to match, sturdily support the eaves which surround the tan and white structure. A wrought iron entrance gate opens to a red-brick courtyard and front porch. Around back is a garden patio, bricks laid in a herringbone pattern, that overflows with climbing roses, trumpet vines and azaleas, all flourishing in the cool ocean climate. Patio tables neatly covered with starched white cloths make this a perfect place to enjoy an afternoon glass of champagne.

Dan and Suzie enlisted the expertise of Dan's sister-in-law, Linda Floyd, an interior designer from San Francisco, to complete the room renovations. The dining room has a semi-circular bay window that originally served as the ticket window. There are no tickets sold, however, for the delicious breakfasts—consisting of homemade muffins, pastries and hot entrees such as Quiche St. Germain, Frittata Nicoise or Tynde Pandekager, served each morning on the unique three-legged, lion-and-paw dining room table—are available only to guests. Suzie told me that the unusual antique table came from the Philippines and was just one of the many pieces Linda had scouted out of antique shops in England and France.

The parlor has a three-sided brocade pouffe, burgandy in color and bordered with lively fringe. An Oriental rug partially covers the dark sheen of the hardwood floor and a gilded Venetian glass chandelier hangs overhead. In addition to the baby grand piano, built-in bookshelves filled with reading material and a cozy fireplace, an abundance of railroad memorabilia captures the era.

"The guestrooms are named and fashioned after different parts of the world, as if you are taking a railway journey and stopping off at different destinations," Suzie explained as I checked in. "All have fireplaces and feather beds, and some have hot tubs. We think Linda did wonders in combining classic European design with a theme from each location."

Leading the way, she informed me I would be staying in the Delft Room, which displays a Dutch influence. The fireplace, already flaming behind glass doors, is faced with blue and white tiles imported from Holland. Varied shades of blue make the room a place of tranquility. Bouquets of orange and red tulips added a hint of brightness. The room has its own private garden and outdoor Jacuzzi, as well as a large marble shower in the adjoining bath.

Each morning I enjoyed a brisk walk along Capitola Beach, only a block from the inn. One evening I heard an outdoor concert at the beach, which are offered weekly towards the end of summer. The town of Capitola offers plenty of shopping and restaurants. For a wider variety, Santa Cruz with its famous Boardwalk is only a short drive away, and less than an hour behind the wheel took me into the Carmel-Monterey area. But shopping was last on my list of things to do, for I became quickly enchanted with the inn and its endless supply of memorabilia on local railroad history.

INN AT DEPOT HILL, 250 Monterey Ave., Capitola-by-the-Sea, CA 95010; 408-462-3376, Fax: 408-462-3697.

Circa 1900 railroad depot converted into a handsome eight-guestroom B&B, each room with fireplaces and unique in design. Overlooking the village of Capitola and Monterey Bay. Breakfast included. Afternoon hors d'oeuvres, wines and tea, plus late evening dessert treats. Mostly queen beds. Some hot tubs. Open all year. Two-night minimum with Saturday. Restricted smoking areas. Santa Cruz, a short drive away, offers fun at the Boardwalk and great shopping. Monterey and Carmel are less than an hour's drive. No pets welcome. CCs: Visa, MC, AE. Suzie Lankes and Dan Floyd, owners/hosts.

DIRECTIONS: Connect from Hwy. 1, 101 or 280 South to Hwy. 17/880 toward Santa Cruz. Take the Watsonville/Monterey/Hwy.#1 South turnoff. Pass the Soquel/Capitola exit, and take the Park Ave., New Brighton Beach exit, going right onto Park Ave. Proceed one mi. to T-intersection of Monterey Ave. Turn left. Driveway of inn is next left on corner of Park and Monterey Aves.

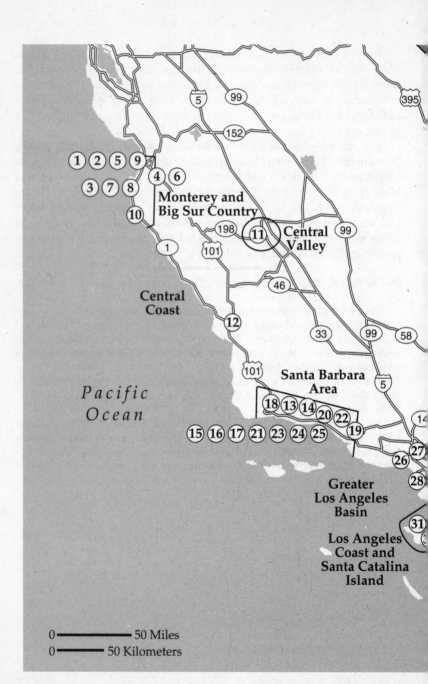

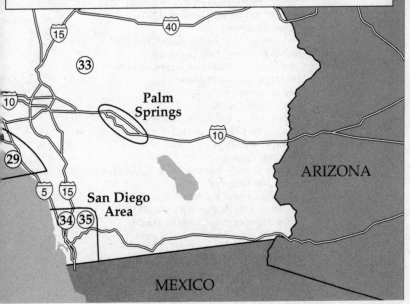

Southern California

1. Pacific Grove, Gosby House Inn
2. Pacific Grove, Green Gables Inn
3. Carmel, The Happy Landing
4. Monterey, The Jabberwock
5. Pacific Grove, The Martine Inn
6. Monterey, Old Monterey Inn
7. Carmel, The Pine Inn
8. Carmel, The Sandpiper Inn At-The-Beach
9. Pacific Grove, Seven Gables Inn
10. Big Sur, Ventana Inn
11. Coalinga, The Inn at Harris Ranch
12. San Luis Obispo, Garden Street Inn
13. Solvang, The Alisal
14. Ballard, The Ballard Inn
15. Santa Barbara, The Bath Street Inn
16. Santa Barbara, The Bayberry Inn
17. Santa Barbara, The Cheshire Cat
18. Solvang, The Inn at Petersen Village
19. Ventura, La Mer

20. Los Olivos, Los Olivos Grand Hotel
21. Santa Barbara, The Old Yacht Club Inn
22. Montecito, San Ysidro Ranch
23. Santa Barbara, Simpson House Inn
24. Santa Barbara, Tiffany Inn
25. Santa Barbara, Villa Rosa
26. Santa Monica, The Channel Road Inn
27. North Hollywood, La Maida House
28. Los Angeles, Salisbury House
29. Dana Point, Blue Lantern Inn
30. Avalon, The Garden House Inn
31. Avalon, The Inn on Mount Ada
32. Seal Beach, The Seal Beach Inn and Gardens
33. Big Bear Lake, Eagle's Nest
34. Rancho Santa Fe, The Inn
35. Rancho Santa Fe, Rancho Valencia

Monterey and
Big Sur Country

Big Sur is about an hour south of the wonderful and quaint towns of Carmel, Pacific Grove and Monterey. Cannery Row, the colorful area that John Steinbeck wrote about, Fisherman's Wharf and the famous Aquarium are all located in Monterey, which was an important Mexican outpost in California's early days. Carmel is as famous for its gorgeous ocean beach as it is for its one-time mayor, Clint Eastwood. Pacific Grove is the winter home of the monarch butterflies, which return to town each October. And the breathtaking coastline drive to Big Sur is a must for every visitor. The area code for the numbers listed below is 408.

EVENTS

JANUARY–FEBRUARY	National Pro-Am Golf Tournament (info: 800-541-9091)
FEBRUARY	Masters of Food & Wine
MARCH	Three-day Dixieland Festival (info: 433-5260)
MARCH	Wine Festival (info: 800-525-3378)
APRIL	Good Old Days Celebration (info: 373-3304)
APRIL	Victorian Home Tours (info: 373-3304)
APRIL	Monterey Adobe Tour (info: 373-2608)
APRIL	Big Sur Marathon
APRIL	Wild Flower Show, Pacific Grove (373-3304)
MAY	Del Monte Kennel Club Dog Show
MAY	Great Monterey Squid Festival (info: 649-6547)
JUNE	U.S. Open Golf Tournament
JULY	Feast of Lanterns (info: 646-0741)
JULY	Bach Festival, Carmel
AUGUST	Historic Automobile Races (info: 648-5111)
SEPTEMBER	Monterey Jazz Festival (info: 373-3366)
SEPTEMBER–OCTOBER	Shakespeare Festival
OCTOBER	Sandcastle Contest
OCTOBER	Monarch Butterfly Festival, Pacific Grove (373-3304)
OCTOBER	Big Sur 10K River Run
DECEMBER	La Posada Candlelight Parade (info: 649-7111)
DECEMBER	Christmas in the Adobes (info: 649-7111)
DECEMBER	Carmel Homecrafters Christmas Market

SIGHTS

Downtown Carmel
Hearst Castle
Mission Basilica
Point Lobos

Monterey Aquarium
San Juan Bautista
17-Mile Drive
Wineries

GOSBY HOUSE INN

Pacific Grove, California

When I set out to visit the Monterey Peninsula, I determined I would stay off the beaten track a bit and picked the town of Pacific Grove. Right in the heart of town I discovered a beautiful historic Victorian landmark called the Gosby House. It shares an entire block with another Victorian that is home to an excellent restaurant featuring continental cuisine.

The Gosby House was lovingly restored from complete disrepair by the Post family. Roger and Sally, along with their four daughters, had been operating the Green Gables Inn in Pacific Grove during summers only and were ready to go year-round when this inn came up for sale. They spent almost two years gutting and remodeling the entire building.

The 22-room inn is completely furnished with antiques. Twelve of the rooms have fireplaces. Handsome armoires, clawfoot tubs, brass beds and stately dressers are just a few of the beautiful pieces in the rooms. The walls are covered with floral papers and the entire inn is fitted with patterned carpet. Each room is named for a local figure; mine was John Steinbeck.

At breakfast I enjoyed a hearty vegetable quiche, lemon poppyseed muffins, a huge platter of fresh fruit, and a selection of cereals, toast, juices and hot beverages. It's served buffet-style, and one can do a lot of damage to the waistline.

GOSBY HOUSE INN, 643 Lighthouse Avenue, Pacific Grove, CA 93950; 408-375-1287.

A 22-room (20 private baths) B&B in the heart of Pacific Grove. Queen & double beds. Open year-round. Lavish afternoon tea. Turndown service. No pets. CCs: Visa, MC, AE. Roger and Sally Post, owners; manager in residence.

DIRECTIONS: From Hwy. 1, go west on Hwy. 68, continue on Forest Ave.; left on Lighthouse Ave. for two blocks.

GREEN GABLES INN
Pacific Grove, California

When Roger and Sally Post purchased the magnificent Green Gables Inn back in 1974, they had no idea they would become two of California's most successful innkeepers. A mortgage banker by profession, Roger had moved his business from southern California just a few years before so his young family could enjoy a smaller community. But he and Sally fell in love with the inn and

when the former owners decided to move, they purchased it. (You'll find the Flatleys running the elegant House of Seven Gables down the street.) Two years later the Posts, with the support of their daughters, aged six through 14, decided to open their home as an inn for the summer. It was so enjoyable that they did it every summer thereafter. Eventually they sold the mortgage bank to concentrate on innkeeping, and in 1984 the inn opened year-round. The Posts now have six inns along the California coast.

The Green Gables Inn has an enviable location on the beautiful, rocky shoreline of Pacific Grove. Built in 1888 by a sea captain, it is an excellent example of Queen Anne Victorian architecture.

I entered the inn through large double doors into an elegant but comfortable parlor, with windows on the sea (some with leaded glass). With its glowing fire, player piano and antique furniture, this room invites romance.

Registration took place in a nook off the kitchen and a charming innkeeper escorted me to my room, decorated with antique furniture and chintz curtains and offering an ocean view.

Breakfast is served for two hours in the morning and guests can dine at a large table, where they meet other guests, or at cozy little tables for two. I had quiche, homebaked bread, fruit and coffee. A lavish afternoon tea with wonderful appetizers is served from 5:00 to 7:00 P.M.

GREEN GABLES INN, 104 5th St., Pacific Grove, CA; 408-375-2095.

An 11-guestroom (7 private baths) B&B. Queen beds (one double). Some rooms with view. Turndown service, bicycles, wonderful beachwalking. Afternoon tea and goodies. Short walk to Aquarium, five-min. drive to Pebble Beach, 15 min. to Carmel. No pets. CCs: Visa, MC, AE. Roger & Sally Post, owners. Manager on premises.

DIRECTIONS: From Hwy. 1 take Hwy. 68 west. Continue on Forest. Left on Ocean View Blvd. to 5th St.

THE HAPPY LANDING
Carmel, California

Just 1-1/2 blocks from Ocean Avenue, the principal shopping street of Carmel, stands the Happy Landing, a collection of English-type pink cottages built around a courtyard with a delightful lily pond and a gazebo, where weddings and receptions are often held.

Built in 1925 as a family retreat, this early Murphy-designed group of buildings has evolved into one of Carmel's entrancing accommodations. They are in keeping with the Carmel tradition of individual and family comfort.

There are seven of these little cottages set amongst the rose trellises, and

almost all of them have cathedral ceilings and individual fireplaces. Some are furnished in wicker and others have antiques and brass. The pink theme is continued throughout, even to the pink towels. When you open your curtains in the morning, it is the signal that you are ready to have breakfast brought to your room. It consists of various breakfast breads, fresh fruit, juice, and coffee or tea. Many guests sit out in the garden enjoying the Carmel sunshine and the ubiquitous birds.

Although the Happy Landing is not on Carmel Bay, it is possible to get a glimpse of the bay through the trees. Views of both the ocean and the garden can be enjoyed from the large reception room with its stone fireplace, where tea is served in the afternoon.

——————————

THE HAPPY LANDING, Box 2619, Monte Verde between 5th and 6th Streets, Carmel, CA 93921; 408-624-7917.

A seven-guestroom (private baths) bed-and-breakfast inn; includes two suites. King, queen and double beds. Open every day of the year. In a very quiet section of Carmel, a short distance from the beach and a pleasant walking distance to shops and restaurants. Conveniently located for drives through Pebble Beach and Big Sur. No pets. CCs: Visa, MC. Dick Stewart, owner; Robert Ballard, manager.

DIRECTIONS: Take the Ocean Ave. exit from Hwy. 1 and continue to Monte Verde. Turn right for 1-1/2 blocks. The Happy Landing Inn is next to the Christian Science Church.

THE JABBERWOCK
Monterey, California

126 -180

The whimsy of Lewis Carroll and his Jabberwock poem from *Alice in Wonderland* is matched by the imagination of Barbara and Jim Allen, proprietors of the Jabberwock. They have turned a towered and turreted former convent, built in 1911, into a seven-bedroom bed-and-breakfast inn. Unique touches abound, starting in the foyer with the gumball machine and shoe-shiner set among antiques and Oriental rugs, along with a needlepoint wallhanging of the Jabberwock poem.

Opened in March of 1982, Jabberwock is one of the very few bed and breakfasts in Monterey. Its unique setting overlooking Monterey Bay offers guests a magnificent view. Situated on a quiet corner, the large lot includes a lush garden with a waterfall and ponds.

The homey living room with its wallpaper, antiques and dark green rug is the place where homemade cookies and milk are set out for guests after dinner. A glassed-in sunporch with comfortable rattan chairs for reading and tables for

3rd floor
120

puzzles and games offers a wonderful view of Monterey Bay. Fresh flower arrangements adorn all the rooms.

The dining room, with its fireplace and charming wallpaper, has a mirror on the table to help guests read the breakfast menu, printed backwards. Breakfast is Barbara's specialty and she uses made-up names, such as "Razzleberry Flabjous" or "Snarkleberry Flumptious." Breakfast can also be served in the guest's room.

A lovely stained-glass window on the landing helps lead the guests to the bedrooms on the second and third floor, each decorated with flowered wallpapers, antique furniture, goosedown quilts and lace-trimmed sheets. Some rooms have fireplaces and <u>telescopes</u> or binoculars.

THE JABBERWOCK, 598 Laine St., Monterey, CA 93940; 408-372-4777.

A seven-guestroom bed-and-breakfast inn (3 rooms with private bath, four share baths) overlooking Monterey Bay. King and queen beds. Open year-round. Minimum two nights on weekends, three nights at special times, *i.e.*, Monterey Jazz Festival, Crosby Tournament. No pets. One dog in residence. V., M.C. Jim and Barbara Allen, owners/hosts.

DIRECTIONS: From San Francisco, take Del Monte Ave. off Hwy. 1 into Monterey, following signs to Cannery Row through the tunnel to Lighthouse Ave. Turn left on Hoffman and left on Laine.

THE MARTINE INN
Pacific Grove, California

125-230
*

The Martine Inn is a grand old home overlooking the spectacular coastline of Pacific Grove on Monterey Bay. The epitome of elegance and luxury, the 10,750-square-foot "palace" was built in 1897 for James and Laura Parke, of Parke Davis Pharmaceuticals.

Purchased in 1972 by Marion and Don Martine, the structure underwent major renovation while keeping the authentic, turn-of-the-century features that make it unique. While the inn's exterior is now that of a rose-colored Mediterranean home, careful attention was paid to restoring the Victorian interior detail. Marion and Don opened the Inn in 1984. Although larger than most bed and breakfasts, the Martines have maintained an atmosphere of intimacy.

Each of the 19 guestrooms is distinctive. A three-piece 1850s American walnut bedroom set with massive carved busts of Jenny Lind dominates one room. Another is furnished with a bedroom set originally owned by costume designer Edith Head. Thirteen rooms are in the main house, some with fireplaces and views of the bay, while the carriage house has six rooms which

overlook the courtyard pond and Oriental fountain. All rooms are furnished in elegant museum-quality antiques and have private baths. An 1890s oak pool table and modern Jacuzzi are also available for guests.

Breakfast and afternoon wine and hors d'oeuvres are served in the family-style dining room. Marion uses the finest Victorian china, crystal and old Sheffield silver pieces—daily. Champagne is served to honeymooners in 1850s Tiffany goblets. Newlyweds are also treated to a tour in Don's 1929 MG, one of his collection of 15 autos that he drives in vintage races. Two are on display in a small auto museum.

The views of Monterey Bay from the dining room and two sitting rooms can bring surprises. Binoculars are placed along the window ledges so guests may scan the water. Watch carefully and you'll be treated to a show by the clown of the sea, the fuzzy brown sea otter. Through the open windows, listen over the crash of the waves and you may even hear the barking of sea lions as they sun their ungainly-looking bodies on the craggy rocks or see whales, otters, dolphins and pelicans.

The Martine Inn, 255 Oceanview Boulevard, Pacific Grove, CA 93950; 408-373-3388, 800-852-5588.

A 19-guestroom (private baths) mansion on the cliffs of Pacific Grove overlooking Monterey Bay. King, queen and double beds. Breakfast included. Open all year. Four blocks from the Monterey Bay Aquarium and Cannery Row. No pets. Smoking restricted. CCs: Visa, MC. Marion and Don Martine, owners/hosts.

DIRECTIONS: Hwy. 1, exit Monterey. Follow signs to Cannery Row. Continue to lighthouse, inn on left.

160-226

OLD MONTEREY INN
Monterey, California

Built in 1929, this three-story, half-timbered English Tudor-style home was converted into an inn 14 years ago and continues to be one of the very best. The proprietors, Gene and Ann Swett, have lived here for more than a decade.

Located in the heart of the city of Monterey, in a quiet residential neighborhood, the acre-plus grounds are studded with old oak, pine and redwood trees, thick ivy, and even a running stream. Secluded outdoor sitting areas invite guests to relax and enjoy the gardens filled with fuchsias, begonias, rhododendrons and a formal rose garden.

In the inn itself, a blend of beautiful antiques and contemporary furnishings reflects an air of casual elegance. Most guestrooms have wood-burning fireplaces, while others have skylights and stained-glass windows. Each room has a view of the peaceful gardens. There are canopied beds (either queen or king), European goose-down comforters and pillows, and visually beautiful color schemes. Outside one guestroom is a flower-filled Mexican fountain; in another is an antique chaise longue and a couple have rocking chairs. A breakfast that might include Belgian waffles, quiche, French toast, homemade muffins or crêpes, among other things, may be enjoyed in bed or downstairs in front of a fire, where early evening wine and cheese is also served.

OLD MONTEREY INN, 500 Martin St., Monterey, CA 93940; 408-375-8284.

A 10-guestroom (private baths) English country house B&B on a hillside in a residential section of Monterey. King, queen and twin beds. Full breakfast and refreshments included. Open year-round. Minimum stay of two nights on weekends. Many golf courses, 17-Mile Drive, seal and whale watching, beaches, Cannery Row with aquarium, Carmel and Monterey shopping nearby. No pets. One dog in residence. No CCs. Smoking outside only. Ann and Gene Swett, owners/hosts.

DIRECTIONS: From Hwy. 1, take Munras Ave. exit heading toward the ocean. Turn left on Soledad Dr., then right on Pacific St. Martin St. is 6/10 mi. on your left.

THE PINE INN
Carmel, California

I found it hard to believe that I was sitting in the oldest commercial building in Carmel as the domed glass ceiling of the Pine Inn's gazebo rolled back to reveal a vibrant blue sky. I also found it difficult to imagine that the original hotel had been rolled on pine logs right down Ocean Avenue to its present location. Yet, it was true. This lovely, authentic Victorian inn, with its subtle updating, has lost none of the classic elegance that has charmed guests for over three generations.

Located in the center of Carmel, within walking distance to the beach, The Pine Inn was originally built in 1890 as the Hotel Carmelo. After the precarious log-rolling move, the hotel opened in 1904 to an overbooking of guests who were finally accommodated in tents pitched on adjoining lots.

Such a whirlwind opening made way for what has become quite a tradition. "See you at the Pine Inn," became an oft-used phrase as the town of Carmel expanded around the inn. From the very beginning, celebrities frequented the guest register. "We can't lay claim to George Washington," manager Hoby J. Hooker told me. "But at least the actor who played him on television slept here." While that actor's name pales against our first president's, the list of celebrated guests is noteworthy: Bing Crosby, Frank Sinatra, Howard Duff, Red Skelton, Ernie Ford, Mel Ferrer, and Tarzan himself, Johnny Weissmuller.

Those who are not quite as well-known receive the same special treatment as celebrities. Each guestroom is decorated with Chinese-style Victorian decor. Pierre Deux fabrics, authentic period furnishings and lovely artworks created a

mood of old-fashioned comfort and charm. Of course, I always feel the height of pampering is excellent room service, an area where the Pine Inn excels. All rooms have private baths and all-size beds are available.

Since World War II, the inn's Red Parlor has been one of *the* places to imbibe. More than a local watering hole, the cozy decor and friendly atmosphere have established it as a traditional meeting place. Subtle lighting and rosy stained glass set an intimate mood. All sorts of rumors abound concerning the clientele. Apparently author John Steinbeck met his second wife here while dipping olives into extra-dry martinis. W.C. Fields is also said to have warmed a bar stool now and then. Sandwiches and evening pub fare are available.

The outdoor patio was converted to a gazebo in 1972 with the addition of the opening dome. Breakfast, lunch and dinner are served here and in the Garden Room. Seafood from the Monterey Bay, fresh local vegetables and the best in California wines make dining a pleasure. The Friday-night buffet and Sunday brunch are more than any epicure could hope for.

After brunch, step just outside the inn's main lobby to the patio complex of Pine Inn Shops. Known as Little Carmel, due to the diversity of unique boutiques, you will find original fashions, men's clothing, antiques and jewelry.

The picturesque town of Carmel can be covered easily on foot. Some of the best art galleries on the West Coast are located in the area, and for those interested in a day "on the links," 17 world-class golf courses are within driving distance. Other points of interest include Fisherman's Wharf, the 17-Mile Drive and the incomparable Monterey Bay Aquarium.

THE PINE INN, Ocean Ave. at Lincoln, Box 250, Carmel, CA 93921; 408-624-3851.

A 49-guestroom (private baths) historic Victorian inn located in beautiful Carmel-by-the-Sea. All-size beds. Open all year. Breakfast, lunch and dinner available. Restaurants, boutiques, galleries and beaches within walking distance. Exceptional golf, Monterey Bay Aquarium and Fisherman's Wharf nearby. No pets. Richard Gunner, owner; John A. Wilson, manager.

DIRECTIONS: From Coast Hwy. 1, take Ocean Ave. west to Lincoln St.

THE SANDPIPER INN AT-THE-BEACH
Carmel, California

90 - 170

Carmel-by-the-Sea! Even the name has a melodious, inviting sound, and I can assure many of our readers who have never visited Carmel that it is an experience to be treasured. South of San Francisco and north of Big Sur on U.S. 1, the California coastal highway, Carmel's gentle weather, beautiful homes and chic shops make it a very popular vacation area and I would suggest that reservations be made well in advance for even a short stay.

The Sandpiper Inn, 50 yards from Carmel Beach, is in many respects similar to a British country house. In fact, both Irene and Graeme Mackenzie are Scottish. There are country house touches, including pots of flowers and window boxes. The inn has 16 furnished rooms. Each room and the common areas are decorated in a wide variety of furniture representing the owners' eclectic

taste. Some have views of Carmel Beach and others have wood-burning fire-places.

Guests congregate in front of a stone fireplace in the living room, which has a distinctive cathedral ceiling. Many of them have come to Carmel to test the challenge of the area's famous golf courses.

Breakfast may be served in a number of different places. For example, it may be enjoyed by the fire in the living room/library or it can be taken on a tray to the bedroom or the rose-garden patio. Breakfast leads off with Swiss cereal and freshly squeezed orange juice, bought pastry, and tea or coffee.

THE SANDPIPER INN AT-THE-BEACH, 2408 Bay View Ave. at Martin Way, Carmel, CA 93923; 408-624-6433.

A 16-room (private baths) bed-and-breakfast inn near the Pacific Ocean. King, queen and king with twin beds. Open all year. Restaurants, shops, galleries, Carmel and Stuarts Cove beaches, Old Carmel Mission Basilica (1770), Point Lobos State Reserve, 17-Mile Drive and Big Sur State Park nearby. Mountain bikes for rent, jogging and walking on beaches. Arrangements to play at nearby private golf and tennis clubs with pools and hot tub. Please no pets. CCs; Visa, MC. Graeme and Irene Mackenzie, owners/hosts.

DIRECTIONS: From the north, on Hwy. 1 turn right at Ocean Ave. through Carmel Village and turn left on Scenic Dr. (next to ocean), proceed to end of beach to Martin Way, and turn left.

SEVEN GABLES INN

Pacific Grove, California

It is difficult to imagine a more dramatic marine outlook than that afforded to the guests of the Seven Gables Inn. Above the shoreline of Monterey Bay, it has an unobstructed view from large picture windows of the bay's half-moon-shaped beach, stretching far, far into the distance. Lucie Chase, a well-to-do civic leader, built this showplace Victorian home in 1886, parking her electric car in front to further display her affluence.

Seven Gables has been the Flatleys' home for many years. Their children, who now operate the house as an inn, have modernized only the baths. The large comfortable rooms are furnished with English and French antiques—carved armoires with beveled pier mirrors, inlaid-wood pieces, chandeliers and Oriental rugs. Most rooms are further enhanced by the filtered light of antique Tiffany-quality stained-glass windows.

Mornings, seated in loge-view seats, savoring a sumptuous breakfast of fresh orange juice, a generous array of sliced seasonal fresh fruits, egg dishes,

crisp croissants, muffins or a hot apple cobbler, guests are treated to a show few people ever see.

Between early December and late February, migratory gray whales cavort below the windows, sending up spouts of vapor, then revealing broad backs before sounding into the deep waters of the bay with a final wave of huge tails. These mammoth creatures use this protected water as a haven to break their long journey between the Sea of Cortez and the Arctic Ocean. Even if your visit is at a different time of the year, you will always enjoy a performance by the frisky California sea otters and the proliferating marine bird life. One can take a pleasant stroll along the ocean path to the world-famous aquarium or Cannery Row.

SEVEN GABLES INN, 555 Ocean View Blvd., Pacific Grove, CA 93950; 408-372-4341.

A 14-guestroom Victorian bed-and-breakfast inn on the ocean front of the Monterey Peninsula. Queen and double beds. All rooms with frontal ocean views and private baths and ocean views. Full breakfast and four o'clock tea in afternoon. Open all year. Wheelchair access. Convenient to Monterey aquarium, Cannery Row, Carmel, Big Sur, Butterfly Trees, 17-Mile Drive. No pets. One dog and one cat in residence. No smoking. CCs: Visa, MC. The Flatley Family, owners/hosts.

DIRECTIONS: From Hwy. 1, take the Pebble Beach-Pacific Grove exit (Rte. 68 west) and continue to Pacific Grove. Continue on Forest Ave. to its end at Ocean View Blvd. Turn right two blocks to Fountain avenue.

Singu cottage
140

VENTANA INN
Big Sur, California

170 - 450

The land on which Ventana is located was once inhabited by Esselen Indians 3000 years ago, as established by radiocarbon dating on charcoal samples from an Indian burial site.

As impressed as I had been with the spectacular coastal views on my winding trip to the small community of Big Sur, nothing quite prepared me for the panorama from the restaurant deck at Ventana Inn. Ventana sits on 243 acres overlooking the Pacific, backed by rolling hills covered with oaks, redwoods and bay laurels. Its 16 buildings built of natural cedar blend well with nature. It has undergone some renovation and additions since its construction in 1975.

As vice president and general manager Bob Bussinger states in the inn's brochure, "We listened carefully to guest comments over the years, and concentrated our effort in the expansion on maintaining the intimate feeling in spite of the increased capacity of the inn."

I saw these changes firsthand as I entered the remodeled and enlarged lobby. There was a fire crackling in the large stone fireplace, with a supply of wood sitting in a basket on the hearth. Two guests seated on the red print couch were enjoying its warmth. The many windows looked out over the natural landscape. Guests were wandering in to share glasses of wine and samplings of fruits and cheeses in the expanded reception area. I decided to deposit my bags in my room and come back to join them.

My room, with a warm cedar interior, was decorated in soft shades of pink and mauve, contrasted by the deep green of several houseplants. It had its own bubbling hot tub and a large private deck. A fire had been laid in the fireplace, and two natural wicker chairs sat nearby. I quickly unpacked and returned to the lobby. As I sipped a delicious Chardonnay, I overheard a young couple describing the two spa areas with swimming pools, a sauna and communal Japanese hot tubs. Protected sundecks were nearby, some with clothing-optional areas.

Intrigued, I finished my wine and set out to do some exploring. I discovered a library with an ocean view, which also serves as an additional breakfast room, and a more secluded reading room decorated to complement its rustic wooden walls. I returned to my room to pick up my bathing suit and head for the spas. The young couple had been accurate in their description. I was to enjoy this spot for the next several days.

Evening found me seated in the romantic restaurant at a table made with three-inch sections of redwood from trees taken off the land. The floors were a shiny tile of dark red. My dinner choice was a light California meal of fresh oysters followed by grilled salmon topped with fennel, pasilla chile and roasted eggplant. I ended the evening with a liqueur in the adjoining bar, another recent addition.

The following morning I returned to the lobby after a brisk walk along the bluffs to the smell of fresh croissants, strudel, cinnamon rolls and muffins baked in the in-house bakery. I poured myself a cup of coffee and grabbed a plate. Striking up a conversation with one of the guests, I learned that she had discovered some wonderful hiking in nearby Andrew Molera State Park at the north end of Big Sur, just eight miles away. She was planning to go into Big Sur to do some shop-hopping. I decided to spend the morning in the Japanese tubs, and ventured into Big Sur after a lunch of Mexican food on the restaurant terrace.

I completed my short stay at peace with the world once again. Ventana is a place for lovers, young and old.

VENTANA INN, Big Sur, CA 93920; 408-667-2331.

A 62-guestroom (some suites) seaside retreat of rustic elegance. King and queen beds. Many rooms with hot tubs, TVs, VCRs and stereos. Continental breakfast included. Complimentary wine & cheese in the afternoon. Lunches and dinner available in restaurant, jackets required for gentlemen. Spa area with pools, sauna, Japanese tubs and sundecks. Open all year. Restricted smoking areas. Walk to beaches. Shopping and state parks nearby at Big Sur. Gift shop at inn. No pets. Major credit cards accepted. Ventana Inn, Inc., owners; R.E. Bussinger, general manager.

DIRECTIONS: 28 mi. south of Carmel on Hwy. 1 at Big Sur.

Central Valley

Interstate 5 is the most heavily traveled San Francisco-to-Los Angeles route. In the midst of the desert which the freeway traverses is the welcome oasis of the Harris Ranch. While in the area, it's worth driving nine miles north of the town of Coalinga to see a group of oil pumps decorated as animals, clowns and assorted imaginary creatures.

THE INN AT HARRIS RANCH
Coalinga, California

The Inn at Harris Ranch and the Harris Ranch Restaurants do not fit my criteria for inclusion in this book; however, an exception is being made because of its high quality and its location as an oasis on the seemingly endless, and often searingly hot, stretch of I-5 joining Northern and Southern California. Located in the fertile San Joaquin Valley, the soft pink stucco inn and restaurant are surrounded by lofty palms. Red tile roofs, stately archways and balconies, along with cool terra-cotta Mexican floor tiles, remind one of the early California haciendas.

The Inn is the newest part of the complex that makes up the legendary Harris Ranch. In the early 1900s, J.A. Harris migrated from Texas to establish one of California's first cotton gins. Two generations later, the ranch has grown to encompass 20,000 acres where cotton, melons, tomatoes and lettuce, as well as an impressive variety of other crops, are grown.

Yet the name Harris Ranch most often connotes beef. The reputation for quality beef has been earned by word-of-mouth more than by advertising. Over 2,000 people a day enjoy breakfast, lunch or dinner in one of the five dining rooms at the restaurant. Today, the beef plant processes more than 200 million pounds of high-quality beef a year. The Harris Ranch country store, which features fresh bakery products, can also pack Harris USDA choice beef to travel.

Entering the inn's double doors, a pink stone fireplace with huge matching columns meets your gaze. The lobby, with its polished granite reservation desk, is softened by antique-pine bookcases, lush plants, cowhide-covered sofas and original oil paintings. Although the inn is large, with 123 rooms, the atmosphere remains intimate and casual. The luxurious guestrooms and suites are designed to create a refreshing country garden theme. Deep pile carpets, high ceilings, scrubbed pine furniture, hickory log chairs and coordinated floral prints combine to make you feel very much at home. The bathrooms are cozy, with overhead heat lamps, double-basin sinks and dressing areas. A state-of-the-art air-conditioning system, designed to be especially quiet, allows comfortable sleeping during the scorching summers. Many of the rooms have private patios or balconies that overlook the terraced courtyard, 25-meter Olympic-style lap pool, fitness center and two Jacuzzi spas.

A continental breakfast can be served in your room, or you can enjoy your meals at one of the ranch restaurants next door. A typical breakfast might include steak and eggs, buttermilk biscuits, hash browns and fresh-squeezed orange juice. Omelets, corned beef hash and other specialty items are also available. My particular favorite is the Harris Ranch *huevos rancheros*.

The Fountain Court Dining Room, the more casual Ranch Kitchen or the intimate Jockey Club offer evening dining at its best. Fresh fruits and vegetables from the ranch farm, along with premium cuts of Harris Ranch beef, are prepared to order. Accompanied by the gentle splash of the courtyard fountain, I had a sumptuous meal of tender roast filet of beef that had been drizzled with a unique dried fruit and cabernet sauce.

Wines and champagne can be delivered to your room, and from May through September there is a poolside bar. A full-service bar/lounge, which offers entertainment on Friday and Saturday evenings, is located in the restaurant.

While you might feel as if you are in the middle of nowhere, a number of activities are available locally: jogging and walking trails are located on the ranch grounds and golf courses, tennis courts and racquetball facilities are only a short drive from the inn.

The Harris Ranch Inn is comfortable, with an attentive staff and beautiful surroundings. Jack Harris would be proud to see that the empire he began in 1937 has not lost its focus: offering the highest in quality.

THE INN AT HARRIS RANCH, 24505 W. Dorris Ave., Rt. 1, Box 777, Interstate 5 and Hwy. 198, Coalinga, CA 93210; 800-942-2333 or 209-935-0717.

A 123-guestroom (private baths) resort featuring a refreshing country atmosphere with elegant styling. Located just off I-5 approximately midway between San Francisco and Los Angeles. Open all year. Breakfast, lunch and dinner available at the ranch restaurants. Nonsmoking rooms available. No pets. Private airstrip. John and Carole Harris, owners; Kirk Doyle, manager.

DIRECTIONS: North or south on I-5, take Harris Ranch exit at the junction of Rte. 198 east.

Central Coast

San Luis Obispo started as a mission in 1772. However, it only became a town when the Southern Pacific Railroad in 1894 completed its route. Make sure you visit the Mission Plaza, a wooded creek and urban setting that offers special events all year. Apple farm is a working millhouse on San Luis Creek where a 14-foot water wheel by way of a series of pulleys and gears powers a gristmill, ice cream maker and cider press. Also to visit is the Mission San Luis Obispo De Tolosa.

EVENTS

JULY, LATE–AUGUST, EARLY	Mozart Festival
SEPTEMBER, EARLY	Central Coast Wine Festival

GARDEN STREET INN BED & BREAKFAST
San Luis Obispo, California

"Listen to the music, then take a guess," hinted Kathy Smith, co-owner of the inn. Strains of the popular show tune *Hello, Dolly!* played from the reproduction radio fitted with a modern tape deck. Kathy was challenging me to guess the name of my room. As Kathy drew open the curtains, I cunningly scanned the room for additional clues. Hmm. . . antique furniture, original stained-glass windows, ornately carved, restored fireplace. . . wait, what's this? I spotted a framed, handwritten paper on the wall entitled "Dollie's House Rules."

"Well, the name Dollie must come into play here," chuckling at my unintentional play on words.

"Right you are! This is the Dollie McKeen Suite. She owned the house for 49 years and rented out rooms, mostly to women. She held strictly to her 'rules'. This is a photo of her." Kathy gestured to an orange-tinged photo of a well-groomed woman standing on the brick steps of a dated version of the inn. "I was a single mom for 12 years. I admire Dollie's spunk, raising four sons and taking care of her tenants. Of course, that was before I met Dan." Kathy was referring to her husband and co-owner, Dan Smith. "You will have a chance to met him this evening. We'll be serving some fine, local wines in the McCaffrey Morning Room." As she closed the door, I began unpacking my suitcase, humming along with Carole Channing.

All of the 13 suites and the two common rooms are named and decorated with different themes. Music from individual radio and tape players highlight that particular theme interlaced with sentimental photos, heirlooms and knick-knacks provided from Dan and Kathy's lives.

The Goldtree Library (named for the original owners) displayed local artwork for sale. The bookshelves were filled with family books. A Vose & Sons grand piano with polished ivory keys, circa 1893, conjured up visions of an evening in the parlor. Ladies in long dresses, delicate china cups raised to their lips, while gentlemen conversed of local politics, cigar smoke drifting up to the high ceilings, as a fire crackled in the fireplace. It was difficult not to get lulled into the past within the walls of the grand Italienate, built in 1887. Pulling a novel off the shelf, I meandered upstairs to find a secluded spot on one of the several outdoor decks. Mozart, a frisky mix of Cocker Spaniel and Lhasa Apso, followed me and waited for my attention, tail impatiently wagging. He certainly follows Kathy and Dan's lead with friendliness.

I sampled some of the promised local wine that evening, then walked a short distance to a wonderful restaurant suggested by a fellow guest. Just a short block from the Inn, I wandered through a farmer's market that displays its wares every Thursday night. The inn was situated conveniently close to downtown, yet none of the hustle-bustle noise followed me to the inn, which is not located on a through street.

Next morning, as I entered the meticulously clean McCaffrey Room, breakfast was being served family style. A steaming crab souffle, one of my favorites, was placed before me, along with homebaked muffins, a juicy selection of fruit and freshly ground gourmet coffee.

I decided to take in the famous Hearst Castle, less than an hour's drive, before I journeyed back home.

GARDEN STREET INN BED & BREAKFAST, 1212 Garden St., San Luis Obispo, CA 93401; 805-545-9802.

Immaculate, restored 1887 Italienate, with 13 uniquely different guestrooms. Mostly queen beds, all have private baths. Open year-round. Minimum two-night stay on weekends and holidays. Full breakfast included. Early evening wine and cheese social in the dining room. No smoking inside the inn. Located on a quiet street, but within walking distance to downtown restaurants, coffee houses, galleries and shopping. Enjoy the Thursday night farmer's market. Drive out to the beaches, Morro Bay or the famous Hearst Castle. Mozart, the family dog, will greet you at the door. Dan and Kathy Smith, owners/hosts.

DIRECTIONS: From Hwy. 101, exit on Marsh St. Travel six blocks and turn right onto Chorro St. After one block, go right onto Pacific St., then right again onto Garden St. Watch for the bright burgundy awning indicating the curbside entrance to the inn.

Santa Barbara Area

An early Spanish settlement, Santa Barbara has become a rich vacation playground. Nestled between the mountains and the ocean, the area offers all kinds of activities, including whale-watching, deep sea fishing, golf and tennis. The climate is always mild to hot and sunny except during the winter months, which usually include several rainy days. Solvang is a fascinating community of Danish immigrants less than an hour's drive north of the city; Ventura, about 25 miles to the south, is a beautiful coastal town. The area code for the numbers listed below is 805.

	EVENTS
JANUARY–MARCH	Whale Watch Programs CINP Visitors Center
MARCH	Film Festival (info: 963-0023)
APRIL	Wine Festival
APRIL	California Beach Party, Ventura
MAY	Strawberry Festival, Ventura
MAY	Mozart Festival, Ventura
JUNE	Fiesta del Sol, Ventura
JUNE	Summer Solstice Parade
JUNE	9-day Amateur Sports Festival
AUGUST	Fiesta Week: Parades, Dancing, Music (info: 962-4469)
AUGUST, MIDDLE TO LATE	Ventura County Fair
AUGUST	Air Show, Ventura
SEPTEMBER	Ventura International Food Fair
SEPTEMBER	Concourse d' Elegance, Santa Barbara (969-2667)
OCTOBER	International Jazz Festival, Santa Barbara (962-0800)
OCTOBER	Oktoberfest (info: 564-5419)
NOVEMBER, MIDDLE	Indian Art Expo, Ventura Fair Grounds
DECEMBER, EARLY	Holiday Street Fair, Ventura
DECEMBER	Christmas Parade (info: 965-3021)
DECEMBER, EARLY	Ventura Parade of Lights, Harbor & Fairgrounds (648-3376)
DECEMBER	Christmas Variety Show-Ventura Fair Grounds
YEAR-ROUND	Theater, Santa Barbara
YEAR-ROUND	Horse Shows, Santa Barbara
YEAR-ROUND	Monthly Ethnic Festivals in Santa Barbara: Greek, Italian, Czech, Yugoslavian, Swiss, German, etc.

SIGHTS
Botanical Gardens
Channel Islands
Lake Casitas
Hispanic Downtown
Ojai
Santa Barbara Mission
Solvang
Ventura Mission
Ventura Harbor
Whale-watching (info: 963-3564)
Wineries at Santa Ynez

THE ALISAL GUEST RANCH AND RESORT
Solvang, California

"Alisal" means "a grove of sycamores" in Chumash, a Native American language dating back to the 1700s. Towering sycamores line the private driveway to the 10,000-acre ranch on the floor of the Santa Ynez Valley. Still a "working ranch," it runs about 4,000 head of cattle in the winter. The ranch, owned by Charles Pete Jackson, Jr., opened its doors to outsiders in 1946. It was an immediate success, welcoming such acclaimed guests as Clark Gable and Doris Day.

Alisal is not lacking in outdoor activities. Its 18-hole, par-72 golf course meanders through the rolling hills, oaks, eucalyptus and sycamores. A 96-acre spring-fed lake offers an abundance of water sports or invites you to just drift on a rubber float in the warm summer sun. Those not liking sand in their shoes or the chilliness of lake water can enjoy the heated free-form pool and whirlpool spa near the ranch quarters. Saddle up and participate in a horseback ride through the trails spotting everything from deer to wild boar, blue herons to stately golden eagles. Those more competitive in nature can face the challenge at one of several tennis courts. Impromptu games of croquet, volleyball or horseshoes develop on the lawn areas. Parents, weary of chasing their charges, can escape to the library which is reserved for adults for indoor reading entertainment.

The guestrooms are of simple taste with no telephones or TVs, a feature I particularly favored. Rooms were equipped with individual coffee makers and a selection of coffee and tea. All had wood-burning fireplaces. The decor in my room had a southwestern flavor.

Dining is reserved for ranch guests only, further insuring privacy during your visit. A buffet breakfast as well as off-menu selections are served each morning in the rustic Ranch Room. In the evening, the Sycamore Room as well as the Ranch Room is opened for dining, where guests savor the hearty cuisine by Chef Scott Douglass. This is a slightly more formal setting, and jackets are required for the gentlemen. The midday meal can be had at the pool snack bar, the Waggin' Tongue Bar or the golf clubhouse, depending on the season. Belly up to the bar in the Oak Room Lounge for entertainment and cocktails.

Services provided are too many to list, but one worth mentioning is the supervised children's program, including an old fashioned hayride, a reptile roundup, square dancing and sing-a-longs.

If you absolutely can't miss watching a sporting event, the ranch provides televisions in the recreation room, the library, the Waggin' Tongue and the Oak Room Lounge for guest viewing.

Area attractions include a visit to the Danish village of Solvang to sample Scandinavian pastries, hiking on park trials, petting Arabians at one of the thoroughbred horse farms or motoring to the beach to do some whale-watching.

I found it impossible to explore everything during my stay, and quickly discovered why guests return to the ranch year after year.

THE ALISAL GUEST RANCH AND RESORT, 1054 Alisal Road, Solvang, CA 93463; 805-688-6411. 73 ranch-style units placed on 10,000 acres. Studios and suites with wood-burning fireplaces. Full American breakfast and four-course dinner are included. Lunch provided at the various snack bars. Cocktail lounge with nightly entertainment. Gentlemen are requested to wear evening jackets to dinner and children not to wear jeans, shorts or T-shirts. Smoking prohibited in the dining rooms. Can accommodate conventions and business groups. Two-night minimum. Ask about seasonal packages. The ranch has horseback riding, lake sports and swimming, heated pool and whirlpool, tennis courts, a special children's program, and an 18-hole golf course. Shopping, wine tours and beach within easy driving distance. CCs: Visa, MC, ANNEX. Jack Austin, Manager.

DIRECTIONS: 40 mi. northwest of Santa Barbara, outside Solvang in the Santa Ynez Valley.

THE BALLARD INN
Ballard, California

My travel schedule had been grueling the past few months, so I decided to combine business and pleasure with a trip to the small community of Ballard, located in the heart of the Santa Barbara wine country. My destination was

the Ballard Inn, which promised respite from the everyday stress. Passing through an opening in the short picket fence, I inhaled the aroma from the flower-laden rose bushes as I approached the steps to the wide veranda. Kelly Robinson, friendly manager of the inn, rose from a white wicker chair, interrupting her conversation with a guest to greet me.

"Larry told me you'd be arriving today," she stated, her hand extending in a welcome. She was referring to Larry Stone, who along with his partner, Steve Hyslop, own this homey establishment. I immediately felt at home, and knots of tension in my neck began releasing on their own accord.

The tan two-story inn, neatly trimmed in white, was built in 1985, yet it fits the general architecture of this small town with only 81 families and still using its one-room school house.

Kelly opened the front door and stepped aside, exposing the lobby. My eyes were immediately drawn to a stunning three-sided fireplace of deep green Italian Marble, bordered with a carved mantle.

"How unusual," I commented, "I've never seen a fireplace like this in my travels."

"It usually brings that sort of reaction from our visitors," Kelly replied.

A carpet runner of matching color unfolded up the hand-polished, oak staircase on the opposing wall.

"I've put you in The Mountain Room," informed Kelly. "I think you'll enjoy the view." I found it had a spectacular view of the surrounding mountains as well as an interior country theme. The room was painted a forest green, complemented with earth tones of gold and brown. A white printed quilt reflected in the brass and iron headboard. A small fire crackled in the brick fireplace. French doors opened to a private balcony providing an even better view of the mountains. Kelly left me to unpack my suitcase, with the promise of a personal tour later that day.

Later, as I shared wine and hors d'oeuvres in the Vintners Room with the other guests, Kelly claimed me to make good on that earlier promise. Glass of local wine in hand, we strolled into The Stagecoach Room. Rich leather sofa, chairs and a round game table furnished this room. The hardwood floors and light chocolate walls provided an atmosphere of warmth while watching the big-screen television. In contrast, the George Lewis Living Room projected a flowery lightness. Comfortable sofas and chairs, upholstered in white linen, surrounded the fireplace and wallpaper speckled with hundreds of tiny flowers covered the four walls. We moved on to the large, cheery dining room. The oak dining room tables were already arranged for the next morning's breakfast. Starched white and pastel tablecloths covered the tables with high-backed chairs bordering each side. With Steve and Larry's background in the restaurant business, breakfast was something to look forward to. Everything was cooked to order, served piping hot, and included in your stay. The spaciousness of the common rooms and the culinary talents of these owners make Ballard Inn a favored choice for weddings and parties, as well as corporate meetings.

I shouldn't fail to mention that there are plenty of activities in the area. Becoming world known for its wines, the area offers great tours and tasting. Bike riding is a favorite hobby. The inn can provide mountain bikes or you can bring your own. Figueroa Mountain is a great test of leg strength. If you have equestrian tendencies, there is the Carriage Classic in April, parading thoroughbred horses drawing intricately designed carriages. Art galleries are open year-round. Breathtaking glider rides provide an opportunity to see the area from above.

The Ballard Inn, 2436 Baseline Avenue, Ballard, CA 93463; 800-688-7770 or 800-638-2466. Friendly small-town inn with 15 guestrooms. King, queen and twin beds. Breakfast selections included. Early evening wine and hors d'oeuvres. No indoor smoking. No pets. Closed Christmas Day. Two-night minimum stay on the weekend. Outdoor activities include wine tours, bicycling, hiking, touring galleries or traveling to nearby lakes or golf courses. Larry Stone and Steve Hyslop, owners; Kelly Robinson, host.

DIRECTIONS: From Hwy. 101, take the Solvang Exit. Follow Rte. 246 east through Solvang, turning left on Alamo/Pintado Rd. Drive three mi., turning right onto Baseline Avenue. Watch for the inn on the right side.

THE BATH STREET INN

Santa Barbara, California

When this 1875 Queen Anne residence was redesigned and reconstructed in order to make it a bed-and-breakfast inn, a great deal of care was taken to preserve the Victorian atmosphere of the original building and at the same time to incorporate security and safety features that conformed to the strictest modern standards.

Each guest accommodation has its individual charm: a small front suite has a quaint flower-hung balcony; a luxurious rear bedroom has a delightful garden bath; the third-floor guestrooms adjoin a library and parlor aerie looking out to Santa Barbara's spectacular Santa Ynez Mountains.

In 1993, two rooms were added with gas fireplaces, air conditioning, TV and one with a Jacuzzi.

In the morning a leisurely full breakfast is served in the sunny dining room or in one of the garden patios. The beach is a short drive or bike ride away, and bikes are provided upon request.

The Bath Street Inn is in a quiet residential area of Santa Barbara, and it is a very warm outreaching place with many, many books and magazines in evidence. The innkeeper, Susan Brown, obviously has a great deal of interest in the arts.

THE BATH STREET INN, 1720 Bath St., Santa Barbara, CA 93101; 1-800-788-BATH.

A 10-bedroom (private baths) bed-and-breakfast inn in a very pleasant residential area of a beautiful southern California city. King and queen beds. Open year-round. Ideally located for all of the historic, natural and cultural points of interest in and near Santa Barbara. A small room with television is on third floor. Abigail, a golden retriever/Lab, visits the first floor. No pets. CCs: Visa, MC, AE. Susan Brown, owner/host.

DIRECTIONS: From Hwy. 101, take Mission St. off-ramp east one block to Castillo, turn right three blocks; left on Valerio one block; right on Bath (Bath is one-way). Inn is on the right, parking in the rear.

THE BAYBERRY INN

Santa Barbara, California

A gilded eagle and two American flags give a Colonial feeling to the imposing white entrance of the Bayberry Inn. Actually, it was built in 1886 as the summer residence for a French diplomat and later served as a finishing school for young ladies. It is now painted a pleasing blue with a white trim.

Completely redecorated by two enterprising innkeepers, one an accomplished designer, the house is furnished in a post-Victorian style reminiscent of the period immediately following the First World War. Victorian furnishings are nicely blended with valuable art objects gathered from many countries. The guest lounge, with welcoming fireplace, has windows that overlook a large, well-manicured lawn, colorful garden and large trees, bordered by a white, lattice fence.

The dining room is resplendent with silk wall coverings rimmed around the top by a wide strip of beveled mirrors that reflect the sparkling crystal chandelier over the table.

LENCH. AUCHTETTER

Just beyond this room is the sun porch with a large bamboo bird cage holding unusual zebra finches. Outside is a lovely garden.

Some guestrooms have fireplaces and tiled baths and others possess canopied beds, thick carpeting and warm comforters. Green plants and cut flowers are refreshing touches in guest areas and rooms.

An excellent complimentary breakfast is included. Hors d'oeuvres and beverages are offered in early evening.

THE BAYBERRY INN, 111 W. Valerio St., Santa Barbara, CA 93101; 805-682-3199.

An eight-guestroom (private baths) inn in the residential area of a seaside town, five min. from ocean beaches. Queen beds. A complimentary full breakfast included. Open year-round. Guidance to fine local restaurants. Hiking and riding available in nearby Los Padres National Forest. Historic courthouse, Santa Barbara Mission, fine art museum are only a short walk. With prior permission small, well-behaved pets. CCs: Visa, MC, AE, DI. Keith Pomeroy and Carlton Wagner, owners/hosts.

DIRECTIONS: From Hwy. 101 take Mission St. off toward the mountains for three blocks to De La Vina, and then right on De La Vina three blocks. Turn left on Valerio.

THE CHESHIRE CAT

Santa Barbara

What owner of what bed-and-breakfast inn in California also owns an 800-year-old castle-hotel in Scotland? The answer is. . . Christine Dunstan! This vivacious and enterprising lady spends her time on both sides of the world; however, if you miss her at the Cheshire Cat, you will find a competent staff including manager Margaret Goeden.

Christine's presence can be felt everywhere in her selection of furnishings and decorations in the two beautiful Victorian houses that make up the Cheshire Cat. The rooms are decorator-splendid, with Laura Ashley fabrics and wall coverings, antiques and many mementos of her native England. Although various versions of "Alice's Cheshire cat" may be found here and there and the names of the rooms are drawn from Lewis Carroll's *Alice In Wonderland*, Christine was probably thinking of Cheshire, the county where she was born, when she named the inn.

When it comes to providing a feeling of luxury and ease, there is little Christine has left to chance. The bathrooms are modern, except for one claw-footed tub preserved from the original home, and have the most elegant appointments and amenities. I was mightily intrigued with the ceramic-tiled double whirlpool bathrub that presided in the Eberle Suite in front of a brick

fireplace. Some rooms have a private patio and others have a fireplace; they all have either a queen- or king-sized bed and a private phone.

There are cushioned bay window seats for cozy reading, and the high-ceilinged living room is divided into several intimate areas for conversation and tête-à-têtes, with a wood-burning fireplace and an old oak English settee.

A pretty, flower-lined brick patio between the two houses has a white latticed gazebo and spa, and when the weather is fine breakfast is served here under a spreading palm at round tables with white wicker chairs. The tables are set with flowered English china on pink tablecloths. On cooler days, there is a buffet breakfast in the dining room, which has a large oak table and handsome sideboard. The full breakfast features fresh ground European coffees, pastries, croissants, fresh fruits and juice.

Santa Barbara is a sunny, mild, very agreeable town on the Pacific Ocean about 80 miles north of Los Angeles. Much of its architecture affirms its Spanish origins. Having a rather resort-like ambiance, it bustles with tourists and sightseers.

The Cheshire Cat offers a charming and romantic respite on a quiet residential street, just a few blocks from all the shops, restaurants and theaters.

THE CHESHIRE CAT, 36 W. Valerio St., Santa Barbara, CA 93101; 805-569-1610.

A 14-guestroom Victorian bed-and-breakfast inn (main house and coach house) on a residential street in a beautiful seaside town, 80 mi. north of Los Angeles. Open year-round. Bicycles on premises. Restaurants, shopping, theater, wineries in Santa Ynez Valley, and all the nautral historic and cultural attractions of Santa Barbara nearby. No pets. No smoking. Christine Dunstan owner; Margaret Goeden, Manager.

DIRECTIONS: From Los Angeles on Hwy. 101, take the Arrelaga St. exit, turning left on Chapala. Continue one block to Valerio. From San Francisco take the Mission St. exit, turning left on Mission. Continue three blocks to De La Vine St. Turn right for three blocks and turn left on Valerio St. and continue one block to inn.

THE INN AT PETERSEN VILLAGE
Solvang, California

Hans Christian Andersen would feel quite at home in Solvang—it's a bit of Denmark in America. Settled by Danish farmers in the 19th century, it has grown into a thriving community with shops of all kinds, bakeries, restaurants, sidewalk cafes, windmills and other tourist attractions. I understand there are good bargains to be had in imported Danish glass and other merchandise.

The village, with its half-timbered buildings, peaked roofs and copper spires, is nestled among the sprawling ranches, farms and vineyards of the Santa Ynez mountains in central California, just north of Santa Barbara.

Playing a vital part in this lively community for the past 30 years, Earl Petersen was the architect for much of Solvang's Old World Village. He personally developed the Petersen Village and Inn, a European-style hotel overlooking an enclave of shops, arcades and a courtyard that makes up the village.

Jim Colvin, manager of the inn and Earl's son-in-law, was on the scene the day of my visit, and he took me all around this picturesque establishment. "Earl and most of the family are in Denmark, attending their oldest son's wed-

ding," he told me, "but almost any other time, you're likely to meet Earl, Delores, Stephanie, Aaron, Nancy, Adam, Jill or Ari. They're all very much involved."

There's much to keep a big family busy in this bustling village within a village. The hotel lobby and guestrooms form a horseshoe around the courtyard and are all, in true European fashion, on the second and third floors above the shops. The inner rooms look down on the courtyard, where trees and flowers are growing and a fountain splashes.

The lobby is tastefully decorated with honey-colored mahogany paneling, groupings of comfortable, Queen Anne-style furniture, some Danish antiques, interesting prints and carpeting imported from England. Because of the architectural design, guestrooms are in various sizes and shapes, with queen- or king-sized canopied beds, chintzes, pretty wallpapers, thick carpeting and handsome tiled bathrooms. All of the rooms have views of either the courtyard or the mountains.

"Our inner courtyard rooms are the most popular, especially on the two weekends before Christmas when we have a pageant reenacting the birth of Christ," Jim explained. "We have choirs and musicians, llamas dressed as camels, Mary rides in on a donkey, and the shepherds have real sheep. Guests with rooms on the inner courtyard can open their windows and enjoy the whole pageant from their rooms."

The pleasing sound of a piano playing "It Had to be You" drifted out of the lounge as we approached it, and there were groups of people chatting and laughing, seated on checkered settees around nice coffee tables. "Our guests are treated to complimentary valley wines and cheese every day at six," Jim said, "and when Frank Engleman is here, he plays the piano. Frank is a delightful retired local gentleman who comes in most evenings. He plays anything anybody requests, and our guests really enjoy him."

Petersen Village has all kinds of interesting shops, a restaurant and a tantalizing bakery, where the delectable pastries for the continental breakfast come from.

Solvang itself has no end of things to do, including horse-drawn trolley rides, tours at 14 wineries, many horse farms in the surrounding hills, and a three-month summer season of Shakespeare, drama and musicals performed under the stars in an outdoor theater one block from the inn.

Midway between northern and southern California, it's really a fun place for a stopover, and I can assure my readers they will find a warm welcome from Earl Petersen and his congenial family.

THE INN AT PETERSEN VILLAGE, 1576 Mission Drive, Solvang, CA 93463; 805-688-3121 (in Calif.: 800-321-8985).

A 40-guestroom (private baths) European-style small hotel over a complex of shops in a Danish village in the Santa Ynez Mountains of central California. Complimentary continental breakfast only meal served; afternoon wine and cheese. Open year-round. All of the attractions of a lively small town, including summer theater, wineries, shopping, gliders and balloon rides, and Santa Ynez mission nearby. No children under six. No pets. The Petersen Family, owners-hosts.

DIRECTIONS: From Hwy. 101, take Rte. 246 two mi. to Solvang.

LA MER
Ventura, California

Entering La Mer is like stepping into a scene from Heidi Comes to America, if there were such a book. Gisela (pronounced GHEE-zel-la) Flender Baida often dons a peasant dress or a *dirndl* to greet her guests; her blond curls, infectious smile and light German accent complete the picture of a Bavarian maiden.

"I used to love to come to Ventura on the weekends and sit in the park, eating an ice cream cone, watching the train go by, and dreaming of owning a home here," she told me as we stood on her front porch looking out at the ocean. She loves the feeling of this charming town beside the ocean, with its hilly streets, its harbor and its fishing boats.

Gisela found the house (circa 1890 and a historic landmark) on the side of a hill above the town and turned part of it into a bed and breakfast. Gisela calls it a Cape Cod Victorian, and she has created a most engaging environment for her guests. Outside, there is a pretty yard with lawns and many flowers and steps leading to the various levels. Parking is up a narrow, winding street, and above and behind the house.

Guests can choose among five rooms, two of which have sea views, decorated to represent different countries. There are many amusing and pleasurable touches, with winsome stuffed animals on cushioned window seats, dried-flower bouquets and wreaths, a pillow with *träume süsse* ("sweet dreams") embroidered on it, interesting old photographs, featherbeds, lace curtains and antiques. The Norwegian room features a queen-size ship's bed, a hanging net with starfish and cork floats, even books of Norse mythology and sailing stories. In contrast, the French Madame Pompadour Room is elegantly decorated with a curved walnut bed from France that is complimented by the Renaissance prints and tapestries on the the walls.

The guests' domain includes a cozy parlor, where a TV is hidden in an antique cabinet, shelves above a roll-top desk are filled with books, and a welcome warmth emanates from a Pennsylvania Dutch stove. The breakfast nook, lined with windows looking out to the sea, has built-in benches around sturdy tables.

Gisela prepares breakfast in the guests' kitchen, and a sumptuous Bavarian buffet it is, with her own muesli, fruit, cheeses, Black Forest ham, eggs, freshly baked croissants, apple strudel, German breads and of course coffee or tea.

Gisela also offers a midweek package that includes an adventure trip to the Anacapa Island, continental dinner and an antique horse-drawn carriage ride to a beautiful lake.

LA MER, 411 Poli St., Ventura, CA 93001; 805-643-3600.

A five-guestroom (private baths) Victorian house on a hillside above town, just blocks from the ocean. King, queen and double beds. Complimentary Bavarian breakfast. Picnic baskets available. Open year-round. Beaches, mineral hot springs, boat rides, nature walks, bicycling, fishing, tennis, golf, antiquing and museums nearby. Therapeutic massages on premises. Smoking restricted to outside. CCs: Visa, MC. Gisela Baida, owner/host.

DIRECTIONS: From the south, exit Hwy. 101 at California St. Turn left at Poli St. From the north, exit Hwy. 101 at Main St. Turn left on Oak St. and follow to Poli St.

INN EVENTS: Mid-week package includes candlelight dinner, buffet breakfast, therapeutic massage, hot mineral bath and carriage ride.

LOS OLIVOS GRAND HOTEL
Los Olivos, California

Night had settled over the Santa Ynez Valley. Lights from the Los Olivos beckoned to my travel-weary bones. A warm meal and soft bed are all a man needs sometimes, I thought, parking the car. I stepped over the threshold and

entered the lobby. Tired as I was, I could not help but be impressed by the elegance and grace of this old hotel. Wall sconces and candelabras casting a soft amber glow over the flowing curves of French Country style furniture, rectangular windows framed with gathered mauve drapes, pulled apart at the center to form a perfect diamond. The glistening black piano with brass tipped legs reminded me of a phrase from the hotel brochure: "luxury resort hideaway."

Michael Healey, owner of the hotel, stepped forward to perform the routine check-in and assist me to my suite.

"I've given you a suite with fireplace and Jacuzzi," he stated. "A business group just departed, leaving it available. Thought you might enjoy a few luxuries! There's complimentary wine on the table. Why don't you settle in, have a glass, and call downstairs when you are ready to come for dinner. A table will be waiting for you in Remington's, the hotel restaurant."

How nice not to have to make any decisions tonight and just enjoy the hospitality. I thanked Michael as he gently closed the door behind him. The theme of my suite was also subtle French Country, accented by bursts of colorful flowers on the fluffy down comforter and drapes. Lush green houseplants were tucked in the corners and atop the armoire. As water filled the Jacuzzi tub, I poured myself a glass of local wine.

As promised, my table awaited me at Remington's. I enjoyed a meal the chef classified as "California Continental." Light, but with great variety, and artistically presented. As I was leaving, my waiter reminded me not to forget the Continental Breakfast served each morning.

Dawn brought the promise of a warm day. After breakfast, with my coffee cup in hand, I wandered out to the patio, through the arched arbor fragrantly filled with climbing vines, down to the pool where I settled at one of the glass-topped tables. My eyes closed, I could hear the whirling noise of the jets from the outdoor Jacuzzi, and the soft voices of its early morning occupants.

My day could include touring nearby wineries, visiting local art galleries, biking or picnicking in the countryside, even a half-hour drive to the beach, but, for now, I would just rest here, breathing the fresh country air and basking in the warmth of the sun.

LOS OLIVOS GRAND HOTEL, 2860 Grand Avenue, Los Olivos, CA 93441; 800-446-2455.

Victorian Hotel with 21 guestrooms. Some with fireplaces and Jacuzzis. King and queen beds. Rooms include TV, phone, wet bar and refrigerator. Open all year, with a two-night minimum stay on weekends. Continental breakfast included. Dining at Remington's, the hotel restaurant. Full bar. Business accommodations available. Smoking restricted. No pets. Pool and outdoor Jacuzzi on premises. Wineries and art galleries nearby, with the beach a short 11-mile drive. Michael and Carolyn Healey, owners/hosts.

DIRECTIONS: North from Los Angeles take Hwy. 101 to Hwy. 154 (San Marcos Pass), approximately 28 mi. to Grand Avenue. South from San Francisco, Hwy. 101 to Hwy. 154, approximately two mi. to Grand Avenue.

THE OLD YACHT CLUB INN

Santa Barbara, California

"We fell under the spell of this old place the minute we found it," said Nancy Donaldson, spokeswoman for the group ownership of the Old Yacht Club Inn. "The house was occupied by two elderly ladies and was a bit neglected but certainly not abused. And it was only a block from the beach! At that time there were four of us, Lu Caruso, Sandy Hunt, Gay Swenson and myself. Although I brainstormed the idea of an inn, we were all looking for a change from working in the Los Angeles school system. We bought the house in June of 1980 and worked our tails off to be open by the fall, becoming Santa Barbara's first bed and breakfast. We figured the worst-case scenario was we would end up owning a fine house near the beach. Gay left the partnership a while back, but the rest of us are still going strong."

I admired their spunk, and was impressed with the outcome. The inn was built in 1912 as a private beach home. Early in 1920, it served as headquarters for the Santa Barbara Yacht Club after their facilities were swept to sea in a tumultuous coastal storm. The building was moved to its present location in 1928. The women have restored the inn and its adjunct building, known as

the Hitchcock House, and furnished both with turn-of-the-century antiques
and lush Oriental rugs. Family memorabilia graces the walls and tabletops. A
well-polished grand piano sits in the corner of the living room, basking in the
warm glow of a fire in the brick fireplace. Late one afternoon, while sipping
wines from the Santa Ynez Vineyards that are offered each day, we had an
impromptu sing-along, accompanied by a talented guest. Shades of burgundy
and beige on the walls and the welcome comfort of the settee and armchairs
create a warm, cozy ambiance in this room.

It was in the adjoining dining room, with its burgundy and white tablecloths over wooden tables and lacy white curtains on the windows, that I was
treated to a gourmet delight on the first morning of my stay. Nancy's culinary
talents are well-known in the area, but are reserved only for inn guests. Fresh
fruit and baked goodies, such as sour cream coffee cake and lemon bread, preceded a deliciously different brie and apple omelet.

Thanks to Nancy's creativity, even if you stayed a week you wouldn't eat
the same thing twice. However, the one-night-a-week dinner is her specialty.
At an additional charge and only on Saturday nights are guests treated to this
experience. I was lucky; I had booked my stay through Saturday. As the sun set
that evening, my appetizer, Artichoke Athena, arrived at my table. This was
followed by a cream of sorrel soup made with fresh sorrel from the herb garden
behind the inn. I rested and sipped some wine before tackling the spinach
salad, tossed with bits of feta cheese, pine nuts, purple onion and a balsamic

vinaigrette dressing. Next came the main course of salmon with beurre blanc sauce and fresh dill accompanied by a rice-shaped pasta called orzo. Full beyond belief, I still couldn't pass up the dessert of rich, chocolate cheesecake.

Satiated, I slowly made my way to my room in the adjoining Hitchcock House. The four rooms in this portion of the inn are named after a member of each innkeeper's family. I was staying in the Belle Caruso Suite (obviously a name from Lu's heritage), which has a king-sized bed, a separate sitting area and French doors that open onto a small deck. This deck conveniently connects to a larger common deck across the back of the house, and afforded me a choice of privacy or mingling with other guests. The common deck is filled with patio tables and chairs, shaded from the southern California sun by large umbrellas. Pots overflow with brilliantly hued flowers.

Sounds of the surf at East Beach, one block away, continually reminded me that the waterfront and its amenities were at my disposal. Borrowing one of the inn's bicycles, I spent one afternoon touring the town. The inn can also make arrangements for a golf game at a nearby private country club. Looking over the brochure in my room, I saw that Santa Barbara has many local events and festivities each month for visitors. I did make time to tour some of the historic missions in the area before my departure.

THE OLD YACHT CLUB INN, 431 Corona Del Mar, Santa Barbara, CA 93103; 805-962-1277, reservations only at 800-549-1676 in CA or 800-676-1676 in US.

A nine-guestroom inn with shades of Spanish design. Breakfast included. Complimentary sherry in each room. No smoking allowed indoors. Five-course gourmet dinner available on Sat. evenings. Most size beds. Open all year. Two-night minimum on weekends if Sat. is included. One block from East Beach. Easy bicycle jaunt to downtown. Abundant in waterfront activities, horseback riding, golfing, touring historic missions. No pets. House pets include two West Highland Terriers, named St. Patrick and Samantha, and Bella Mia Barbone, a toy poodle. CCs: Visa, MC, AE, DC. Lucille Caruso, Sandy Hunt and Nancy Donaldson, owners/hosts.

DIRECTIONS: Take the Cabrillo Blvd. exit from left lane of Hwy. 101. Turn west toward ocean. Travel approximately one mi. and turn right onto Corona Del Mar Dr.

SAN YSIDRO RANCH
Montecito, California

Waiting to check in at San Ysidro Ranch's reception desk, I was certain that I had seen famous chef Julia Child stroll through the cozy Hacienda Lounge. The Ranch's general manager confirmed my suspicion. "Oh, yes, she's one of our guests. A large number of celebrities have considered the Ranch a second home since it opened in 1893," she said. I was impressed with the list, which included honeymooners John and Jacqueline Kennedy, Paul Newman and Joanne Woodward, Bruce Springsteen, and Barbra Streisand. Writer Somerset Maugham used the haven of the Geranium House to complete some of his finest works. Sinclair Lewis wrote in the closet of the Oak Cottage, away from the spectacular but distracting ocean views. Sir Laurence Olivier and Vivien Leigh plighted their troth in the old-fashioned wedding garden.

It's easy to see why San Ysidro Ranch attracts romantic couples and those who just want to retreat to the rustic residential atmosphere. Nestled at the foot of the Santa Ynez Mountains, 43 cottages are tucked into the 540-acre grounds, of which the main grounds and garden remain virtually unchanged since the original land grant adobe was built in 1825. Hundred-year-old trees and wide terraces of pungent citrus, flowers and herbs surround the lawns. Hedges heavy with flowering jasmine and honeysuckle perfume the air.

Each cottage has its own personality. California-country charm is enhanced by polished antiques, cozy upholstered pieces in soft yellows and blues, fluffy pillows and coverlets and cushioned wall-to-wall carpeting. Thirteen bungalows have private outdoor Jacuzzis, and all have wood-burning fireplaces and wide sun decks for lounging. King and twin beds are available, and

all cottages have full baths with tub/shower combos. A special touch: Your name is engraved on a wooden sign outside your cottage to make you feel at home.

Complimentary morning coffee, newspapers and an Honor Bar, where guests mix their own drinks, are located in the Hacienda Lounge. The rooms have TV and videos, as does the Hacienda.

I had difficulty choosing among the outdoor entertainment possibilities. Tennis at one of two courts, hiking, swimming in the sunny Ranch pool or horseback riding? I chose to mount up and explore the resort's 500 acres of canyon wilderness trails that wind through forests, bubbling creeks and chaparral. I felt gloriously invigorated by the unspoiled beauty that surrounded me.

After a soak in my private Jacuzzi, I dressed for what I knew would be a special dining experience. Formerly the Plow and Angel, the Ranch restaurant took on a new name with the arrival of chef Gerard Thompson. Now known as the Stonehouse, Thompson characterizes the restaurant's cuisine as "fresh." The fixed menu is adapted every three months to make maximum use of fresh ingredients in the Ranch garden. "It makes it interesting and motivates me to try new things," Thompson told me. He has his own herb garden, and cures the restaurant's meat and fish in a smoker. Breakfast and lunch are also available, and all meals can be served in your cottage.

San Ysidro Ranch is just five minutes from downtown Montecito and Santa Barbara. Few inns can provide such privacy, comfort, calmness and personalized service so close to the hustle and bustle of civilization.

SAN YSIDRO RANCH, 900 San Ysidro Lane, Montecito, CA 93108; 805-969-5046.

A 43-guest cottage (private baths) California-country retreat at the foot of the Santa Ynez Mountains. King and twin beds available. Open year-round; two-night minimum. Very private. European plan. Breakfast, lunch and dinner available. Tennis, swimming, horseback riding, hiking. Five min. from Santa Barbara. Pets allowed with deposit. Claude Rouas and Bob Harmon, owners; Janis Clapoff, General Manager.

DIRECTIONS: Take the San Ysidro exit off Hwy. 101; head toward the hills. Follow San Ysidro Rd. to San Ysidro Lane, which ends at the Ranch.

SIMPSON HOUSE INN
Santa Barbara, California

It's 1874, and you have just received an engraved invitation to a housewarming party for Scotsman Robert Simpson's recently completed Eastlake-style Victorian in beautiful Santa Barbara. The Civil War has been over for nine years, and Ulysses S. Grant is serving his first term in office. You prepare a

large picnic basket for the 36-hour stagecoach journey from your home in San Francisco.

As you arrive, you enter through wrought-iron gates and follow a curved path through tastefully landscaped grounds. Seated in a white wicker chair on the large, wraparound teak-floored veranda, your host is waiting to greet you. The house is charming, you say. He tells you that it is Italianate Victorian in style. Your stay has begun.

Yes, you are at the Simpson House, and no, it isn't 1874, but 1994. Your hosts are Glyn and Linda Sue Davies. Other than those differences, all else remains true to the style of the 1870s. Secluded on an acre of English gardens, and just a five-minute walk from Santa Barbara's downtown, the Simpson House retains its place as one of the most distinguished Victorian homes in southern California.

The sitting room is spacious and elegant, with a fireplace and book-lined walls. The adjoining dining room has windows and French doors that open onto the garden. Both rooms are furnished with antiques.

In the uncluttered guestrooms, chintz and an abundance of English lace combine for a mood of elegance. European goose-down comforters cover comfortable beds. All rooms have private baths, some with clawfoot tubs.

The garden cottages have hand-sponged and stenciled walls, river rock wood-burning fireplaces, Jacuzzi tubs and private courtyards with fountains.

The veranda is a lovely spot to enjoy a breakfast of baked pears with crème fraiche, strawberry crepes, muffins and scones with homemade lemon curd. Hors d'oeuvres, tea and local wines are served in the evening. Croquet on the lawn and bicycles are provided.

A stay at the Simpson House Inn is a wonderful way to recapture, for a short time, the elegance and luxury of the Victorian age.

SIMPSON HOUSE INN, 121 East Arrellaga St., Santa Barbara, CA 93101; 805-963-7067. 1-800-676-1280.

A 13-guestroom (private bath) Victorian on a secluded acre. Four of the rooms with fireplaces and private decks are in the newly restored barn, three in the cottages. King, queen and double beds. Open all year. Breakfast included. Five blocks to town; one mi. to beaches. Smoking restricted. No pets. CCs: Visa, MC. AE. Dis. Glyn and Linda Sue Davies, owners; Gillean Wilson, manager.

DIRECTIONS: North on Hwy. 101 to Arrellaga St. exit; turn right. Go 6-1/2 blocks. South on Hwy. 101, exit at Mission St., go left six blocks to Anacapa, turn right four blocks to Arrellaga, turn left.

TIFFANY INN
Santa Barbara, California

I walked up the steps to the Tiffany Inn with the excited expectation that I was going to be able to talk antiques with owners Carol and Larry MacDonald. I wasn't disappointed. The MacDonalds are antique dealers, and their inn is a showcase for some of their prize finds.

The 1898 Colonial Revival home is a stately structure with three stories, a front gable and a balcony on the second floor. The MacDonalds have preserved the historic home's authenticity, original charm and ambiance.

Colonial diamond-paned bay windows and a century-old wood staircase are featured in the elegant interior. Of course, the rooms are all furnished with antiques. The living room is comfortable, with couches in front of the fireplace and a table on which to play cards.

Guestrooms have been decorated with antiques and colorful fabrics. Wallpapers in prints of bright peach, rose and green create a cheerful atmosphere and enhance the rich, dark wood trims. Each room has unusual accents and queen-sized beds. I was enchanted by the honeymoon suite, with its lovely secluded garden, fireplace, brass-canopied bed and double Jacuzzi. Some of the other rooms also have fireplaces, and most have lovely views.

After a breakfast of juice, fresh fruit, artichoke-spinach pie and fresh-baked carrot muffins, Larry invited me out to the sun-dappled veranda where we settled into the comfortable wicker furniture to talk "shop."

Fine restaurants and exclusive stores are within walking distance from the inn, and the beach is only 13 blocks away. Historic landmarks like the Old Spanish Mission and Stearn's Wharf are nearby. The MacDonalds are happy

to help you set up arrangements for a winery tour or an evening at the theater.

During the evening I enjoyed complimentary wine and cheese in front of the fire with the other guests. We all commented on the warmth and hospitality of the Tiffany Inn and agreed that our stay had been memorable.

TIFFANY INN, 1323 De la Vina St., Santa Barbara, CA 93101; 805-963-2283.

A six-guestroom (4 private baths) charming Victorian close to the beach, shopping and restaurants. Open all year. Breakfast included. Wine and cheese in the evenings. Smoking restricted. No pets. Carol and Larry MacDonald, owners/hosts.

DIRECTIONS: From the south, take Hwy. 101, exit at Mission St., turn right. Go three blocks to De la Vina. From the north, take Hwy. 101, exit at Mission St., and turn left onto Mission. Go three blocks to De la Vina.

VILLA ROSA
Santa Barbara, California

This delightful inn was formerly a small apartment-hotel. The present owners, a young architect and a young builder, each with a talented wife, removed complete sections of the ground floor during the inn's renovation to provide both a large comfortable lounge with a working fireplace and a separate breakfast room.

French doors in the lounge open directly onto a secluded solar-heated pool protected by tall hedges, a Jacuzzi and a fountain terrace where the continental breakfast may be enjoyed. Colonial Spanish furniture with a contemporary flair, used throughout the inn, offers complete comfort and is complemented by pots and baskets of tropical plants.

Guestrooms include lounge areas; their fabrics and carpeting are soft-textured in warm, soothing tones. The queen- and king-sized beds are very comfortable and room accessories are of the finest. Such amenities as turn-down service, pool robes and towels are some of the niceties offered.

The Pacific Ocean is nearby. Sit and enjoy the inn's red tile roofs, colorful bougainvillea and squat banana palms.

VILLA ROSA, 15 Chapala St., Santa Barbara, CA 93101; 805-966-0851. Fax: 805-962-7159.

An 18-guestroom (private baths) two-story Spanish-style inn. Short walk to a wide, sandy beach. King and queen beds. Continental breakfast. Minimum two-night stay on weekends. Pool, Jacuzzi, TV on request, room telephones. Bicycling, picnics, shopping, arts and crafts shows on weekends, excellent restaurants. Stearn's Wharf with attractions nearby. No pets. CCs: Visa, MC, AE. Annie Puetz owner/host.

DIRECTIONS: From the north take Hwy. 101 south to Castillo St. Turn right at the stop light and follow Castillo to Cabrillo. Turn left at the stoplight and take Cabrillo to Chapala. Turn left on Chapala. From the south take Hwy. 101 north to the Cabrillo Blvd. exit. Turn left at stop sign and follow Cabrillo Blvd. to Chapala St. Take a right on Chapala St. Inn on left.

Greater Los Angeles Basin

This area features beautiful beaches, tourist attractions for the whole family (including Universal City, Disneyland and Magic Mountain), sporting events and almost perpetually clear weather. But on the practical side, be aware that you'll spend a great deal of time in smog and on the freeway during your visit.

EVENTS

JANUARY	Japanese New Year
FEBRUARY	Chinese New Year
FEBRUARY	U.C.L.A. Gymnastics Invitational
MARCH	Marathon
APRIL	Hispanic L.A. Fiesta
MAY	Venice Art Walk

SIGHTS

Farmer's Market
Gene Autry Museum
Getty Museum
Griffith Park Observatory
Hollywood Bowl
Huntington Gardens & Library
La Brea Tar Pits
L.A. County Museum
L.A. Museum of Art
NBC Studios
Norton Simon Museum
Olvera Street
Universal Studios
Watts Towers

THE CHANNEL ROAD INN
Santa Monica, California

When Susan Zolla and Jean Root met the old McCall House, they could see beyond its dilapidated condition to a structure of historical character and charm. The two combined talents, and Channel Road Inn was born.

A rare example of shingle-clad Colonial Revival architecture, the McCall House is listed in architectural guidebooks. The large, blue-shingled home was built in 1910 by oil magnate Thomas McCall, and the family lived in the home until 1962. The building was then moved to its present location and essentially abandoned for 12 years. Jean and Susan, along with a group of friends, bought the house in 1988. "Other bed-and-breakfast inns use European features," Susan said. "We wanted people to see what Santa Monica looked like in 1910. We spent months looking for [authentic] door hardware, fixtures and furnishings." They have done a remarkable job and were just recently granted the Historic House of the Year restoration award from the Pacific Palisades Historical Society.

The entire house is light and airy. The living room, cozy library and breakfast room are furnished in authentic 1920s decor. Original birch and pine bookshelves, French doors, small-paned windows and inlaid paneling were painstakingly restored.

The 14 guestrooms and suites are all distinctive, many with canopy beds, antiques and unusual accessories. Two suites offer sitting rooms and separate bedrooms. All have private baths, and most have glorious ocean views. Despite the inn's street location, the walls have been heavily insulated, so the rooms remain quiet.

A breakfast of homebaked breads, muffins and fresh fruits is served in the sunny breakfast room, furnished in mint-green wicker. Additionally, afternoon brings wine, tea and hors d'oeuvres.

The inn is only one block from the beach and within driving distance to the wonderful Getty Museum and Will Roger's Home and Park. A real bonus for weary travelers is its proximity to the L.A. airport, just 20 minutes away.

THE CHANNEL ROAD INN, 219 W. Channel Rd., Santa Monica, CA 90402; 310-459-1920.

A 14-guestroom (private baths) beach-house inn in a quaint residential section of Pacific Palisades. All size beds. Open all year. Breakfast included. Wheelchair access. No pets. Near restaurants, shops, museums. CCs: Visa, MC. Susan Zolla, owner/host.

DIRECTIONS: Contact inn for directions.

LA MAIDA HOUSE
North Hollywood, California

Megan Timothy happily goes through life perfecting one skill after another: sculpting, photography, painting, carpentry, landscape planning, interior design, gourmet cooking, folk singing, horsemanship and innkeeping. She has creatively embroidered each into a tapestry called La Maida House.

A native of Zimbabwe, Megan came to the United States as a folk singer. She purchased the 7,000-square-foot mansion nearly two decades ago. Set in a quiet residential neighborhood, the 1926 Italianate-style home typifies the Hollywood mansions of the 1920s, with arched windows, white stucco walls, red-tiled roof and wrought-iron gates.

As you enter the expansive courtyard, you will be greeted by a bubbling fountain. The oak staircase that dominates the interior hallway is illuminated by a magnificent stained-glass window of a peacock, one of Megan's 97 stained-glass creations.

The public rooms are luxurious, with marble, oak, mahogany, tile and stained glass. Many antiques, Oriental rugs and primitive art works decorate the rooms. The atmosphere is refined and relaxed.

Guestrooms are airy hideaways. Every comfort has been provided, from terry robes matched to the room's color scheme to private telephones and answering machines on request. All of the guest quarters are unique. Some are elegant, some cozy. Many have private patios or gardens, and all have elegant baths, some with Jacuzzis.

La Maida's continental breakfast is served on bone china in one of two dining rooms or the solarium. Homemade pastries, fruit juices blended in unusual combinations and fresh fruits from the garden are arranged with a creative flair. A four-course exotic dinner served on gold-rimmed Limoges is by advance request only.

While La Maida is convenient to film studios, Beverly Hills and down-town L.A., there is much to occupy you right on the grounds, with a pool, gymnasium and resplendent gardens to explore.

Megan has adopted an African custom called *padkos*, which means "vict-uals for the road." Each guest receives some small gift as a farewell: a basket of fresh eggs from her chickens, homemade jams or perhaps cookies. Megan Tim-othy practices innkeeping as an art.

LA MAIDA HOUSE, 11159 La Maida St., North Hollywood, CA 91601; 818-769-3857, Fax (818) 753-9363.

An 11-guestroom (private baths) villa with privacy and refinement. All size beds. Two-night minimum. Breakfast included. Centrally located. No smoking or pets. Numerous cats in residence. CCs: Visa, MC. Megan Timothy, owner.

DIRECTIONS: Call inn for directions.

SALISBURY HOUSE
Los Angeles, California

I was looking forward to meeting innkeepers Sue and Jay German, the new owners of Salisbury House, after a recent letter in which Sue said, "We hope to bring our enthusiasm for people, places and food to our new life and to pro-mote the Salisbury House as a unique piece of quiet and turn-of-the-century charm in a city so full of concrete and metal." The spacious 1909 California Craftsman house is located in the historic residential West Adams section, an area rapidly being restored to its original elegance.

A walkway framed by roses led me to the wood-shingled inn. The magnificent hand-carved, leaded-glass front door opens to a stately home decorated with original stained and leaded glass, wood-beamed ceilings and an abundance of wood paneling, all set off by airy white eyelet curtains and antique furnishings. The living room is dominated by a large, rustic fireplace. Jay told me the home has often been used for movies and commercials.

All guestrooms are light and airy, with antiques and starched white curtains. I was given my choice and picked the Attic Suite. The pine floors, walls and gabled ceilings are enhanced by bright red plaids and prints. A braided rug draws together the wing-back settee and table and chairs in the sitting area. For real country atmosphere, the antique clawfoot tub sits open in one gable. As I snuggled under the down comforter, I felt like a kid in my secret room.

A full gourmet breakfast featuring juice, fruit, homebaked goods, a hot entree and Sue's blend of coffee is served in the formal dining room.

The Salisbury House is two blocks from the Santa Monica freeway and minutes from downtown Los Angeles, the Convention Center, Hollywood, Beverly Hills and the beach. After a busy day of window shopping on Rodeo Drive and star-watching at every turn, you'll be glad to return to the "piece of quiet" Sue and Jay have waiting at the Salisbury House.

SALISBURY HOUSE, 2273 W. 20th, St., Los Angeles, Ca. 90018; 1-800-373-1778 or 213-737-7817.

A five-guestroom (three private baths) charming B&B in L.A.'s historic West Adams district. All size beds. Open all year. Breakfast included. No pets. One cat in residence. Smoking restricted. CCs: Visa, MC, AE. Sue and Jay German, owners/hosts.

DIRECTIONS: Take the Santa Monica Freeway (#10), exit on Western Ave., and go north to 20th St. Turn left one block.

L.A. Coast and Santa Catalina Island

The coast is noted for its clean sandy beaches, warm to hot climate and carefree spirit. Catalina, an island 28 miles long and eight miles wide, is 22 miles from the mainland. The island is well preserved and is protected as an open wilderness by a special conservancy. Cars are not allowed here; when you visit, you'll get around in a golf cart, on a bicycle or on foot. Avalon, the principal town, is thronged during the summer—but if you come in the spring or fall, you'll have its old-fashioned seaside charm all to yourself.

EVENTS

MARCH (ST. PATRICK'S DAY)	Afternoon Big Band Dancing, Avalon
JULY 4TH	Dana Point Celebration
JULY, LATE	Dixeland Jazz Festival, Avalon
JULY–AUGUST	Sawdust Art Festival, Laguna Beach
AUGUST	Sunday Afternoon Big Band Dancing, Avalon
AUGUST	Sea Festival, Dana Point
SEPTEMBER, MIDDLE TO LATE	Art Festival, Avalon
OCTOBER	Sunday Afternoon Big Band Dancing, Avalon
OCTOBER 31	Halloween Parade, Avalon
NOVEMBER, EARLY	Triathalon Marathon, Avalon
DECEMBER, MIDDLE TO LATE	Casino Christmas Party, Avalon
DECEMBER 31ST	New Year's Eve Dance & Party, Avalon

SIGHTS

Disneyland
Knott's Berry Farm
Lion Country Safari
Long Beach Music Center
Long Beach Playhouse

BLUE LANTERN INN
Dana Point, California

When Roger and Sally Post began to design their sixth inn, they did so to take advantage of one of the most beautiful sites in Southern California. The Blue Lantern Inn sits on a high bluff overlooking the Dana Point Yacht Harbor and the Pacific Ocean. What's more, 25 of the rooms have at least some of that spectacular view.

Although this inn is new, it has the traditional feel of a Cape Cod inn. The colors of the inn are cool and calming: periwinkle blue, seafoam green and lavender. The public areas are spacious and inviting. The library has a fireplace, a backgammon table, comfortable sitting areas and a small bar where wine and hors d'oeuvres are served each afternoon. When I visited, a wonderful cream cheese spread was tasted by all, as well as a mustard peppercorn dip.

The parlor has a huge stone fireplace with a beautiful hand-made quilt hanging above. The dining room has large glass doors that open out with tables both inside and outside.

The inn has definitely become "the place to go for a romantic weekend," according to the young manager. Forty-five minutes from Disneyland, one hour from San Diego and the charming art galleries and cafes of Laguna Beach, this is a nice destination spot.

The guestrooms all have gas fireplaces, Jacuzzi tubs, mahogany furniture, refrigerators and huge bathrooms. Many rooms have a deck or balcony with chairs to enjoy the view. The tower suite has a 180-degree view, vaulted ceilings, a king-sized four-poster bed, a telescope and a deck—complete with complimentary champagne. Additional amenties include a morning paper, an exercise room, bicycles, concierge, breakfast in bed and evening turndown with towel change.

Those sensitive to traffic and street noise should make that clear when making their reservation.

BLUE LANTERN INN, 34343 Street of the Blue Lantern, Dana Point, CA 92629; 714-661-1304. Fax: 714-496-1483.

A 29-room (private baths) inn on bluff overlooking yacht harbor and Pacific; Cape Cod style with white trim, gabled room, balconies, panoramic views. King, queen and double beds. Open year-round. Many artistic shops in town, driving distance to Disneyland and San Diego. No pets. Roger and Sally Post, owners; manager in residence.

DIRECTIONS: From Hwy. 1 go left on Street of the Blue Lantern one block.

THE GARDEN HOUSE INN
Avalon, California

I couldn't believe I was actually swooping over the Pacific Ocean in a helicopter, but I was in the able hands of an Island Express pilot and on my way from Long Beach to Catalina Island, approximately 20 minutes away. As we landed, I noticed the odd absence of cars and asked about transportation to the Garden House Inn, where I had reservations. I was told that cars are generally not allowed on the island, and those that are usually had an eight-year wait for licensing. In a manner slightly reminiscent of the transportation in the classic television series "The Prisoner," the island residents travel by golf cart. Unlike the series, there is a relaxed sense of freedom here: a lazy lifestyle and beautiful surroundings even though the town can get a little noisy.

The Garden House Inn is located in the Mexican-flavored village of Avalon, just steps from the beach. The three-story 1920s home was purchased in 1987 by Jon Olsen and his family, who restored it to its present elegant state.

Decorated in French country style, the sunny guestrooms have an early 1930s theme. Floral bedspreads and quilts are enhanced by matching wallpapers. Several have ocean and harbor views. All have private baths, cable television and VCRs. With its white wicker umbrella tables and rose cushions, the adjoining garden patio is a lovely place to relax surrounded by masses of colorful flowers.

The lovely living room, with its walnut-panelled fireplace, is a cozy place to enjoy a hearty buffet breakfast. At 5:00 P.M., you can meet other guests at the wine and cheese hour.

Located on a main thoroughfare for early-morning barge off-loading, the inn offers a unique opportunity for those who are awake to enjoy the dawn. Climb to the third-floor sun deck and you can see what most people sleep through. You will also be treated to the graphic outline of the mainland as the sun rises.

Convenient to restaurants, shops and entertainment, the inn provides an excellent home base. After a full day of scuba diving or a glass-bottom-boat tour, you will return to find sherry, taffy and cookies to enjoy before bed.

THE GARDEN HOUSE INN, Third and Claressa, P. O. Box 1881, Avalon, CA 90704; 213-510-0356.

An eight-guestroom (private baths) inn on the island of Catalina, 1/2-block from the beach. Queen beds. Open all year. Breakfast included. No pets or smoking. The Olsen Family, owners/hosts.

DIRECTIONS: Transportation to Catalina by Island Express helicopter service, or by boat or plane.

THE INN ON MOUNT ADA
Avalon, California

In 1921, when chewing gum magnate/philanthropist William Wrigley, Jr. stood back and, in his mind's eye, saw a vision of a summer home, he pulled out all the stops. Located on 5-1/2 acres of the lovely island of Santa Catalina, high atop hills overlooking Avalon Harbor, the compound covers nearly 7,000 square feet, which includes a main house ornamented with elaborate columns, arches, panel work and handmade moldings. The den, sun room, living room, card lounge, dining rooms and butler's pantry complete the first level. Six bedrooms fill the second floor.

Eventually the property was donated to the University of Southern California for use as a marine institute. The university funded rehabilitation to meet electrical and plumbing codes, as the building had been vacant for more than 25 years prior to the university's possession.

In February 1985, a 30-year lease was signed by USC and the Mt. Ada Inn Corporation, composed of island residents Susie and Wayne Griffin, Marlene McAdam, and ex-residents Suzie and Scott Wauben, and the property was transformed into a B&B inn.

With backgrounds in home economics, restaurant management, computer bookkeeping services, interior design and civic affairs, the partnership had the necessary combination of business experience to operate such an undertaking. "Everyone in Avalon has chosen to live here as an alternative lifestyle to the mainland," explained Susie Griffin, the assistant innkeeper and conference center coordinator.

The Georgian home, listed on the National Register of Historic Places, offers the stately architecture of detailed French doors and paneled insets and dentil molding. Thought to commemorate the Bay of the Seven Moons, the L-shaped terrace is composed of seven configurations of local terra-cotta tile.

The common rooms are classical, restful and custom-designed by the best in the business. Views to the ocean are commonplace, and sumptuous couches and rattan furniture invite conversation. Crafts indigenous to the area are found in the form of rare Catalina pottery, an art practiced by island craftsmen in the 1920s.

The six guestrooms are detailed with old-world antiques. Chandeliers, carpeting, drapery fabrics and bedding are thoughtfully created and coordinated by specialty designers. The installation of acoustical insulation to provide adequate privacy was one aspect of upgrading that took place when the rooms were prepared for guests. Most rooms have queen-sized beds and all have private baths.

A hearty breakfast is included with the room tariff and may offer bran muffins; freshly squeezed orange juice; poached pears with strawberry glaze; a mushroom, onion, jack and cheddar cheese omelet; bacon; and bagels. Hot and cold appetizers, freshly baked cookies, a coffee and tea tray, soft drinks, fresh fruit and mixed nuts are available at all times. Late-afternoon relaxation is accompanied by red and white wines, sherry, port, beer, and champagne. A deli-style lunch and traditional country inn dinner is also included.

The owners call their style of food "simple." They've found that the rich foods they once served were too much for guests who stayed more than one night, so they listened to their repeat guests and simplified the cooking. I had a lovely salad with creamy vinaigrette, a roasted leg of lamb served with roasted new potatoes Provencale, sauteed cabbage and baked poppy seed rolls. The dessert was a blackberry custard tart.

The Inn on Mount Ada is a five-minute drive from town, by golf cart only, if you please. The island only allows travel by such unintrusive means. In fact, I had one of the most serene mornings of my life as I stood on my balcony at 5

A.M. watching a spectacular sunrise, with the sounds of small birds and the sea to keep me company.

THE INN ON MOUNT ADA, 398 Wrigley Rd., P.O. Box 2560, Avalon, CA 90704; 213-510-2030.

A six-guestroom (private baths) elegant Georgian Colonial on the fabled island of Santa Catalina. Queen and double beds. Open all year, except Christmas. Breakfast, lunch and dinner. No pets. CCs: Visa, MC. Susie Griffin and Marlene McAdam, owners/hosts.

DIRECTIONS: Boat or helicopter from mainland.

INN EVENTS: JULY 4TH—Fireworks Celebration

DECEMBER, MIDDLE—Christmas Party

THE SEAL BEACH INN AND GARDENS

Seal Beach, California

Over the years, Marjorie Bettenhausen has developed her inn into a showplace that welcomes guests from all over the world, as well as stars from nearby Hollywood.

Here are some observations from Marjorie herself about the inn: "It is a fairyland of brick courtyards, old ornate street lights, blue canopies, objects

d'art, fountains, shuttered windows, window boxes and vines. We are a family-run inn, a place of character, a thoughtfully designed place where guests are pampered and our service is friendly and caring.

"From the very start we saw the opportunity to create an inn that would have the ambiance of inns that we have visited in southern France. We've been very fortunate since 1980, when you first visited, in having been discovered by many feature writers and also in having been on TV many times."

The French Mediterranean appearance is enhanced by the truly extraordinary gardens. All of the lodging rooms are named after flowers, including fuchsia, gardenia and camellia. The full-time gardener keeps the flowers blooming even in winter with considerable aid from the mild year-round weather in this part of California. There are rare vines, climbing vines, flowering bushes, sweet-smelling bushes, deciduous trees, evergreen pear trees and a wonderful variety of a cascading willowy tree that looks like a weeping willow but really isn't. It stays green all year.

Lush plantings and antique newel posts are beside each guestroom door, and in the rooms, lovely luxurious comforters and dust ruffles set off the wrought-iron headboards. The bridal chamber, with its very own veranda beside the pool, is much in demand.

In addition, there are the Royal Villas, six of the most romantic, lavish suites imaginable.

The entrance to the inn from the street is through a three-sided square, around which the guestrooms are situated, and this is indeed a flower-filled courtyard, lit by street lamps that were rescued from the scrap pile at nearby Long Beach. There is a red English telephone booth in one corner, and a kiosk (that would be quite at home in Nice) has notices of all the nearby attractions. The library is an elegant guest salon with an impressive fireplace, books and games.

"We never stop improving, adding, changing, embellishing and fine tuning, since we view innkeeping as an art form. We continually seek to enhance our impact on the guests' senses through new ways of exciting them, especially visually."

Some bathrooms have been done with beautiful Roman tubs and hand-painted tiles. The fireside Victorian dining room has been enlarged. The library has many historical books inherited from Marjorie's grandfather and father's estates. Some of the new features include feather comforters, triple sheeting, afternoon tea, handsome imported Italian leather chairs in several suites, a wind chime in a tree outside the reception room, a fountain splashing water outside the library and a tea room.

Breakfasts are lavish, with quiche or other interesting egg casseroles, freshly squeezed juices, homebaked pastries, bread, cereals, their own granola, seasonal fruits, cheeses, freshly ground Viennese coffee and an assortment of imported teas. A special treat is the giant chocolate chip cookie presented to each arriving guest.

THE SEAL BEACH INN AND GARDENS, 212 Fifth St., Seal Beach, CA 90740; 310-493-2416 or 213-430-3915.

A 23-guestroom (private baths) village inn located in a quiet residential area of an attractive town, 300 yds. from beach. King, queen and double beds available. Breakfast only meal served. Restaurants within walking distance. Open all year. Catalina Island is 20 mi. offshore; California mountains and lakes two hrs. away. Long Beach Playhouse, Long Beach Music Center nearby. Swimming pool on grounds. Tennis, beach, biking, skating, golf nearby. No pets. Marjorie and Jack Bettenhausen, innkeepers.

DIRECTIONS: From Los Angeles Airport take Hwy. 405 south to Seal Beach Blvd. exit. Turn left toward the beach, right on the Pacific Coast Hwy., left on Fifth St. in Seal Beach, which is the first stoplight after Main Street. Inn is on the left, two blocks toward the beach on Fifth St.

Big Bear Region
(San Bernardino County)

EAGLE'S NEST BED & BREAKFAST
Big Bear Lake, California

Sipping hot chocolate, I was sitting on the hearth of the huge river rock fireplace located in the living room. The fire snapped and sparked next to me. Heavy cedar beams braced the rustic log walls of the main house. Dark clouds hung heavy in the late afternoon sky. There was still a chill in the air. Leftover smatterings of snow created a natural patchwork quilt on the lawn surrounding the log home and adjacent cabins. The surrounding mountains still donned white winter caps. Ski season was winding down, and guests, like myself, were here more for the early spring scenery and solitude.

Cordial owners Jack Draper and Jim Joyce, once weekenders to the area, now claim this place as home year-round, taking time off now and then to ski the nearby slopes.

The log cabin lodge was built in 1983 and has five guestrooms. The additional five private cabins date back to the 1930s and 1940s. All have been renovated but retain that comfortable, log cabin feeling. The cabins have TVs, telephones, fireplaces and some Jacuzzis. One even has a full kitchen, perfect for a small family. The main house features a TV and VCR in the living room.

This is definitely a "blue jeans" place, especially if you want to spend time outdoors enjoying Jim and Jack's animal menagerie, consisting of two horses, two dogs, a goat and some ducks, a real attraction for two of the younger guests. The animal area is a distance from the lodge, keeping in mind that not everyone is an animal lover.

The lodge is centrally located on two acres, just one mile from the conveniences of Big Bear Village. A half-mile hike takes you to the shores of Big Bear Lake, and Snow Summit Ski area is close by.

In addition to the natural beauty of the surroundings, two things remain etched in my mind about Eagle's Nest. . . pre-breakfast coffee delivered to my door each morning and a mint on my pillow with blankets turned down each night. Such attention to detail!

EAGLE'S NEST BED & BREAKFAST, 41675 Big Bear Blvd., P.O. Box 1003, Big Bear Lake, CA 92315; 909-866-6465.

Rustic cedar-log lodge sheltered on tree-studded two acres. Five guestrooms in the main house. Five cabins, one with kitchen. Jacuzzis in some rooms. Most have fireplaces and TVs. Large living room featuring a river rock fireplace. Complimentary continental breakfast and late afternoon hot chocolate, wine and hors d'oeuvres served. Check for minimum stays. No smoking. Small pet can be accommodated in one unit with increased deposit. Short walk to Big Bear Lake. Close to village shopping and ski areas. Horses, dogs, goat and ducks on property, but away from guest area. No CCs accepted. Jim Joyce and Jack Draper, owners/hosts.

DIRECTIONS: From Los Angeles, take I-10 East to Redlands. Exit at Orange Street and go left. Turn right onto Lugonia (also Highway 38). Proceed approximately 50 miles to Big Bear Valley. At first stop light in Big Bear Valley, Hwy. 38 becomes Hwy. 18. Travel through stop light approximately 4-1/2 mi. Lodge is on left side.

San Diego Area

This city is a popular year-round resort, due to its beautifully warm climate and family attractions like Marine World, Sea World, and the San Diego Zoo. There are wonderful beaches, and many visitors make shopping or restaurant excursions across the Mexican border.

EVENTS

MARCH	St. Patrick's Day Parade
APRIL	San Diego Crew Classic at Mission Bay
MAY	Cinco de Mayo Celebration
MAY	American Indian Cultural Days Pow Wow
JULY	Blue Angels
SEPTEMBER	Gold Cup Races
NOVEMBER	Dixieland Jazz Festival

SIGHTS

Balboa Park

Old Town

San Diego Zoo

Sea World

THE INN
Rancho Santa Fe, California

Aromatic eucalyptus trees, orange trees, bougainvillea, acacias, palm trees and Brazilian pepper trees—fragrance and color. That was my first impression of this elegant but unassuming inn, spread out in hacienda-style cottages with red-tile roofs amid terraced gardens, shaded by the towering eucalyptus trees. Six gardeners keep the 20 acres verdant and manicured, with broad lawns, clipped hedges and shrubs, and ornamental flowers of all kinds, including gorgeous roses.

This is a quiet haven, where the atmosphere, though conservative, is not at all stuffy. The mood is set by the Royce family, including Duncan Royce Hadden, who is a fourth-generation hotelier and is very much in evidence.

They see to it that everything runs like clockwork for their guests, who are usually found around the pleasantly sheltered heated swimming pool; on one of the three tennis courts or one of the two nearby 18-hole golf courses; down at the Del Mar beach cottage, where there are dressing rooms and showers, or in their whites playing a serious game of croquet on the regulation English croquet lawn.

There are several dining areas in the main building, and I was assured that gentlemen wear coats at dinner. The Garden Room overlooks the pool and gardens and is decorated with lattice and painted murals; the Vintage Room is modeled after a traditional tap room, the charming Library Room is lined with over 4,000 books, and the Patio Room opens out onto a patio flanked with brilliant poinsettias and hanging plants. On some summer weekend evenings there's dinner and dancing on the patio under the stars.

Before and after dinner, guests usually gather in the lounge area, a huge 30-by-40-foot room, with a high-beamed cathedral ceiling, handsome fireplace, comfortable sofas and chairs, and filled with Royce family heirlooms. There are some exquisite Oriental objects d'art, collected by the family during their travels in China—wall tapestries, dolls, vases and bowls. Duncan pointed out the collection of very intricately tooled antique ship models mounted on the walls around the room.

Guestrooms in the main building and cottages are individually decorated with family antiques. The cottages contain from two to ten guestrooms, some with kitchens, fireplaces and private patios.

The town of Rancho Santa Fe is one of the most attractively designed that I have ever visited. It has been well described as a "civilized planned community." The homes, estates, shops and buildings have been created in perfect harmony with nature's generous endowment of climate and scenery. One of the dominating factors is the presence of the gigantic eucalyptus trees.

One of the most useful and gratifying amenities at the inn is a map showing many short motor trips to points 50 miles away, including Temecula to the north and Tijuana, Mexico, to the south. I am personally acquainted with the rolling ranch and orchard country to the east as far away as Julian. All of these trips make a stay at the inn worth several extra days.

THE INN, P.O. Box 869, Rancho Santa Fe, CA 92067; 619-756-1131, 800-654-2928. A 90-guestroom (private baths) resort-inn, 27 mi. north of San Diego Freeway #5 and five mi. inland from Solana Beach, Del Mar. European plan. King and twin beds available. Breakfast, lunch and dinner served to travelers daily. Open year-round. Wheelchair access. Pool, tennis and six-wicket croquet course on grounds. Golf, Delmar and ocean nearby. Day trips to Balboa Park, San Diego Zoo, Wild Animal Park, Sea World, harbor cruises, La Jolla shops and galleries, Old Town San Diego and backroading. Duncan Royce Hadden Innkeeper.

DIRECTIONS: From I-5, take the Lomas Santa Fe Dr. exit and drive inland about four mi. The inn is on the righthand side of the road.

RANCHO VALENCIA RESORT
Rancho Santa Fe, California

It had been an evening to remember. First, I sat aloft in a hot air balloon viewing the Pacific Coast sunset. Then back to Rancho Valencia to change for ele-

gant dining in the resort restaurant. Finally, I ended my evening by dancing under the stars in the Fountain Courtyard. I could become accustomed to this lifestyle!

This was my first visit to Rancho Valencia, set high on a 40-acre plateau overlooking the San Dieguito Valley. Reminiscent of early California haciendas, the architecture is Spanish-Mediterranean. Tiled roofs and sprawling stucco buildings are connected with broad walkways of Spanish pavers. Casitas contain the 43 suites, each with a fireplace, private terrace, wet bar, fully stocked mini-bar and a coffeemaker complemented with a basket full of fresh ground coffee. A thick terry robe hung in the luxurious bathroom, which even included a hair dryer.

While working out in the Health Center one morning, I overhead two businessmen expressing positive comments about the facilities for the conference they were attending. The resort has several meeting and banquet rooms to accommodate such functions. The Hacienda, a large private residence, is ideal for smaller groups. Once a private residence, it has been elegantly restored to three suites, each with private baths, a common kitchen, dining room and living room. Outdoor features include a private pool, Jacuzzi and several cabanas.

I was perfectly content with my suite, and particularly impressed with the staff's attention to detail. Each morning, outside my door, I would find freshly squeezed orange juice (from the property's 4,000 citrus trees), the daily newspaper and a single rosebud. After a relaxed beginning to the day, I would wander down to the dining room and partake of the complimentary breakfast al fresco.

Choices of activities then ranged from laying by one of the pools, playing a round of golf at the adjacent championship course, signing up to play on one of the 18 tennis courts, and viewing a game of croquet on the world-class court. Venturing off the grounds, I could head for the beaches of La Jolla or Del Mar, take in horse races at the famous Del Mar Racetrack, take the 20-minute drive to San Diego Zoo and Sea World, or even head over the border to Tijuana to barter in their marketplace. Disneyland is a 1-1/2-hour drive.

As the sun went down, I would stroll the grounds. The subtle splashing from the water fountains and chirping of crickets filled the warm night air.

RANCHO VALENCIA RESORT, 5921 Valencia Circle, P.O. Box 9126, Rancho Santa Fe, CA 92067; 800-548-3664 or 619-756-1123. Reminder of California's Spanish history with this 43-suite, hacienda-style resort. Ideal for business groups as well as private guests. Spacious and private. View of the San Dieguito Valley from 40 acres. Complimentary breakfast. Lunch and dinner selections in the resort restaurant. Inquire about guest packages. Open all year. Travel to the beach, visit Sea World, take in horse races at Del Mar or view it all from above in a hot air balloon. Most major credit cards accepted. Auberge Associates, managers; Lorraine Dasker, Regional Director.

DIRECTIONS: From Los Angeles, take Interstate 5 to Del Mar. Go east on Via De La Valle (S-6) and turn left at San Dieguito Rd. Turn right at Rancho Diegueno Rd., and take an immediate left at Rancho Valencia Rd. Then turn left onto Rancho Valencia Drive.

Indexes

Property Index

AGATE COVE INN, Mendocino 10
ALAMO SQUARE INN, San Francisco 97
ALISAL GUEST RANCH, Solvang 164
AMBER HOUSE, Sacramento 52
APPLE LANE INN, Aptos 128
APPLEWOOD, THE, Guerneville 56
ARCHBISHOPS MANSION INN, San Francisco 98
ABIGAIL'S BED & BREAKFAST, Sacramento 53
BABBLING BROOK INN, THE, Santa Cruz 129
BALLARD INN, THE, Ballard 165
BATH STREET INN, THE, Santa Barbara 168
BAYBERRY INN, THE, Santa Barbara 169
BEAZLEY HOUSE, Napa 75
BENBOW INN, Garberville 3
BLUE LANTERN INN, Dana Point 192
CAMPBELL RANCH INN, Geyersville 57
CARTER HOUSE, Eureka 5
CASA DEL MAR, Stinson Beach 91
CHANNEL ROAD INN, THE, Santa Monica 187
CHATEAU DU SUREAU, Oakhurst 44
CHATEAU VICTORIAN, Santa Cruz 130
CHESHIRE CAT, Santa Barbara 170
CLIFF CREST BED AND BREAKFAST INN, Santa Cruz .. 132
COUNTRY ROSE INN BED AND BREAKFAST, Gilroy .. 133
COURT STREET INN, Jackson 35
DUNBAR HOUSE 1880, Murphys 46
EAGLE'S NEST, Big Bear Lake 200
FOOTHILL HOUSE, Calistoga 76
FOXES, THE, Sutter Creek 36
GARDEN HOUSE INN, THE, Avalon 193
GARDEN STREET INN, San Luis Obispo 159
GATE HOUSE INN, Jackson 37
GINGERBREAD MANSION, Ferndale 6
GLENDEVEN, Little River 11
GOSBY HOUSE INN, Pacific Grove 141
GREEN GABLES INN, Pacific Grove 142
GRAPE LEAF INN, Healdsburg 59
HANFORD HOUSE, THE, Sutter Creek 39

HAPPY LANDING, THE, Carmel 143
HARBOR HOUSE, Elk 12
HAYDON HOUSE, Healdsburg 60
HEADLANDS INN, THE, Mendocino 14
HEART'S DESIRE INN, Occidental 62
HEIRLOOM, THE, Ione 40
HENSLEY HOUSE, San Jose 122
HOPE-MERRILL HOUSE, Geyersville 63
INN, THE, Rancho Santa Fe 203
INN AT DEPOT HILL, Capitola by the Sea 135
INN AT HARRIS RANCH, THE, Coalinga 156
INN AT PETERSEN VILLAGE, THE, Solvang 172
INN AT SARATOGA, THE, Saratoga 123
INN AT UNION SQUARE, THE, San Francisco 100
INN ON MOUNT ADA, Avalon 195
INN SAN FRANCISCO, THE, San Franciso 101
JABBERWOCK, THE, Monterey 145
JOHN DOUGHERTY HOUSE, Mendocino 16
JOSHUA GRINDLE INN, Mendocino 18
JUGHANDLE BEACH COUNTRY BED & BREAKFAST, Mendocino 19
LA MAIDA HOUSE, North Hollywood 188
LA MER, Ventura 174
LARKMEAD COUNTRY INN, Calistoga 77
LOS OLIVOS GRAND HOTEL, Los Olivos 175
MADRONA MANOR, Healdsburg 64
MANSION AT LAKEWOOD, THE, Walnut Creek 102
MANSIONS, THE, San Francisco 103
MARTINE INN, THE, Pacific Grove 146
MEADOWOOD RESORT HOTEL, St. Helena 79
MENDOCINO FARMHOUSE, Mendocino 21
MILL ROSE INN, Half Moon Bay 118
MURPHY'S INN, Grass Valley 31
OLD MONTEREY INN, Monterey 148
OLD THYME INN, Half Moon Bay 119
OLD WORLD INN, THE, Napa 81
OLD YACHT CLUB INN, THE, Santa Barbara 177
PETITE AUBERGE, San Francisco 106
PINE INN, THE, Carmel 149
PUDDING CREEK INN, Fort Bragg 22
RACHEL'S INN, Mendocino 23
RANCHO VALENCIA RESORT, Rancho Santa Fe 204
ROUNDSTONE FARM, Olema 92

RED CASTLE INN, THE, Nevada City   32
SALISBURY HOUSE, Los Angeles   189
SANDPIPER INN AT-THE-BEACH, THE, Carmel   151
SAN YSIDRO RANCH, Montecito   179
SCOTT COURTYARD AND LODGING, Calistoga   83
SEAL BEACH INN & GARDENS, THE, Seal Beach   197
SERENITY, Sonora   48
SEVEN GABLES INN, Pacific Grove   152
SHERMAN HOUSE, THE, San Francisco   107
SILVER ROSE INN, Calistoga   84
SIMPSON HOUSE INN, Santa Barbara   181
SPENCER HOUSE, THE, San Francisco   108
STANFORD INN BY THE SEA, Mendocino   25
TEN INVERNESS WAY, Inverness   94
TIFFANY INN, Santa Barbara   183
TIMBERHILL RANCH, Cazadero   66
UNION STREET INN, San Francisco   110
VENTANA INN, Big Sur   154
VICTORIAN GARDEN INN, Sonoma   68
VICTORIAN INN ON THE PARK, San Francisco   112
VICTORIAN ON LYTTON, THE, Palo Alto   125
VILLA ROSA, Santa Barbara   184
VINTNERS INN, Santa Rosa   70
WASHINGTON SQUARE INN, San Francisco   114
WEDGEWOOD INN, THE, Jackson   41
WHALE WATCH INN BY THE SEA, Gualala   27
WHITEGATE INN, Mendocino   28
WHITE SWAN, San Francisco   115
WINE COUNTRY INN, THE, St. Helena   86
YE OLDE' SHELFORD HOUSE, Cloverdale   72
ZINFANDEL INN, St. Helena   87

Rates

Space limitations preclude any more than a general range of rates for each inn, and these should not be considered firm quotations. All inns serve full breakfasts unless noted as CB which is a continental breakfast, AP which is American Plan (must purchase your meals separately) and MAP which is Modified American Plan (Breakfast & Dinner included in rate for two.)

Please check with the inns for their various rates and special packages. It should be noted that many small inns do not have night staffs, and innkeepers will appreciate it if calls are made before 8:00 P.M.

Aptos, APPLE LANE INN	$85–125
Avalon, THE GARDEN HOUSE INN	$125-250
Avalon, THE INN ON MOUNT ADA	$230—590 AP
Ballard, BALLARD INN,	$155–185
Big Bear Lake, EAGLE'S NEST	$75-165
Big Sur, VENTANA INN	$170–450 CB
Calistoga, FOOTHILL HOUSE	$125–250
Calistoga, LARKMEAD COUNTRY INN	$125
Calistoga, SCOTT COURTYARD	$100—135
Calistoga, SILVER ROSE INN	$115–195
Capitola, INN AT DEPOT HILL	$145–225
Carmel, PINE INN	$85–205 AP
Carmel, THE HAPPY LANDING	$90–145
Carmel, THE SANDPIPER INN AT-THE-BEACH	$90–170
Catalina Island, INN ON MOUNT ADA	$190–580 AP
Cazadero, TIMBERHILL RANCH	$296–350 MAP
Cloverdale, YE OLDE' SHELFORD HOUSE	$85–110
Coalinga, THE INN AT HARRIS RANCH	$80–150 AP
Dana Point, BLUE LANTERN INN	$135–250
Elk, HARBOR HOUSE	$160–245 MAP
Eureka, CARTER HOUSE	$75-$165
Ferndale, THE GINGERBREAD MANSION	$105–175 CB
Fort Bragg, PUDDING CREEK INN	$65–115
Garberville, BENBOW INN	$88–180
Geyersville, CAMPBELL RANCH INN	$100–145
Geyersville, HOPE-MERRILL HOUSE	$65–125
Gilroy, COUNTRY ROSE INN BED AND BREAKFAST	$72–169

Grass Valley, MURPHY'S INN	$74–123
Gualala, WHALE WATCH INN BY THE SEA	$165–275
Guerneville, APPLEWOOD	$100–150
Half Moon Bay, MILL ROSE INN	$150–275
Half Moon Bay, OLD THYME INN	$65–190
Half Moon Bay, ZABALLA HOUSE	$65–150
Healdsburg, GRAPE LEAF INN	$90–145
Healdsburg, HAYDON HOUSE	$70–120
Healdsburg, MADRONA MANOR	$135–210 CB
Inverness, TEN INVERNESS WAY	$110–140
Ione, THE HEIRLOOM	$60–91
Jackson, COURT STREET INN	$75–125
Jackson, GATE HOUSE INN	$75–120
Jackson, THE WEDGEWOOD INN	$85–120
Little River, GLENDEVEN	$85–130
Los Angeles, SALISBURY HOUSE	$75–100
Los Olivos, LOS OLIVOS GRAND HOTEL	$160–225 CB
Mendocino, AGATE COVE INN	$69–155
Mendocino, HEADLANDS INN	$98–165
Mendocino, JOHN DOUGHERTY	$95–145
Mendocino, JOSHUA GRINDLE INN	$95–145
Mendocino, JUGHANDLE BEACH COUNTRY	$80–100
Mendocino, MENDOCINO FARMHOUSE	$75–100
Mendocino, RACHEL'S INN	$96–165
Mendocino, STANFORD INN BY THE SEA	$160–250
Mendocino, WHITEGATE INN	$95–165
Montecito, SAN YSIDRO RANCH	$185–540 AP
Monterey, OLD MONTEREY INN	$160–220
Monterey, THE JABBERWOCK	$120—180
Murphys, DUNBAR HOUSE 1880	$105–145
Napa, BEAZLEY HOUSE	$110–165
Napa, OLD WORLD INN	$95—140
Nevada City, THE RED CASTLE INN	$70–140
North Hollywood, LA MAIDA HOUSE	$90–210
Oakhurst, CHATEAU DU SUREAU	$250–350
Occidental, HEART'S DESIRE INN	$95–195
Olema, ROUNDSTONE FARM	$115-125
Pacific Grove, GOSBY HOUSE INN	$85–130
Pacific Grove, GREEN GABLES INN	$100–160
Pacific Grove, SEVEN GABLES INN	$105–205
Pacific Grove, THE MARTINE INN	$125–230

Palo Alto, THE VICTORIAN ON LYTTON	$95–175
Rancho Santa Fe, THE INN	$80–450 AP
Rancho Santa Fe, RANCHO VALENCIA	$295–350
Sacramento, AMBER HOUSE	$80–195
Sacramento, AUNT ABIGAIL'S BED & BREAKFAST	$75–135
St. Helena, MEADOWOOD RESORT HOTEL	$225–265 AP
St. Helena, THE WINE COUNTRY INN	$130–202 CB
St. Helena, ZINFANDEL INN	$125–200
San Diego, HERITAGE PARK BED & BREAKFAST	$85–125
San Francisco, ALAMO SQUARE INN	$85–175
San Francisco, ARCHBISHOPS MANSION INN	$115–285
San Francisco, THE INN AT UNION SQUARE	$110–400
San Francisco, THE MANSIONS	$89–350
San Francisco, PETITE AUBERGE	$105–215
San Francisco, SHERMAN HOUSE	$190–650 AP
San Francisco, THE INN SAN FRANCISCO	$75–175
San Francisco, THE SPENCER HOUSE	$95–155
San Francisco, UNION STREET INN	$115–225 CB
San Francisco, VICTORIAN INN ON THE PARK	$94–154
San Francisco, WASHINGTON SQUARE INN	$85–180
San Francisco, WHITE SWAN	$145–250
San Jose, HENSLEY HOUSE	$95–125
San Luis Obispo, GARDEN STREET INN	$90–160
Santa Barbara, THE BATH STREET INN	$70–125
Santa Barbara, THE BAYBERRY INN	$85–135
Santa Barbara, CHESHIRE CAT	$110–190
Santa Barbara, THE OLD YACHT CLUB INN	$65–135
Santa Barbara, SIMPSON HOUSE INN	$80–200
Santa Barbara, TIFFANY INN	$75–175
Santa Barbara, VILLA ROSA	$90–190
Santa Cruz, CHATEAU VICTORIAN	$100–130
Santa Cruz, CLIFF CREST BED AND BREAKFAST INN	$80–125
Santa Cruz, THE BABBLING BROOK INN	$85–150
Santa Monica, THE CHANNEL ROAD INN	$85–210
Santa Rosa, VINTNERS INN	$118–195
Saratoga, INN AT SARATOGA	$150–265 CB
Seal Beach, THE SEAL BEACH INN & GARDENS	$88–155
Solvang, THE ALISAL GUEST RANCH & RESORT	$270–350 MAP
Solvang, THE INN AT PETERSEN VILLAGE	$95–155
Sonoma, VICTORIAN GARDEN INN	$79–135
Sonora, SERENITY	$85

Stinson Beach, CASA DEL MAR	$100–225
Sutter Creek, THE FOXES	$95–140
Sutter Creek, THE HANFORD HOUSE	$60–110
Ventura, LA MER	$80–155
Walnut Creek, THE MANSION AT LAKEWOOD	$85–225

Index by Activity

Boating

    HARBOR HOUSE, Elk
    THE INN AT SARATOGA, Saratoga
    MILL ROSE INN, Half Moon Bay

Cycling

    CAMPBELL RANCH INN, Geyserville
    FOOTHILL HOUSE, Calistoga
    THE GINGERBREAD MANSION, Ferndale
    GRAPE LEAF INN, Healdsburg
    GREEN GABLES INN, Pacific Grove
    HARBOR HOUSE, Elk
    HERITAGE PARK BED & BREAKFAST, San Diego
    LA MER, Ventura
    THE SANDPIPER INN AT-THE-BEACH, Carmel
    THE SEAL BEACH INN AND GARDENS, Seal Beach
    VILLA ROSA, Santa Barbara

Fishing

    HARBOR HOUSE, Elk
    LA MER, Ventura
    MADRONA MANOR, Healdsburg
    MILL ROSE INN, Half Moon Bay

Golf

    BENBOW INN, Garberville
    GATE HOUSE INN, Jackson
    HARBOR HOUSE, Elk
    THE HEADLANDS INN, Mendocino
    THE INN, Rancho Santa Fe
    LA MER, Ventura
    MADRONA MANOR, Healdsburg
    MEADOWOOD RESORT HOTEL, St. Helena
    MILL ROSE INN, Half Moon Bay
    THE OLD YACHT CLUB INN, Santa Barbara
    THE PINE INN, Carmel
    THE SANDPIPER INN AT-THE-BEACH, Carmel
    SAN YSIDRO RANCH, Montecito
    THE SEAL BEACH INN AND GARDENS, Seal Beach
    TIMBERHILL RANCH, Cazadero

THE WINE COUNTRY INN, St. Helena

Hiking
THE BAYBERRY INN, Santa Barbara
BENBOW INN, Garberville
CAMPBELL RANCH INN, Geyserville
CASA DEL MAR, Stinson Beach
FOOTHILL HOUSE, Calistoga
HARBOR HOUSE, Elk
THE HEADLANDS INN, Mendocino
THE INN AT SARATOGA, Saratoga
MADRONA MANOR, Healdsburg
SAN YSIDRO RANCH, Montecito
TIMBERHILL RANCH, Cazadero

Horseback riding
THE BAYBERRY INN, Santa Barbara
THE INN AT SARATOGA, Saratoga
MILL ROSE INN, Half Moon Bay
THE OLD YACHT CLUB INN, Santa Barbara
SAN YSIDRO RANCH, Montecito

Skiing
GATE HOUSE INN, Jackson

Swimming
BENBOW INN, Garberville
CAMPBELL RANCH INN, Geyserville
FOOTHILL HOUSE, Calistoga
HOPE-MERRILL HOUSE, Geyserville
THE INN, Rancho Santa Fe
THE INN AT SARATOGA, Saratoga
MEADOWOOD RESORT HOTEL, St. Helena
THE PELICAN INN, Muir Beach
SAN YSIDRO RANCH, Montecito
THE SEAL BEACH INN AND GARDENS, Seal Beach
TIMBERHILL RANCH, Cazadero
THE WINE COUNTRY INN, St. Helena

Tennis
THE BABBLING BROOK INN, Santa Cruz
BENBOW INN, Garberville
CAMPBELL RANCH INN, Geyserville

GRAPE LEAF INN, Healdsburg
THE INN, Rancho Santa Fe
THE INN AT SARATOGA, Saratoga
LA MER, Ventura
MADRONA MANOR, Healdsburg
MEADOWOOD RESORT HOTEL, St. Helena
THE SANDPIPER INN AT-THE-BEACH, Carmel
SAN YSIDRO RANCH, Montecito
THE SEAL BEACH INN AND GARDENS, Seal Beach
TIMBERHILL RANCH, Cazadero
THE WINE COUNTRY INN, St. Helena

Wheelchair access
THE BABBLING BROOK INN, Santa Cruz
BEAZLEY HOUSE, Napa
THE CHANNEL ROAD INN, Santa Monica
THE HANFORD HOUSE, Sutter Creek
HEART'S DESIRE INN, Occidental
HOPE-MERRILL HOUSE, Geyserville
THE INN, Rancho Santa Fe
THE INN AT UNION SQUARE, San Francisco
JOSHUA GRINDLE INN, Mendocino
THE PELICAN INN, Muir Beach
SEVEN GABLES INN, Pacific Grove
STANFORD INN BY THE SEA, Mendocino
TIMBERHILL RANCH, Cazadero
VINTNERS INN, Santa Rosa

Let Me Hear From You. . .

Please use this page to let me know about your reactions—positive and negative—to your stay at any of the inns recommended in COUNTRY INNS AND BACK ROADS: CALIFORNIA, and to tell me about the inns you've enjoyed that I may have overlooked. Just tear out this page and send your comments to me at the address below.

_____

_____

_____

_____

_____

_____

_____

_____

_____

_____

Name:_____

Address:_____

_____

Thanks for your help, and happy traveling!

Jerry Levitin
1565 Partrick Road
Napa, CA 94558

Please use this page to let us know about your experiences with ___ or share with your friends any of the lines you've read. And if you ___ FILMS AND BECOMES A MAJOR MOTION PICTURE, a feature we think we may ___ to __ involved in the new lines overlooked, just tear out this page and mail your comments to us at the address below.

_____

_____

_____

_____

_____

_____

_____

_____

_____

Address _____

_____

Thanks for your help. And happy reading.